Text, Community and Christian Origins

Biblical Hermeneutics Rediscovered

The Series as the name suggests will focus on Biblical Hermeneutics, i.e., literary works concerned with methods of interpreting the Old and New Testaments of Bible via different stream of topics like Literature & Poetry, Indigenous Philosophizing, Ethical response towards Ecology, Health & Healing, Science & Technology, Feminist Theology, Sociological approach towards Human Rights, Law & Politics, Arts, History of Ideas, Ancient Civilizations, Cultural Contiguity, Religious Cosmologies & Mysticism, Appraisal of various Theologians, World Peace & Harmony, Global Capitalism, Network Marketing, Cybertheology, Population & Demographics, Epigraphic Studies, Contextualized Education, and many others. We welcome a Mss. on any topic/s mentioned, whether they are original works, scholarly monographs, collections of conference papers, revised dissertations, or translations of historical documents. Through the Series we, the Publishers, are striving to put forward published works that may help Institutions, Academic Bodies, Researchers, Scholars and the World at large in furthering their respective knowledge and understanding on the concerned subject. We welcome your comments on our efforts and further suggestions on how we can enshrine new ray of analysing & explaining the written Texts through our upcoming books.

Biblical Hermeneutics Rediscovered - 15

Text, Community and Christian Origins

Searching the Rhetoric of Identity Description in the Markan Gospel

Cyprian E. Fernandez

CWI

Christian World Imprints™

First Published in 2018 by

Christian World Imprints(TM)
Christian Publishing & Books from India
H-12 Bali Nagar, **New Delhi-110015**
info@christianworldimprints.com
www.ChristianWorldImprints.com
Phone: +91 11 25465925

ISBN: 978-93-5148-285-7 (HB) ISBN: 978-93-5148-292-5 (PB)

Cataloging in Publication Data--DK

Courtesy: D.K. Agencies (P) Ltd. <docinfo@dkagencies.com>

Fernandez, Cyprian E., 1974- **author.**

Text, community and Christian origins : searching the rhetoric of identity description in the Markan Gospel / Cyprian E. Fernandez.

pages cm. -- (Biblical hermeneutics rediscovered ; 15)
Includes bibliographical references.
ISBN 9789351482857 (HB)
ISBN 9789351482925 (PB)

1. Bible. Mark--Criticism, interpretation, etc. 2. Identification (Religion) 3. Christianity--Origin. I. Title. II. Series: Biblical hermeneutics rediscovered ; 15.

LCC BS2585.52.F47 2018 | DDC 226.306 23

Cover image description by author:
A stone carving image of parade with Menorah, on the first century AD honorific Arch of Titus located on the Via Sacra, Rome, commemorating the siege of Jerusalem and destruction of the temple by Titus in AD70.

Printed in India.

Contents

FOREWORD-I

Dr. Cyprian E. Fernandez, in his recent book *Text, Community and Christian Origins*, makes a commendable effort to articulate the identity of the audience of the gospel of Mark or the first readers of the gospel of Mark. In order to arrive at a convincing conclusion regarding the community addressed by Mark in his gospel, he puts to use various methodological tools. Hence, his research and the conclusions deserve honest appreciation and polite evaluation from the scholars of the Markan studies.

Nevertheless, ever since I started my specialization on the gospel of Mark, the question that bothered me was regarding the ineptness of some of our researches. Can we reach a conclusion with some kind of a certitude regarding the first readers or the audience or the community of the gospel of Mark? The current state of research that Fernandez presents in the first chapter and the conclusions he summarises at the end, do not encourage a positive answer to this question. Hence, I intend to approach the whole matter, viz., the Markan readers/audience/community, from a different angle.

Gospel, at first, was not just read, but rather proclaimed. One person proclaims the gospel and others listen to the proclamation. The written gospel of Mark, at first, might probably have been a tool to facilitate the act of proclamation of the same.

The purpose of such proclamation was to bring about conversion (Mk 1:15) in the listener and thereby to transform his/her life. In other words, the objective of the gospel proclamation was to generate apt responses in the listener, because of the attentive listening to the proclaimed gospel story. In that spectacle of the proclamation of the gospel story, the characters of the gospel turn out to be sheer ploys by whom the reader is provoked to respond, in the process of listening to the gospel. In other words, the listener is invited to respond to the characters of the story, at each moment of the development of the gospel story.

In the gospel of Mark, one encounters the repeated failures of the disciples of Jesus. Since the focus of this volume of Dr. Fernandez is on the listeners/audience, let us focus on the listener responses, primarily to the failures of the disciples of

Jesus, they meet in the gospel. In order to actualize this objective, we shall make use of the reader-response criticism as our methodological tool.

Reader-Response Criticism as Methodological Tool

Reader-response criticism[1] focuses on the interaction between the text and its receiver in contrast to the focus of the earlier methods, i.e., on the text and the author. It views the text as a literary communication employing rhetorical devices and means of argumentation intended to persuade its recipients to feel, think or act in specific ways. It focuses on those mental moves/responses, the author is trying to evoke in the intended audience through the rhetoric of his/her narration. It attempts to articulate how the text as a literary rhetorical communication works upon the audience and what persuasive effects it would generate upon its implied readers.[2]

R. M. Fowler's *Let the Reader Understand* (1991) is ranked among masterpieces in the history of gospel reader-response criticism.[3] It is significant, because it is not only a meticulous and systematic study on the subject, but also the first book-length discussion on the theoretical constituents of the reader-response methodology, exemplifying them in the context of the gospel of Mark. Hence, for the textual construct of the implied reader[4] and the principles of reader-response criticism,[5] I mainly follow Fowler.

Progressive Stages of the Story

When the gospel had been proclaimed or written, it was not divided based on chapters and verses. That came much later. Consequently, the gospel of Mark was the story of Jesus, continuously proclaimed from the beginning to the end, viz., 16:8, without a break.[6] Therefore, in order to go through the responses of

---

[1] For introductions to Biblical reader-response criticism, see: R.M. Fowler, "Reader-Response Criticism: Figuring Mark's Reader," in *Mark and Method: New Approaches in Biblical Studies*, in J.C. Anderson-S.D. Moore (ed.), Minneapolis, Fortress, 1992, 50-83; S. Brown, "Reader Response: Demythologizing the Text," *NTS* 34 (1988), 232-237.

[2] Introductions to reader-response criticism in general: S.R. Suleiman, "Introduction: Varieties of Audience-Oriented Criticism," in *The Reader in the Text: Essays on Audience and Interpretation*, (ed.) S.R. Suleiman – I. Crosman, Princeton, Princeton University Press, 1980, 3-45.

[3] R.M. Fowler, *Let the Reader Understand: Reader-response Criticism and the Gospel of Mark*, Minneapolis, Fortress, 1991.

[4] Fowler, *Let the Reader*, 26-40. See also R.M. Fowler, "Who is the Reader of Mark's Gospel?," *SBL SP* 22 (1983), 31-51; P.L. Danove, *The End of Mark's Story: A Methodological Study* (BibInterpS 3), Leiden, Brill, 1993, 167-191. For a detailed bibliography on the "reader" of the Markan narrative, see J.C. Naluparayil, *The Identity of Jesus in Mark: An Essay on Narrative Christology* (SBFAnalecta 49), Jerusalem, Franciscan Printing Press, 2000, 301, n. 54. Hereafter I shall use the term "reader" in the sense of "the implied reader."

[5] See Fowler, *Let the Reader*, 61-227.

[6] On the text critical problems regarding the ending of the gospel: B.M. Metzger, *A Textual Commentary on the Greek New Testament*, Stuttgart, United Bible Societies, 1975, 122-128; J.K.

the reader at any specific moment of the story, we need to have a division of the progress of the story into various stages. Interestingly, the author of the gospel gives an indication in the development of the story by creating change in its spatial setting. Hence, on the basis of the change in the spatial setting in the narration, we divide the development of the story into the following stages:

The first part of the story (1: 2-13) unveils in the wilderness. John preaches repentance and confers baptism in the Judean desert (1:4).[7] Again, the baptism of Jesus and his temptation happens against the background of the desert (1:9, 12-13). Hence, the *locale* of the first part of the Markan gospel story is the desert.[8]

In 1:14, the Spatial setting shifts from "the wilderness" to "Galilee" and it continues to be the main setting until the next setting of "on the way" which appears in 8:27.[9] Galilee is the general setting where all the events of this block take place. This narrative block (1:14-8:26) could be easily divided into two, viz., 1:14-3:6 and 3:7-8:26, based on the shift in spatial setting and plot.[10] The principal event of 1:14-3:6 is the arrival of the reign of God through the words and deeds of Jesus. Thereafter, in 3:7-8:26, Jesus reveals the mystery of the reign of God to the insiders, viz., his disciples.

A shift in the spatial setting occurs in 8:27, at the very opening of the new block and in the new setting is "on the way." This phrase appears for the last time in 10:52.[11] The principal narrative event of this block (8:27-10:52) is the presentation of the ultimate destiny of the Son of Man – his suffering, death and resurrection. It is a teaching that explains the 'Christhood' of Jesus.

In 11:1, the spatial setting shifts from "on the way" to "Jerusalem" and it continues to be so, until 15:41.[12] Moreover, all the activities of Jesus in Jerusalem appear in 11:1-15:41. This narrative block could easily be divided into two phases, based on the change in the setting and in the development of the story

---

Elliot, "The Text and Language of the Endings to Mark's Gospel," in *The Language & Style of the Gospel of Mark: An Edition of C.H. Turner's 'Notes on Markan Usage'* (SupplNT 71), ed. Idem, Leiden, E.J. Brill, 1993, 203-211.

[7] Cf. F.J. Matera, "The Proloue as the Interpretative Key to Mark's Gospel," *JSNT* 34 (1988), 4-15; S.H. Smith, *A Lion with Wings: A Narrative-Critical Approach to Mark's Gospel* (BibS 38), Sheffield, Sheffield Academic Press, 1996, 96.

[8] Naluparayil, *The Identity*, 306-307.

[9] E.S. Malbon, "Galilee and Jerusalem: History and Literature in Markan Interpretation," *CBQ* 44 (1982), 242-255; Naluparayil, *The Identity*, 310-311.

[10] On the particular setting of sea and boat, see Naluparayil, *The Identity*, 323, n. 161, 162, 163.

[11] For a detailed list of its appearance, see Naluparayil, *The Identity*, 344, n. 286.

[12] See Naluparayil, *The Identity*, 366, n. 393.

– 11:1-13:37[13] and 14:1-15:41.[14] The principal event of 11:1-13:37 consists of presenting Jesus, the Christ, as the eschatological divine Son, who comes into conflict with the religious establishment. Besides, he demands vigilant adherence to his way from his followers in view of the *parousia*. Whereas, the principal event of 14:1-15:41 is that Jesus undergoes suffering and violent death, proclaiming his Christhood, divine Sonship and Kingship.

The tomb operates as the spatial setting of 15:42-16:8.[15] The principal narrative event is the announcement to the women that the crucified Jesus has risen from the dead, and their failure in perceiving this mystery. Based on these tentative divisions of the story, let us focus on the responses that the narratives generate in the reader at each stage of the story.

Reader as the privileged informee (1:1-13)

At the first stage of the gospel, none of the disciples of Jesus enters into the scene. As a result, some of the outstanding revelations provided at this stage, regarding the protagonist of the story, are kept incognito from the disciples. These revelations are: (a) Jesus is Christ, the Son of God (1:1), (b) God speaks with the protagonist regarding the sending of his forerunner (1:2-3), prior to his earthly arrival, (c) God declares to Jesus that he is His beloved Son and He empowers him with His Spirit (1:10-11), and (d) He encounters Satan in his domain (1:12-13).

These revelations, hidden to the human characters of the story, are secretly revealed to the reader.[16] Thereby, the narrator intends to show the reader that Jesus of Nazareth is a divine person - designated as the 'Lord' and called by God 'My beloved Son' – who has come on earth to fulfil the divine promises revealed through the prophets. These privileged informations enable the reader from the very beginning of the story, to be in a better position, to evaluate and judge the characters of the story, especially the disciples of Jesus.[17]

Reader aligns with the disciples (1:14-3:6)

The principal event of this narrative block is the arrival of the God's Kingly Rule as the eschatological liberation being realized through the person and ministry of

---

[13] Temple and its surroundings as the spacial setting of this narrative block: K. Bollmann, "Die Rolle des Tempels im Neuen Testament (Mk 11:1-13:2). Beitrag zur Diskussion über 'Die Einheit der Bibel,'" *TK* 7 (1980), 19-31; E.L. Schnellbächer, "The Temple as Focus of Mark's Theology," *Horizons* 5 (1983), 95-112.

[14] Danove, *The End*, 144-147 has a three-way division, viz., 11:1-12:44; 13:1-37; 14:1-15:41.

[15] See Naluparayil, *The Identity*, 366, n. 662. E.S. Malbon, *Narrative Space and Mythic Meaning in Mark*, San Francisco, Harper & Row, 1986, 128-129.

[16] On the privileged knowledge of the reader, see Matera, "The Proloue," 5-6.

[17] J.A. Camery-Hoggatt, *Irony in Mark's Gospel: Text and Subtext* (SNTS MS 72), Cambridge, University Press, 1992, 93.

Jesus.[18] Jesus accomplishes it through his ministry of preaching (1:14-15, 38-39; 2:2), teaching (1:21-22, 27; 2:8-11, 13, 17, 18-22, 23-28; 3:1-5), exorcism (1:23-28, 32-34, 39), healing (1:29-34, 40-45; 2:3-12; 3:1-6), forgiving sins (2:5) and the calling of his disciples (1;16-20; 2:14). Members of Jesus' audience are thus invited to change their minds and place their belief in the Good News that Jesus brings in (1:15).

In this section, the disciples respond generously to Jesus' invitation to partake in his mission of catching men for the Kingdom of God (1:18, 20; 2:14; cf. also 3:13-19). The people who encounter the inbreaking of the eschatological reign of God through his preaching, teaching, liberating exorcisms and healing, salvific forgiving, and the insight into the correct practice of the Law, crowd around him wherever he goes (1:32-33, 37, 45; 2:2, 13, 15). They remain amazed at the extraordinary activities of Jesus (1:27; 2:10), but they fail to comprehend the real significance of his ministry. The Jewish leaders consider him as one who blasphemes (2:7), and take counsel to kill him (3:6).

The reader not only responds to the invitation of Jesus but also reacts to the responses of the characters of the story. Since s/he has been provided with the privileged informations (1:1-13), s/he knows that Jesus is the divine Son of Man sent by his Father to establish the salvific reign of his Father on earth though his ministry. Consequently, the reader adjudges the response of the Jewish leaders as wrong, and that of the crowd as insufficient. In contrast, he acknowledges the response of the disciples to the invitation of Jesus as the most laudable. Consequently, s/he aligns himself/herself with them.[19]

Reader begins to distance himself/herself from the disciples (3:7-8:26)

The principal event running through this section of the narrative[20] constitutes 'the mystery of the reign of God' (4:10-12; cf. 4:13-20, 34; 7:17-23) and that of 'the divine identity' and the Messianic function of Jesus. In addition, 'the insiders' are privileged to receive this message (4:35-41; 5:1-13, 25-34, 35-43; 6:30-44, 45-51; 8:1-10).

The 'insiders' are those who do the will of God and thereby become the true family members of Jesus. 'The twelve' and 'the three' are privileged to be set apart as the 'insiders' and the 'participants' of Jesus mission of proclaiming the reign of God (3:13-19; 4:0; 5:37; 6:7-13, 30). They are provided with additional explanations of the parables (4:10, 13-20, 34; 7:17-23) and private manifestations of the divine person of Jesus (4:35-41; 5:1-13, 25-34, 35-43; 6:30-44, 45-53; 8:1-10) in order that they may recognize the divine identity and mission of Jesus (8:17-21).

---

[18] For a detailed discussion on this section, see Naluparayil, *The Identity*, 340-322.

[19] Camery-Hoggatt, *Irony*, 101-102.

[20] For a detailed discussion on this section, see Naluparayil, *The Identity*, 323-345.

Correspondingly, those who fail to do the will of God constitute 'the outsiders' who do not have access to 'the mystery of the reign of God.' Here, the implicit invitation of Jesus is to do the will of God (3:31, 34) and thereby perceive the mystery of the reign of God (4:11-12) and the Messianic role of Jesus (8:17-21; cf. 8:22-25, 29).

The disciples, viz., the insiders, who have received the privileged hearing of the mystery of the reign of God and private disclosures of Jesus' divinity and his Messianic role, are expected to recognise and accept his divine identity and his Messianic role.[21] However, it is unfortunate that the responses of the disciples are not satisfactory because they fail repeatedly in their responses (4:40; 6:49-52; 8:17-18), whereas the people who listen to him, appear to admit some kind of an eschatological role in him (6:14-16; 7:37).[22] Subsequently, Jesus makes the disciples to revaluate 'the bread-miracles' and invites them to recognize the 'bread-provider in the desert' who takes care of his people with divine compassion (6:34; 8:2). This opens the eyes of the disciples and they perceive Jesus as the Christ (8:29).

The reader, who is already confirmed in the faith that Jesus of Nazareth is God's Son (1:14-3:6), in the knowledge that he is the divine person sent by God witnesses to Jesus' repeated attempts and the disciples' recurrent failures (4:40; 6:49-52; 8:17-18). This invites the harsh judgement of the reader against the disciples' obduracy. Each time the reader reacts to the failure of the disciples, s/he gets reinforced in her/his perception of the mystery of the reign of God and the divine identity of Jesus.

Reader assimilates the divine point of view (8:27-10:52)

The principal narrative running through this block[23] is the presentation of the Son of Man's destiny of suffering, death and resurrection, that explains the Christhood of Jesus. The narrator demonstrates the destiny of the Son of Man as the good news by means of the phrase "and he was saying (*ton logon*) plainly" (8:32a).[24] As a result, the good news of the previous block (3:7-8:26), which constituted the mystery of the reign of God and the mystery of the person of Jesus, transforms into the Son of Man's destiny of suffering, death and resurrection.[25] At

---

[21] "The mystery" given to the insiders is two-dimensional. That is, the mystery concerning the kingdom of God and the mystery concerning the divine identity of Jesus: see J. Marcus, *The Mystery of the Kingdom of God* (SBL DS 90), Atlanta, Scholars, 1986, 51-52; M.A. Beavis, *Mark's Audience. The Literary and Social Setting of Mk 4:11-12* (JSNT SS 33), Sheffield, JSOT Press, 1989, 146.

[22] The failures of the disciples are highlighted against the success of the minor characters, who place trust in Jesus (5:21-43; 7:24-30) and the popular recognition of some eschatological role to Jesus (6:14-16; 7:37).

[23] For a detailed discussion on this section, see Naluparayil, *The Identity*, 345-367.

[24] See Naluparayil, *The Identity*, 350, n. 307.

[25] D.O. Via (Jr.), *The Ethics of Mark's Gospel: In the Middle of Time*, Philadelphia, Fortress, 1985, 190.

the same time, the Son of Man's destiny of suffering and death is introduced as 'the way' to discipleship and to the reign of God.[26]

Jesus explicitly calls for a "change of mind" (8:33) in this central section of the gospel. Literally what Jesus demands from his disciples is a shift from "thinking the things of men" to "thinking the things of God" (8:33).[27] In other words, Jesus attempts to transform the disciples' human perspectives on daily realities and to bring them to the divine perspective. With this aim in mind, he teaches them repeatedly, three times, God's plan about the Son of Man, how he would actualise his Christhood. Unfortunately, when Jesus resolutely tries to get rid of the disciples 'spiritual blindness, they regularly fail to accept the way of the Son of Man.[28] His appeal is to exchange their human point of view with his divine point of view. The fundamental transformation he proposed, must bring about corresponding changes in the different areas of their life.[29]

However, there is a gradual decline in their resistance against Jesus' endeavour. They move from total rejection (8:32-33), through lack of understanding (9:32), to understanding with fear, and following him with proclaimed readiness to die with him (10:32, 38-39). Thus, at the end of this section, the disciples seem to perceive the destiny of the Son of Man's suffering and death, and follow him to Jerusalem, the place of his death.[30]

The reader observes both Jesus' teaching on the necessity of his suffering and death and the disciples' repeated failures, and s/he adjudges such failure as excessive and unreasonable. By pronouncing judgement over the disciples, the reader has been in a way moulded to accept and assimilate the Son of Man's way of suffering and death into her/his life. Moreover, the reader gets herself/himself initiated into the perspective of the Man's by observing Jesus training his disciples to apply the evaluative system of the Son of Man on the different aspects of life: real greatness (9:35); service to the insignificant equals to service to God (9:36-37; 10:13-16); appreciation of the goodness in others (9:38-40); necessity of freedom from riches (10:17-27); greatness of serving others (10:41-43); and the nobility of dying for others (10:45).

A transformed reader, who has assimilated the divine perspectives of Jesus, who understands the real significance of the Son of Man's Christhood, and who accepts the divine necessity of Jesus' death, follows Jesus and his disciples to

---

[26] J. Marcus, *The Way of the Lord: Christological Exegesis of the Old Testament in the Gospel of Mark*, Louisville, Westminster, 1993, 33.

[27] J.D. Kingsbury, *The Christology of Mark's Gospel*, Philadelphia, Fortress, 1989, 47-48; Naluparayil, *The Identity*, 452-453.

[28] "The way of the Son of Man" is "the way" to discipleship and the way to the reign of God.

[29] For a detailed discussion on these conflicting points of view, see Naluparayil, *Identity of Jesus*, 452-461, 480-494.

[30] C.D. Marshall, *Faith as a Theme in Mark's Narrative* (SNTS MS 64), Cambridge, University Press, 1989, 139-140; Via, *The Ethics*, 162.

Jerusalem. In that sense, one can say that the eye-opening of Bartimaeus and his following Jesus symbolizes the perception of the reader and his following.[31]

Reader gets prepared for the middle time (11:1-13:37)

In this narrative lock, the narrator demonstrates the intensification of the conflict between Jesus and the Jewish leaders centred on his apparent claim to be the Christ.[32] This conflict supplies the background for his persisting demand for the faithful following of his Way. For, both the consequences of this conflict, i.e., the expected destruction of the protagonist and the antagonists, operate with the scope of inculcating in his followers, a faithful adherence to the Son of Man's way of life. In other words, Jesus instructs his disciples to be constantly watchful for the eschatological coming of the Son of Man by being faithfully dutiful in following him in his way of suffering and death (13:32-34).

The Jewish leaders react to Jesus' claim of his Christological identity of being the Son of God (11:29-12:11) and his Christological prerogative concerning the Temple (11:12-21), by intensifying their plan to destroy him (11:18; 12:8, 12, 13). The reader is tempted to make harsh judgements against the antagonists and thereby to side with the protagonist, Jesus. The narrator does not sketch the response of the disciples who are asked to be watchful and dutiful in their anticipation for the coming of the Son of Man (13:28-37). But the invitation in the story, operates as a direct appeal to the reader to follow the way of the Son of Man, in the present time, to get ready his eschatological arrival later.[33]

The reader, who has been hitherto led to the conviction that the divine person sent by God is the Son of Man (1:14-3:6), that the Son of Man on earth is the Christ (3:7-8:26/29), and that his Christhood consists of his suffering and death, in obedience to his Father (8:27-10:52), is now convinced that The Christ is to come again in *parousia*. He understands that the unqualified following of "the way of the Son of Man" (cf. 8:34-38) is expected from the followers as a prepared readiness for the imminent coming of the Son of Man (13:26, 34-37).

Reader, the faithful follower of Jesus (14:1-15:41)

The principal event of this narrative block is that of Jesus' suffering and violent death, thereby proclaiming his Christhood, divine Sonship, and Kingship in the reign of God.[34] Here, Jesus persuades his disciples to partake in the mystery

---

[31] On the identification of the reader with Bartimaeus, see J.F. Williams, *Other Followers of Jesus: Minor Characters as Major Figures in Mark's Gospel* (JSNT SS 102), Sheffield, JSOT, 1954, 151, 166, 170-171; E.S. Malbon, "Fallible Followers: Women and Men in the Gospel of Mark," *Semeia* 28 (983), 31.

[32] For a detailed discussion on this section, see Naluparayil, *The Identity*, 367-389.

[33] Camery-Hoggatt, *Irony*, 167-168; T.J. Geddert, *Watchwords: Mark 13 in Markan Eschatology* (JSNT SS 26), Sheffield, JSOT Press, 1989, 194.

[34] For a detailed discussion, see Naluparayil, *The Identity*, 389-418.

of his divine person. He invites them to accept it, appropriate it, and participate in his suffering and death in their role as his disciples. Jesus' attempts for winning over the disciples appear in his interpretation of the anointing by the woman as the anointing for his burial (14:3-9), in his prediction with precision, of his betrayal by one of his disciples (14:18-21) and of Peter's denial (14:27-30). What Jesus strives for is a shift in the disciples' behavioural pattern, i.e., a change from human reluctance for suffering to divine readiness to die for the sake of others, a change from self-centeredness to other-centeredness.

The Jewish leaders, who in the previous narrative block (11:18; 12:12, 13), intensify their attempt to entrap and destroy Jesus, now succeed in executing their plot (14:1-2). With the help of one of his disciples (14:10-11) they arrest Jesus (14:43-46), put him on trial, condemn him to death (14:53-64), make him face trial before Pilate (15:1-15), mock and persecute him (14:65; 15:15, 16-20, 31-32), and finally crucify him (15:21-27).

The disciples, who, in the previous narrative block, have been provided with the revelation that Jesus the Son of Man is the Christ, the Son-Heir of God (11:1-13:37), are led to see the nucleus of his divine Sonship in the current narrative block (14:1-15:41). The reader comes across the total failure of the disciples here. The decisive moment of their failure happens at Gethsemane, when they fail to watch and pray.[35] They miss to partake in Jesus' prayer, which unveils the nucleus of Jesus' Sonship (14:32-42). As a result, they abandon him in front of death-threat, flee from him (14:50-52), and deny him (14:66-72). By now, their failure seems to be total and devastating.

The reader, who witnesses the progress of these story lines, exercises his critical judgement against the plot of the antagonists and the failures of the disciples. Moreover, the disciples' failures highlight the unique role of the reader because at the conclusive failure of the disciples, the reader emerges as the sole companion of Jesus during his passion. Each failure of the disciples works as a device that deepens the reader's commitment to stand by Jesus in his suffering, to partake in it, and to die, following his way.

The reader, who has witnessed Jesus' conflict, prayers, obedience, and his divine Sonship at Gethsemane,[36] accompanies Jesus on his way of suffering and death. At his trial before the Sanhedrin (14:53-64), the reader hears Jesus confessing himself as the Christ, the Son of God, the Heir of God's reign, and the eschatological Judge - as the Son of Man (14:61-62). Subsequently, s/he closely accompanies Jesus during his trial before Pilate (15:2-15), at the mockery by the soldiers (15:16-20), and at the time of his crucifixion (15:21-32). Finally, the reader is there at the foot of the cross, when Jesus breathes his last, experiencing the intense forsakenness by all, including even God (15:33-37).

---

[35] M.A. Tolbert, *Sowing the Gospel: Mark's World in Literary-Historical Perspective*, Minneapolis, Fortress, 1989, 213, 217-218.

[36] Fowler, *Let the Reader*, 219: "The naratee is turned into the narrative's only insider."

As a result, the reader is really transformed, by the suffering and death of Jesus, as the ideal disciple to the extent that s/he hears his own inner voice speaking through the confession of the centurion (15:39).[37] For, the centurion is – in the story world – the closest witness and partaker of the death of the Son of Man, just like the reader at the discourse level.

Reader as the sole messenger of the good news of Jesus (15:42-16:8)

After the complete failure of the disciples in the passion narrative, the narrator continues the imagery of discipleship through the women-followers. They have followed Jesus in Galilee, come up with him to Jerusalem, and have witnessed to his death (15:40) and burial (15:46-47). Further, they have been conferred the good news of Jesus' resurrection, along with an injunction to convey it to his disciples and the news of his imminent meeting with them (16:6-7). Unfortunately enough, they too fail (16:8).

The failure of the women-disciples to fulfil the entrusted mission of the announcement implies their fundamental failure to comprehend the mystery that the crucified Jesus of Nazareth has risen from the dead. This failure of the women-disciples in the story-world incites the reaction of the reader. His harsh judgement on the failure of the women intensifies her/his perception and appropriation of the culminating mystery of the person of Jesus, which transforms her/him as the messenger of the good news of the Son of Man.

Thus the total failure of the human characters of the story, epitomized in the failure of the women, begets success at the discourse level by engendering an ideal discipleship in the reader. In other words, the reader is induced to substitute the failures of the disciples and the women, by appropriating the way of the Son of Man and becoming the messenger of His Good News. Therefore, the failed finish of Jesus' story in Mark, rhetorically generates a successful beginning of the Good News in the reader.

Conclusion

Our attempt here was not to attempt at identifying the readers/audience of the gospel of Mark, rather to attempt at spotting the decisive responses of the reader at the listening of the narrative. In fact, this was the prime goal of the proclamation of the gospel itself, viz., to generate responses in the reader, often articulated as conversion. In the act of reading the gospel, the reader would surely side with the protagonist and his point of view (8:31, 33). As a result, the reader evaluates the words and deeds of other characters of the story form this point of view. Each time the reader reacts to the behaviour of the characters, he aligns himself with Jesus and his point of view. Thus, as the story progresses, Jesus' perspectives take roots in the reader because of the spontaneous responses that the

---

[37] Naluparayil, *The Identity*, 415.

story generates in her/him. As a result, the reader turns out an ideal follower of Jesus and eventually, the messenger of his Good news.

Dr. Jacob Naluparayil
Divya Karunya Ashram
Thannipuzha, Okkal P.O.
Kaladay, Ernakulam (Dist)
Kerala

FOREWORD-II

The *Text, Community and Christian Origins* is a genius creation of long and tireless efforts of a virtuoso scholar. Each and every chapter of the book clearly discloses mastermind of Cyprian Fernandez. As mentioned in the introduction of the book, the scope of the subject is vast, and this book is yet another attempt to focus on a missing perspective of the subject concerned which seriously unattended so far by the Markan scholars. So, the author should be appreciated primarily for the newness of the subject. He is striving to find out the real identity of the community of Mark, to whom the Gospel according to the Mark was addressed.

In order to cram the identity of the community, author studies individual characters of the community. He discovers two major areas of internal crises confronted by the community as his research advances. They faced Christological crisis and Ecclesial crisis. The identity and position of each member of the community was questioned. The basic unity of the community was disturbed. So, Mark presents a solution to the issue. According the author, Mark presents few model characters ("*Possible Selves*" in the terminology of the author) to be followed by the members of his community. In the words of the author, "through the presentation of prototypes and antitypes of discipleship, he addresses his community what they should believe and what they should not; how they should behave and how they should not; and how they should relate to each other and how they should not respectively." Ultimately, Mark hopes for a society that is bound by strong love for one another. Harmony and unity are the results of such following of prototypes presented by Mark.

Through making a comprehensive study on the community of Mark, Cyprian tries to broadcast to the world of today that there is always a possibility to be united even in the midst of multiplicity and division. The book must be read between the lines. Just as Robert Frost depicts in his *Mending Wall* where the incongruity of the fence is criticized, Cyprian illustrates how people in the society should always be able to interact with one another and not only when there are problems to be solved.

Bringing out the colours of communion, he hopes for a better world where human beings live in peace and harmony, all men and women are treated with respect and dignity, human rights are considered primarily, justice is considered as the backbone of the human relationship and mercy is enshrined in the hearts of all men and women.

The efforts of Cyprian are praiseworthy and the result, innovative. I wish him the very best and to you the reader, a soothing and fruitful time of learning and living. My wish is that let the Markan concept of unity come true and the world enjoy peace and harmony.

✠ Stanley Roman
Bishop of Quilon

PREFACE

Whenever we make the effort to return to the source and to recover the original freshness of the Gospel, new avenues arise, new paths of creativity open up, with different forms of expression, more eloquent signs and words with new meaning for today's world.
(Pope Francis, *Evangelii Gaudium*, 11)

The reading and re-reading the Gospels to understand the community which they were addressed to has much relevance today and many studies about historical audience of the NT writings are coming out. Such efforts are encouraged by the needs of the time that loses sight of an authentic Christian identity when a return to the source and recovering of the original charisma of the nascent Christianity becomes a necessity. This book is perhaps helpful to serve that purpose by way of casting some light on the origins of Markan community.

This work can be considered as a corollary to my earlier work *Identity in Conflict: A Socio-rhetorical Reading of the Markan Story of Jesus,* a study that outlined the implicit and ideal image of identity which the Markan community was expected to live up. The aim of this work was not just to arrive at that image of identity rather it must have to facilitate the reader in probing the socio-historical situations which provoked for such imprints of identity. Having explored the implicit image of the social identity of Jesus-movement within the story world, one was encouraged further to answer the following questions. Why this implicit ideal image of the social identity was directed by Mark to the readers of his time? What might have been the real situation that provoked Mark to propose this new social identity for his audience? This present book is just a sample work that carries over those questions to be answered therefore it has gone a step further from my previous work.

I strive in this book to introduce interpretations of discipleship, Christian identity and community of Mark in a simple and intelligible language to any kind of readers, without diluting their scientific traits. It explores the social characteristics of the group reflected in the Markan Gospel with the help of social scientific models. The study is more socio-cognitive than sociological because, its approach is emphatically endeavored not to merely enumerate certain social features and peripheral data of a group, for example, literacy, demography, topography, art, culture, religion or political and economic status of a group, rather to extract the social identity of a community that would indispensably be constituent and represented by a stream of ideological categories within the Markan text. Hence, this research has to go in search of the social spirit of the Markan community and subsequently, a set of values, norms, attitudes and point of views will be importantly held dear while treating the Gospel text. Moreover, this book can meekly serve as an attitudinal guide to anyone who wishes to be transformed as an authentic disciple of Jesus or as a motivational guide for Markan-students and researchers. A book can be worth reading not only when it offers instant solutions but also when exposes certain problems to be solved. Even if not meant to offer perfect solutions, indeed, this book will have in store at least some puzzles for the serious minds of the Gospel studies.

I owe thanks to Dr. Santiago Guijarro Oporto, Head of the NT Studies of the University of Salamanca (Pont.), for the seed of thoughts sown in me for this work. It had its origin as a tiny idea during the project of my Master and Doctoral studies, which was enriched by the scholarly guidance of Prof. Guijarro. This book came into being during my time as teacher of NT in the Pontifical Institute of Alwaye. My interactions in the bible class rooms with the post graduates students, seminarians and with the lay faithful who are passionate for the Word of God really motivated me to shape this book. Moreover, my pursuit of this work was enhanced by the comfortable ambience of the Carmelgiri Seminary, Pontifical Institute of Alwaye and its library. For that, I sincerely thank my colleagues and students.

I want to thank Rev. Dr. Jacob Naluparayil, an eminent scholar and authority of Markan studies, who happily obliged to extend a forward to this book. I owe much gratitude to my Bishop Most Rev. Stanley Roman of the Diocese of Quilon for his endless encouragement and gracious support.

I wholeheartedly thank Rev. Dr. Soosamma Kavumpurath CTC, the retired Principal of Fatima Mata National College, Kollam, for her meticulous reading of the manuscript and observation of corrections. My heartfelt thanks go to Miss Bincy Maria, Assistant Professor at the University of Pondicherry, for her patient proofreading and correction of its language.

I have always enjoyed my opportunity in spending time in the library of the University of Salamanca, and herein express my heartfelt appreciation for the dedicated service rendered by the librarians of UPSA. I also take this opportunity to thank the Episcopal Commission of the Carmelgiri Seminary for having extended my probation period as the Staff, which gifted me with a golden time to pursue this work without delay. I thank my family, well-wishers, and dear ones who supported me in this humble effort.

ABBREVIATIONS

AB	The Anchor Bible
ABD	Anchor Bible Dictionary
ABR	Australian Biblical Review
Ant	Flavius Josephus, *Antiquities of the Jews*
BibInt	*Biblical Interpretation*
BIS	Biblical Interpretation Series
BTB	*Biblical Theology Bulletin*
CBQ	*Catholic Biblical Quarterly*
CE	Common Era (AD)
DENT	Diccionario Exegético del Nuevo Testamento
Did.	Didaché
Eccl.Hist.	Eusebius, *The Church History of Eusebius*
EDNT	Exegetical Dictionary of the New Testament
EICS	Enciclopedia Internacional de las Ciencias Sociales
ESCA	Encyclopedia of Social and Cultural Anthropology
Esd	Esdras
EstBib	*Estudios Biblicos*
Gos.Thom.	Gospel of Thomas
HELOT	Hebrew English and English Lexicon of the Old- Testament
HTR	*Harvard Theological Review*
IBT	International Bible Translators
IESS	International Encyclopedia of the Social Science
Int.	*Interpretation*
JBL	*Journal of Biblical Literature*
JBS	*Journal of Biblical Studies*
JSNT	*Journal for the Study of the New Testament*
JSNTsup.	*The Journal for the Studies of the New Testament, Supplement Series*
JSOTsup.	*Journal for the Study of the Old Testament, Supplement Series*
JSP	*Journal of Social Psychology*
JTS	*Journal of Theological Studies*

JW	Flavius Josephus, *The Jewish War*
LNTS	*Library of New Testament Studies*
LW	*The Living Word*
Nat. Hist.	Pliny, *Natural History*
NGEINT	New Greek-English Interlinear New Testament, UBS.
NovT	*Novum Testamentum*
NovTsup.	*Novum Testamentum Supplement Series*
NT	New Testament
NTS	*New Testament Studies*
OT	Old Testament
Pan.	Ephipanius, *Panarion*
RBL	Review of Biblical Literature
RevBib	*Revue Biblique*
RIBLA	*Revista de Interpretación Bíblica Latinoamericana*
SBL	Society of Biblical Literature
SCT	Self Categorization Theory
SF	*Social Forces* (Journal)
SIT	Social Identity Theory
SJT	*Scottish Journal of Theology*
SMT	Social Memory Theory
ST	*Sociological Theory* (Journal)
TPI	Theological Publications of India
WBC	Word Biblical Commentary
ZNW	*Zeitschrift Für die neutestamentliche Wissenschaft und die Kunde der älteren Kirche*

- This work follows *The New Revised Standard Version*, Catholic Edition for India, TPI, Bangalore 1993, for abbreviations of the books of Bible.

INTRODUCTION

Mark breaks a Christian perspective confined to the present by creating the vision of a temporal continuum, consisting of past, a present interval and a future.

(Kelber, *The Kingdom in Mark,* 141)

An active quest for the Markan community has been commenced ever since the Gospel of Mark was begun to be read critically and scientifically. By the advent of redaction criticism, a good deal of New Testament Scholarship has tried to explain the historical and socio-temporal settings of the Markan Gospel. A few of those studies have shed much light on the nature of the Markan Community from the sociological and ideological perspective.

It could be said in preview that the scholars are unanimous on the opinion that the knowledge of the real historical audience of Mark is an important base for any kind of interpretation of the Markan text. However, among them there is "...no consensus on the setting of Mark, nor is there a method agreed upon for describing the social makeup of a given community on the basis of a text."[1] They admit the insufficiency of the search in this area of scholarship. W. R. Telford after treating the same topic so briefly, referring to the similar mind of J. R. Donahue, opines that the "features such as these are not sufficient of course, to provide a definitive clue to the identity of the Markan community. This, like the provenance, still remains an open question."[2] This statement itself is enough and more to give an impetus to dedicate a study in this area.

It will become a presumption of our research when we agree with the unanimous opinion of scholars that the community of Mark is the grid on which the text is to be placed and understood, as well as to presume further that the same text reflects the historical circumstances of the community. This has been a seriously discussed topic in the recent scholarship of the Markan community

[1] J. R. DONAHUE, "Windows and Mirrors: The Setting of Mark's Gospel", *CBQ* 57 (1995), p. 2.

[2] W. R. TELFORD, *The Theology of the Gospel of Mark*, Cambridge University Press, UK, 1999, p. 17.

quest.[3] Without becoming pessimistic to believe in the impossibility of knowing about the Markan community, we give here a try for the search of it even without sweeping under the carpet the *status quo* of the so far investigations, for they will certainly cast meaning on our study.

As Peterson says, "the inferring and reconstruction of Markan communities from the text of the Gospel in order to provide sure footing for its interpretation is highly problematic practice indeed."[4] In addition to this, we would suppose that our search for a social identity in itself is a vast topic. The identity of a group is constituted with different planes of social realities, like psychological, ideological, topographical, geo-political and cultural dimensions. Therefore, this study on the Markan community needs to delimit the scope of its theme, hence the attempt here will be to view not the whole of the identity dimensions of the community, but a part, that is, the ideological dimension of the social identity of the Markan group. Many of the scholarly studies, as we would see in the first chapter, concentrate on the socio-historical settings rather than viewing the identity of the Markan community in an ideological plane. Indeed Kee and Kelber[5] are exceptions to this regard, who are explanatory in their views regarding the social nature of the community. As I was in search of bibliography, I could not come across at least a few topics or titles of this sort treating exclusively the social identity of the Markan community; certainly a few works are there treating on it at random.[6] It does not mean that recent scholarship is mute on this topic, the Markan community, for Incigneri's and Roskam's[7] studies reveal its great relevance in the biblical scholarship. This growing interest is an incentive that motivates this work to see this topic in different perspective with the backing of those scholars.

This study is also incited much by the current quest that began since a few decades regarding the question of Christian origins and the community formation. The freshness of this quest was the welcoming of the new exegetical methods and analytical approaches accompanied by the new literary criticisms and its accessory schools, in reading the communicative elements of ancient texts. The social scientific and anthropological approaches have collaborated in this search at the quest of knowing the boundaries, social images, functions and developments,

---

[3] cf., Review of Peterson's Book, *The Origin of Mark*, in C.A. Evans, *RBL* 12/05/2001, http://www.bookreviews.org, (accessed 03-08-2006).

[4] cf., *Ibid.*

[5] H. C. KEE, *The Community of the New Age: Studies in Mark's Gospel*, The Westminster Press, Philadelphia – Pennsylvania, 1977; W. H. KELBER, *The Kingdom in Mark: A New Place and a New Time*, Fortress Press, Philadelphia, 1974.

[6] cf., J. S. SUH, *Discipleship and Community: Mark's Gospel in Sociological Perspective*, Nexus Monograph series 1, Claremont, CA, 1991; H. WAETJEN, *A Re-ordering of Power; A Socio-political Reading of Mark's Gospel*, Fortress Press, Minneapolis, 1989.

[7] B. J. INCIGNERI, *The Gospel to the Romans: The Setting and Rhetoric of Mark's Gospel* (BIS 65), Brill, Leiden, 2003; H. N. ROSKAM, *The Purpose of the Gospel of Mark in Its Historical and Social Context*, Brill, Leiden, 2004.

operation of collective memory, authorities, conflicts and responses and such of the earliest Christian groups. As we would see below, some studies intimate us that the use of traditional exegetical methods in the Markan studies are found inadequate and in turn it necessitate for a newer approach of coherent and holistic reading of the text and interpretive strategies. This work here is just collaboration-in-test with this quest and search for the origin and identity of an early Christian community – the Markan community.

The genre of the Gospels being distinct to that of the letters opens up the question of identity of their community. The Gospels are clandestine in exposing the nature of their real audience and the crisis dealt with, in contrast to the Pauline letters. It is curious to know that, if evangelists were addressing certain problems or crisis by shaping a communal identity for them, why they did so in a muffled way than doing that so straight. Some scholars have satisfied this curiosity by untying the Gospels from the 'single-community-thought' for a wider horizons of first century churches and by explaining the Gospel-purposes with an implication of less authorial interest in the pressing problems but more in the preservation and presentation of the communities' tradition of Jesus. Even though Bauckham and Michael Bird, because of the absence of physical evidence of a community within the text and that Gospels generates itself to be a new genre versus epistles, argue for a wider readership, they never deny an existence of a community to the Gospels.[8] What their studies really bring in is a division in the Markan world by cutting the 'umbilical cord' of the Markan Gospel from the Markan community. We are taken up by the curiosity generated by this division and its corresponding debate, to see on the 'clandestine' community behind the Gospel of Mark.

Above all, it is truly natural that 'the fruit comes from within.' This study is a fruit that comes much out of my personal interest in Mark and the quest to know the origin of Christianity. Personally, I have been fascinated by the compactness and the literary quality of the Markan Gospel. Added to that, considering its primacy of origin as a new literary genre among the Gospels, I have presumed that the origin of Christianity and its related importance could not be accounted without reading and studying Mark. It seems to be a universal phenomenon that various ethnic groups of today show the desire for having a convergence in knowing and reviving their identity and roots of existence in the fast growing pluricultural world, and by all means relevant it is to say of the Christianity. In this changing global world of trends and pompousness, all the ethnic groups are wanting of their identity being untouched of those sweeping ideologies and transient values. It is sure that Christianity, to which this experience is not new for it has been born out of a multireligious and cultural milieu of the first century, is also in want of this sort of search for its true identity in this postmodern world.

---

[8] cf., M. F. BIRD, "The Markan Community, Myth or Maze? Bauckham's "The Gospel for All Christians" Revisited", *JTS* 57 (2006), p. 476.

It is doubtless, the Word of God is the cornerstone of any reconstruction of the Christian identity.

It should be reminded again that this study is not different from that of the scholars, yet would be sparsely distinguished in the usage of modern social scientific tools and analytical methods to define the social shape of the Markan community. The above-mentioned scope and relevances of the theme persuade us to re-ask the questions of the past, which are plain and fundamental to any search of the Markan community. Hence, this study as such will try to answer the following three questions. 1. What is the social identity of the Markan community intrinsic to the Gospel of Mark? 2. What occurred to the Markan community to have a Gospel at the particular point of time? 3. What could have been the location of the Markan community? These questions presuppose that Mark was not explaining the 'identity-in-repair' of his community rather his orientation was to reconstruct a new identity – a new way of being – of his community through his intelligent work.

Hermeneutical task

There are two wings of method chosen in order to pursue this study; the social scientific criticism and the narrative criticism. As the text is the point of departure of our search for the community of Mark, on one hand, the narrative criticism jointly with the redaction criticism will guide us to explore the textual analysis. On the other hand, the social scientific criticism will guide the interpretation of the social identity of the group from the already explored textual data with the aid of a model. They would do justice to this study to render a satisfying guidance for both the empirical and interpretive task of this work respectively.

As J. H. Elliott defines, "social scientific criticism of the Bible is that phase of the exegetical task which analyzes the social and cultural dimensions of the text and of its environmental context through the utilization of the perspectives, theory, models and research of the social sciences."[9] This method has the over all control on this study by offering verified presuppositions and by guiding the hermeneutical function facilitated with the use of models and theories. The reason for the use of this method is due to one of its strong presuppositions that the text is conditioned by the cultural properties and social characteristics from which it has been emerged.[10] As Botha suggests, "...a text and a possible context within an environment link up illuminating each other, and that this give and take is made possible by the 'texture' (the linguistic features) of the text...it must be emphasized that a text gains cognitive meaning only in its relationship to an environment and other texts. In other words, [social] context is more than a necessary aspect of

---

[9] J. H. ELLIOTT, *What is Social-Scientific Criticism?*, Fortress Press, Minneapolis, 1993, p. 7.

[10] cf., *Ibid.*, pp. 3-15.

interpretation it is the very essence of the process of understanding."[11] These views regarding the use of social scientific methods empowers us to approach the text as a communicative medium as *reflection of* and *response to* the social and cultural settings of the community in which the text was produced.[12] We will discuss in detail the relevance and application of model and social scientific criticism as preface to the second chapter.

While the social scientific criticism steers the interpretation of the context, the internal analysis of the text is controlled by the criteria of the narrative criticism. Again, the text-context intimacy is to be underscored. These two methods are sister-concerns in our field of methodology. The synchronic method of narrative criticism is a branch of literary criticism that will guide the empirical phase of this study. It has only an internal operation of exploring the basic textual properties for the interpretation of the context (community). With its direction, we will have a typical way of approaching and reading the text and discovering the basis for the final hermeneutics. The text is considered not as parts or pericopes but as coherent, finished story as a whole unit.[13]

Much of the work that led to the development of narrative criticism was undertaken in the Markan Seminar of the Society of Biblical Literature, chaired first by Norman Perrin and then by Werner Kelber between 1971 and 1980. In course of its development, David Roadhs, in his paper called "Narrative Criticism and the Gospel of Mark", coined the term "narrative criticism" to describe the investigative areas of literary criticism in application to the study of the Gospels.[14]

Narrative Criticism analyses the story world of a narrative and of its implied rhetorical impact on readers. It is to be underscored importantly that the text is considered as whole, not "piecemeal".[15] The Gospel is viewed as dramatic

---

[11] P. J. J. BOTHA, "The Historical Setting of Mark's Gospel: Problems and Possibilities", *JSNT* 51 (1993), p. 53.

[12] cf., *Ibid.*, p. 8.

[13] We said that narrative criticism takes the text as coherent and complete in itself in the stricter sense. It becomes a matter of suspicion when the Gospel is evident for its incoherencies, disconnections between pericopes, gaps to be filled up and the lack of unity. The narrative critics would answer this, that the unity and coherence is a good sign of a quality literature, similarly the lack of the same is also considered as the authorial artistry for the rhetoric functioning of the literature, leaving some space for the creativity of the reader to fill up the gaps and find adequate connections. The intentional gaps are suggestive rather than exhaustive, while unintentional gaps become real to the reader because of the temporal width between the real reader and the twenty-first century reader. cf., D. RHOADS - J. DEWEY - D. MICHIE, *Mark as Story: An Introduction to the Narrative of a Gospel* (2nd ed.), Fortress Press, Minneapolis, 1999, p. 4 ; D. RHOADS – K. SYREENI (eds.), *Characterization in the Gospels: Reconceiving Narrative Criticism* (JSNTsup.), Sheffield, 1999, pp. 15, 30, 270.

[14] cf., MERENLAHTI – HAKOLA, *Reconceiving Narrative Criticism*, in D. RHOADS – K. SYREENI (eds.), p. 17.

[15] cf., J. A. GRASSI, *The Rediscovering the Impact of Jesus' Death: Clues from the Gospel Audience*, Sheen &Ward, Kansas City, 1987, p. i.

performance with unified plots with consistent characters that play their parts to bring out a full emotional impact of the whole narrative in the implied audience so that they can identify with the whole story and become deeply involved in it.[16] To make it clear, the analysis of the story world focuses on the world inside the narrative with its own times and places, characters, past and future, sets of values, and series of events moving forward in some meaningful way. This story world is neither the historical world depicted by the story nor the historical world of the situation in which the story was first told.[17] The goal of the narrative criticism is to read the narrative from the perspective of the implied reader.

Real author and reader are historical Mark and his original reader of the first century respectively, while the implied author and implied reader are independent of any historical real readers and authors. The implied reader or the Gospel audience, as J. Grassi defines, is "an ideal audience [reader] in the author's mind, who would listen to the Gospel and respond to it in a desired way. This "ideal audience" does not always correspond to an actual audience either in ancient times or today."[18] To understand the meaning of the textual elements, we must become part of the implied audience. The reading of the characters from the implied reader's position would lead our study to find out the fictive community that Mark reconstructs for his actual historical group. The fictive social identity he suggests is a bridge through which we pass to the historical situations and predicaments of the community.

How the implied author guides the implied reader in his/her reading of the text? It is important that the implied reader is guided by the evaluative point of view of the implied author through various rhetoric patterns. M. A. Powell has enumerated almost fifteen categories of narrative patterns found in the biblical narratives that were originally proposed by David Bauer. They are repetition, contrast, comparison, causation and substantiation, climax, pivot, particularization and generalization, statement of purpose, summarization, interrogation, inclusion, interchange, chiasm and intercalation.[19] Roadhs and Michie identify particularization as the most pervasive stylistic feature of Mark while Dewey considers chiasm.[20] In the Markan story, the narrator is omniscient and knowledgeable reporting all the public and private events, outer and inner world of the characters, which renders credibility and reliability to what he says

[16] cf., D. RHOADS - J. DEWEY - D. MICHIE, p. 3.

[17] cf., K. SYREENI, *Peter as Character and Symbol in the Gospel of Mathew*, in D. RHOADS – K. SYREENI (eds.), p. 265.

[18] J. A. GRASSI, p. ii.

[19] cf., D. RHOADS - J. DEWEY - D. MICHIE, pp. 47-49; J. DEWEY, "Mark as Interwoven Tapestry: Forecasts and Echoes for a listening Audience", *CBQ* 53(1991), pp. 221-236, 224; M. A. POWELL, *What is Narrative Criticism?*, Fortress Press, Minneapolis, 1990, pp. 32-43.

[20] cf., J. DEWEY, "The Literary Structure of the Controversy Stories in Mark 2:1-3:6", *JBL* 92 (1973), pp. 394-401.

and narrates to the implied reader. He guides the narratee. He becomes the agent of the identity suggestion and makes the reader to respond positively to the story.[21] The reader gets into the story world and assumes the evaluative point of view by the implied author. The evaluative point of view is the standard of judgement that consists of author's norms, values and general worldview, which is established as operative for the discourse of the story. This suggestion of the point of view is to make the reader to get close to and identify with the good values and to get distanced from counter antagonistic values.

Taking into account these rhetorical principles and approaches of a story and discourse, for the purpose here, we need to analyse only the characters of the Markan story. The narrative criticism will animate the textual reading to decode the Markan characterization of characters, their roles, distinct positions and responses, values and viewpoints represented by them and their impact in the implied reader, by understanding the analogical tapestries that build characters in the story unit. As the social identity theory proposes, the characterisation of the individuals in a group sociologically leads us to the characterization of the group to which they belong and that would subsequently pave the way for categorising them as in-groups and out-groups according to the values they represent. Since we need an immediate introduction to the application of this analytical method in reading the Markan text, the more of its relevance and operations in making of the Markan characters will be outlined as a preface to the fourth chapter of this work.

Before ending this introductory part, it is quite a need to clarify a suspicion, that is, why the literary mode of exegesis becomes relevant to Mark instead of the traditional method of redaction criticism. After assessing the investigations of three major scholars[22] on radactive elements in Markan disciples, Black C. Clifton suggests that, "... [the] redaction criticism does not work when applied to the second Gospel."[23] The main objection is that, there is no evident and prior source of tradition to which Mark would have dependent on. So, it would be mere hypothetical to distinguish between what is traditional and what is redactional. Mark in itself is self-evident of its tradition. The tradition and the interpretation or the radactive act of Mark are 'overlapping and influencing one another that makes it impossible to discover clear cut original sayings.'[24] This contention leads us more closely to the fundamental rule of the biblical exegesis that, "the interpreter must be obedient to the text itself; that is, he or she must allow the texts to

---

[21] cf., M. A. POWELL, pp. 25-26.

[22] Robert P. Meyer, Ernest Best, Theodore J. Weeden.

[23] B.C. CLIFTON, *The Disciples According to Mark: Markan Redaction in Current Debate*, JSOT Press, Sheffield, 1989, pp. 246-255.

[24] P. J. J. BOTHA, p. 41.

determine their interpretation. The understanding of a text must be "standing under", listening to, and hearing the text, not one's own voice."[25]

The above opinion does not sound any making of the redaction criticism impaired, as Norman Perrin has commented, this new literary criticism is the heir to the redaction criticism, mutating into "a genuine literary criticism."[26] Both are complimentary to each other because the intra-textual meaning resulted by the narrative criticism and the extra-textual referents used by the historical critical method, together contribute a holistic meaning to the text. Integration of the two methods is adopted in this research. It will infer the meaning of the discipleship intended by the evangelist with the help of the Redaction Criticism when the narrative criticism employs to disclose the characters and their viewpoints. Despite his expression of non-appreciation for the redaction criticism in Mark, B. Clifton appreciates the nuanced and cogent redactional exegesis of Ernest Best than of others, so that, this study is a bit lenient to Best in perceiving the Markan redactional hand.

Plan of this Book

The first chapter is an exposition of the scholarly views on the Markan community. The most representative authors are classified into three categories according to their position regarding the location of the community: Roman, Galilean and Syro-Palestinian audience.

The second chapter explains the social identity model especially the essential elements that would interpret the identity of a group: valorative, cognitive and emotional aspects. Since, the text is the point of departure of search for the group identity from where we are led to the context of the group, this chapter is dedicated to explain what the social/collective memory is and how it functions in the formation of the ancient texts. The social memory theory will elucidate that Mark is using the collective memory of Jesus' tradition to articulate the identity of his group at a particular point of time.

The third and fourth chapters concentrate on the reading of the text. The third chapter will evince out the meaning of discipleship (what Jesus speaks about following him, mainly the discourse on discipleship 8:34 -10:45) as the main category assumed of the Markan community. Here, the norms, values and attitudes of following Jesus that mark the constitutive factors of group identity are explained in general. The fourth chapter will deal with the characterization of disciples, crowd, minor characters along with the opponent characters (Jesus' family, priests) and show how some configure with the norms of discipleship and how the others are indifferent. The principle of social comparison will help

[25] G. M. TUCKER, "Editor's forward" in KRENTZ, *The Historical-Critical Method*, (Guides to Biblical Scholarship: Old Testament Series) Fortress Press, Philadelphia, p. v., in B.C. CLIFTON, p. 250.

[26] J. R. DONAHUE, p. 4.

this study to expose the conflicting tension between the in-group (disciples and minor characters) and out-group and further more to expose how Mark creates prototypical figures (mostly minor characters of in-group) as paradigms of the discipleship to his community. The literary situations in the text that Mark uses to expose those exemplary paradigms will mirror in turn the concrete situation, crisis and challenges of the community that had probably made Mark to teach the 'lessons of following' to his group.

The last chapter will be a synthesis of the whole study to define the social identity of the community. There we try to answer the basic questions corporately. What is the social identity of the Markan community intrinsic to the Gospel of Mark? What occurred to the Markan group to have a Gospel at the particular point of time? What could have been the immediate historical context of the Markan community?

Chapter 1

AUDIENCE OF MARK: A BRIEF SURVEY ON SCHOLARLY VIEWPOINTS

Reconstructed communities behind Gospels are hermeneutically necessary to read Gospels rightly.

(Peterson, *Origin of Mark*, 202)

This chapter is a presentation of the scholarly research on the community of Mark with their variegated colors of approaches, arguments and positions in an encapsulated manner. Their positions on the provenance of the Markan Gospel and the social and religious identity, demarked through diverse exegetical methods, would certainly guide this study. Here, I do not claim to have an exhaustive account of all the authors and viewpoints on the Markan community but only an attempt to present some representative authors and their remarkable viewpoints, especially the recent developments of the research. The inquiry of the scholarly survey prevails upon this section to classify their hypothetical positions mainly on three divisions; Roman audience, Syrian/Palestinian audience and Galilean audience of the Gospel of Mark. In short, "most scholars think Mark wrote to a community or communities comprised of both Judeans and Gentiles."[1] The same materials narrated in the Synoptic Gospels with changes and differences, says that those redactions and additions were due to the priorities that evangelists had for their community.[2] If this were the opinion of the majority, what would be its

[1] D. RHOADS - J. DEWEY - D. MICHIE, *Mark as Story: An Introduction to the Narrative of a Gospel* (2nd ed.), Fortress Press, Minneapolis, 1999, p. 2.

[2] E. BEST, *Mark: The Gospel as Story*, T & T Clark, Edinburgh, 1983, p. 4.

contrasting minority-opinion? This question is to be clarified before we set for the scholars' major opinion for a single historical community of Mark.

The Community or Communities?

Richard Bauckham, challenging the standard assumption in the NT scholarship of respective communities for each Gospel, proposes a groundbreaking thesis that 'the Gospels were written with the intention that they should circulate all the churches and not for a specific definite group. He attributes a wider readership for the Gospels with due evidence, locating it in the various scattered Christian communities or groups of the first century.'[3]

His proposition is based on some presumptions and reasons as follows. Firstly, as Bauckham says, the context out *of which* and the context *to which* the Gospels were written, should not be assumed to be one and the same. In short, *the model for* and *the model of* motifs of the Gospels are different. Secondly, so far scholars were misguided because of the Pauline letters that were addressing to particular communities. The Pauline letters were a substitution for his presence, but regarding the Gospels, they were formed out of the oral tradition of the communities in which they had been residing, so there would not have been the need to write what was already present in the community. Thirdly, Bauckham's positive evidence for the encyclical Gospels is the 'cosmopolitanism' of the ancient world and the 'ecumenical' consciousness of the ancient churches.[4] The Gospel authors were not 'insulars of sectarian communities but belonged to a world of networks of communication, for the transmission of their messages for all the 'nations' according to the spirit of *the Gospel*' (13:10). In his own words, "...all the evidence we have for early Christian leaders (the kind of people who might have written Gospels) shows them to have been typically people who traveled widely and worked in more than one community at different times, the outlook and concerns of neither the early Christian communities not their teachers would have been locally confined. Both had a lively and informed sense of participation

[3] R. BAUCKHAM (ed.), *The Gospels for All Christians: Rethinking the Gospel Audiences*, Eerdmans, Grand Rapids, 1998, pp. 1-48.

[4] cf., *Ibid.*, p. 26. His position was shown affectionate by a few authors like Michael F. Bird and recently Hengel. Bird argues for a wider readership because, firstly, there lacks internal evidence and exists ambiguity in the text that if it was written 'for' or 'about' or 'in' a community; secondly, John Mark had a wider experience of communities by his missionary journey as tradition attests; thirdly, never a narrative like Markan Gospel is adequate to address crisis and challenges. Because of the imprecision of date and location of the Gospel, "the possibility of identifying and retrieving a markan community from the Markan text remains virtually impossible..." cf., M. F. BIRD, *The Markan Community, Myth or Maze? Bauckham's* "The Gospel for All Christians Revisited", *JTS* 57 (2006), pp. 474-486. M. Hengel says, "contrary to a widespread view, none of the four Gospels was written only for one particular community; far less do they simply reproduce the views of on individual community". M. HENGEL, *The Four Gospels and the One Gospel of Jesus Christ: An Investigation of the Collection and Origin of the Canonical Gospels,* Trinity Press International, Harrisburg, 2000, p. 106., in the review of the book by J. West in *JBS* 3/2 (April 2003), pp. 63-66.

in the worldwide movement...Would not an author who believed so strongly in the necessity of worldwide proclamation have been interested in seeing his own encapsulation of the good news travel as far a field as possible?"[5]

We have to understand Bauckham's position rightly. He does not challenge the existence of a Markan community, as Michael Bird says, but "...merely challenges the notion that the Gospels were addressed to single communities with no thought of wider disseminations."[6] The relevant question of Bauckham, to put in our transcribed phrase, is, did Mark write the Gospel for his particular community? Though he speaks of all the Gospels in general terms, we look at the response to his thesis, in view of our theme – Markan community. We would herein look at some scholarly responses and rebuttals to his position.

As Philip Esler evaluates, Bauckham is doing an anachronistic and ethnocentric retrospection of modern assumptions onto ancient data, which accompanies it. It weakens his thesis. In view of the group-oriented culture of the Mediterranean world, it is socially realistic to imagine such traveling of evangelists but was to represent the views of the congregation with which he was closely related, than to think that he was largely an independent free agent.[7]

According to Joel Marcus, it may be right to speculate that eventually the Gospel would reach to a wider readership as Matthew and Luke had used it but it is not right to say that Mark had this as his sole intention. The Gospel was a teaching tool, for first instance, to his community. The analogy of the Shepherd of Hermas, as used by Bauckham, is relevant, but primarily it was written for the pastors in Rome before it was circulated. It was customary that even the Jewish counterparts of the Gospel communities had writings written particularly for them as, for example, Qumran scrolls were written for the community of Essenes in the Judean wilderness.[8]

The plurality of synoptic Gospels and its similarities suggest that they were written in and for different churches, addressing specific crisis and predicaments of the community to which evangelists belonged. The churches were independent. The existence of local manuscripts stands as evidence for this (eg. Alexandrian, Western, Byzantine) in spite of their obvious debt to a common tradition. Moreover some proper names in the Gospel like Alexander, Rufus that refer to the persons of a particular community whom known to their compatriots.[9]

We can argue here in anticipation for a particular community of Mark because the Gospel addresses certain particular crisis and situations confronted by

---

[5] R. BAUCKHAM, pp. 3, 26.

[6] M. F. BIRD, p. 476.

[7] cf., P. F. ESLER, "Community and Gospel in Early Christianity: A Response to Richard Bauckham's 'Gospel for All Christians'", *SJT* 51 (1998), pp. 235-248.

[8] cf., J. MARCUS, *Mark 1-8*, (AB) – Double day, N.Y. – London – Sydney – Auckland, 2000, pp. 26-27.

[9] cf., *Ibid.*, pp. 25-28.

the community and Markan Gospel had become an agenda of meeting them in a specific context rather than meeting the universal problems. The author wouldn't necessarily be well cognizant of all the problems of all the communities and also he had not probably been authorized in status to address other communities to which he did not belong. The problems of the communities though might have had some global nature, varied locally according to the particular cultural and religious situations.

Philip Esler's strongest rebuttal is that, Bauckham's position is based on only two possibilities – evangelists wrote for a specific community or for circulating for a wider communities – missing to consider the third one, 'that each evangelists might have primarily shaped their Gospel in accordance with the faith and understanding of their respective local community, predicting that it would travel further afield, in which case they hoped that their version would compete with and even supplant the unsatisfactory Gospel of others.'[10]

The NT scholarship of the Markan community construction is in no way at stake by the Bauckham's position, rather it remains an instigation and contributive for a more thorough search for it. Now we switch on to the opinions of the majority who believes that Markan Gospel was meant for a particular community.

A Roman Audience to Mark

It is traditionally believed that the first readers of the Gospel of Mark were Roman gentile Christians. Martin Hengel[11] is one of the pioneers in this regard, to mark out its location and date with precision. His task was out of conviction on the availability of both external and internal evidences.

Argument for Authorship and Date

Normally the testimony of Papias[12] is dismissed as an attribution of apostolic authority to the Mark's Gospel in 120-130 C.E. But, Hengel looks at it differently as a critical remark of Mark's Gospel which was written without "order". This critical view of Papias at the apostolic tradition becomes ironically, for Hengel, an authentic evidence for the location of Mark's audience and for the authorship of the same. As Peter's interpreter, Mark recollected his instructions, which had already been adapted to his audience in Rome. Moreover, Clement of Alexandria

---

[10] cf., P. F. ESLER, pp. 235-248.

[11] M. Hengel develops his argument of Roman location for Mark in his work "Studies in the Gospel of Mark." cf., M. HENGEL, *Studies in the Gospel of Mark*, Fortress Press - SCM, Philadelphia - London, 1985 ; D. SENIOR, ""With Swords and Clubs ...": The Setting of Mark's Community and His Critique of Abusive Power", *BTB* 17 (1987), pp. 10-20; P. J. J. BOTHA, "The Historical Setting of Mark's Gospel: Problems and Possibilities", *JSNT* 51 (1993), pp. 27-55; J. MARCUS, "The Jewish war and the Sitz im Leben in Mark", *JBL* 111(1992), pp. 441-462 ; E. P. SANDERS – M. DAVIES, *Studying the Synoptic Gospels*, SCM Press – Trinity Press, London – Harrisburg, 1989, pp. 3-24.

[12] *Eccl. Hist.*, 2:15.1,2; cf., Eusebius' reference to Clement and Papias; (1 Pet 5:13).

and Origen bolster Mark's link to the direct witness of Peter and this link between Mark and Peter insists Hengel to conclude that John Mark in antiquity is the same Mark of the second Gospel (Acts 12:12; 1Pet 5:13; Dialogue, Justin 106:3). Hence, this external evidence makes Hengel to say that Mark's origin was after late sixties C.E. at the end of Peter's career in Rome. He enumerates enough internal evidences to show that Mark had a pre- 70 C.E. setting.[13] Moreover, the chapter thirteen is not a *vaticinium ex eventu* but inspired by the Jewish apocalyptic motifs and scenario in the Book of Daniel, as well as the chaotic political and cultural situation of the time. The text does not show any familiarity with the actual event of the Judean war and destruction of the temple, as in Mathew and Luke (Mt 21:33-43 ; Lk 19:41-44). Best differs from Hengel in his opinion on date of Mark, for he holds that, it had origin in Rome and addressed to Roman household Christians probably after the fall of Jerusalem in 70 C.E. Similarly, Incigneri's latest monograph also advocates for a post 70 C.E. Roman provenance of Mark.[14]

The internal linguistic[15] evidence like Aramaism and Latinism are contributing textual elements to tell about the authorship and location. Aramaism argues for a Palestinian Jewish Christian author and Latinism rules out any provenance of the Gospel from Syria. The geographical inaccuracies of the Markan Gospel regarding Galilee, is a proof that author is John Mark who is from Jerusalem unknown very well of Galilee, and who have been absent from his native for years at the time of writing the Gospel.

---

[13] For this early date, Hengel shows some internal evidence. They are as follows: it was written in Jesus' generation because in Mk 9:1 , "some" will not taste death before the coming of the son of Man , is contrasted with 1 Cor 15:6 which dated around 53-54 C. E. ; Mk 13:30 speaks about the parousia before the generation is passed away; Alexander and Rufus as the sons of Simon the Cyrene (15:21; Rom 16:13) known to the Markan community; High Priest by name which is dropped by Matthew and Luke indicates that it was written within thirty to forty years of the passion events; there is little traces of hierarchical order of the Church in Mark than Matthew and Luke. The strong evidence for this extracted from the text, is the reflection of interrelationship of various fractions of pre-70 Judaism. "Scribes and Pharisees are not lumped together as in Matthew. The scribes come to Galilee from Jerusalem (3:22; 7:1; 11:18, 27) – prior to 70 C. E. Jerusalem was the most important centre for study of the Torah. Pharisees are introduced along with the Baptist's disciples, both groups characterized as having rigorous piety (2.18). Sadducees are completely absent from the Galilean scene. Herodians are assigned to the territory of Antipas (3:6). The main opponents of Jesus in Jerusalem are members of the Sanhedrin: priests, elders, scribes. All of these alignments, Hengel notes, were destroyed or radically altered after 70 but Mark's tradition still accurately reports the subtle pre 70 differences." cf., D. SENIOR, pp. 11-12.

[14] cf., B. J. INCIGNERI, *The Gospel to the Romans:The Setting and Rhetoric of Mark's Gospel*, Brill, Leaden-Boston, 2003.

[15] Aramaic words : Mk. 3:17 (*boanerges*); 5:41 (*talitha cum*); 7:11, 34; 10:46; 15:22; Latin words : *aulé, legión, spekoulatóra, dénarion*, (7: 4 ;12:14;15:15; 15:39, 44-45; 12:42 ; 2:23 ; 3:6 ; 3:17; 7:11, 34 ; 12:42; 15:16, 42 ; 15:15; 15:19). Other Latin influences are the Mark's references to "Syro-Phoenician" (7:24), a linguistic usage of West especially of Rome; Alexander and Rufus as the sons of Simon the Cyrene (15:21; Rom 16:13).

Argument for Location

For Hengel, the location of the Markan community is Rome. The dominant theme of persecution and suffering make Hengel to position the Markan community as such. The illustration of Mk 13, especially the enigmatic 'anti-christ' figure (13:14) is explained as cryptic figure of Nero.[16] After the massive persecution of Christians under Nero,[17] after the martyrdom of Peter and Paul in Rome, John Mark, following the style and preaching of Peter, created his own unique "precedent-setting presentation of the Kerygma in narrative form."[18]

When he advocates for Rome, he finds due reasons for rejecting the preceding argument to him of Howard Clark Kee for a Syrian audience.[19] Kee argued for the late 60 and pre 70 similar to the proposal of Hengel with the same evidence but parts with him for an alternative location. Kee's strong foundation of arguments was his link of the 'Jewish–Hassidic –Essene – apocalyptic' tradition in Palestinian Judaism with the cynic stoic itinerant style of life in order to construct a rural Syrian setup for the community. Hengel refutes by telling that Kee's construction is by avoiding valuable tradition of Papias and he fails to take into account the presence of Latinism, which would be a great stumble to the Kee's argument. Iersel after his dissecting analysis of the prior studies concludes for Latinism as strong evidence for locating Mark. "My conclusion is that there are no reliable external data about the date and place of composition, and that none of the internal indications provides conclusive evidence either. Still, what evidence there is – the influence of spoken Latin on the Greek of Mark and especially the book's focus on persecutions – seems to support the hypothesis that Rome is the most likely place of the origin of Mark's Gospel? Even if Mark was not written in Rome but on the east coast of the Mediterranean basin in 65 CE, there is little doubt that the Gospel was read by Roman Christians in the seventies."[20]

---

[16] Incigneri is also much fond of decoding the cryptic symbolic meaning of the text in favour of Roman audience, historical figures and socio-political situation.

[17] The reference to war and rumors in chapter 13 reflects the situation of 68-69 C. E. in Rome. Tacitus in *Annals* 15:44.4 describes the Neronian strategy of persecuting the Christians. He used the denunciation of Christians by their fellow Christians as basis for persecution. It reflects Markan account of betrayal of family. Famine, earthquakes are reported in antiquity, in Italy.

[18] D. SENIOR, p. 13.

[19] cf., H. C. KEE, *The Community of the New Age: Studies in Mark's Gospel*, The Westminster Press, Philadelphia – Pennsylvania, 1977, pp. 75-105.

[20] cf., B. M. F. VAN IERSEL, *Mark: A Reader Response Commentary*, T & T Clark, London – N.Y., 2004, pp. 30-49. Also see, B. WITHERINGTON III, *The Gospel of Mark: A Socio-Rhetoric Commentary*, Eerdmans, Grand Rapids – Cambridge, 2001, pp. 20-36. Helmut Koester is also in favour of the Roman provenance of the Gospel, because of its gentile- Christian environment. He points out specific reasons like, insignificance to Peter's authority in Mark; the priority of the passion Christology to the 'divine man' belief prevalent in Syria as another point unfavorable to Syrian provenance; the urgency of the expectation for the Son of man; the Christology as the ordering principle according to which the materials are arranged and the Cross perspective under which the

Argument for the Situation and Purpose of the Community

At the backdrop of Hengel's proposition, D. Senior constructs the hermeneutical presentation of the Gospel and its historical purpose. The Gospel is a prototype for the community deploring the oppressive powers of the ruling authorities against the life-giving power of Jesus, the Son of God. Ched Myer's political reading of the Markan Gospel, who also advocates for Roman location,[21] is closer to this reading of Senior. This theological importance becomes effective to a community that had been torn apart from within and outwith due to the situation of persecutions and apostasy. The frightened and divided community, that lost two pillars of leaders and uncertain about the future due to the political chaos, had to be consoled at the situation of temor. By reading this Gospel against the abusive political power and religious authority contra-positioned to the pronounced hope in the dominion of God's reigning power, Senior finds the Roman location appropriate for its community.[22] So far, the purpose of the Gospel was influenced by the outside factors to the community but Ernest Best's explanation would be slightly distinct from this view, in finding out the concrete situation within the community that necessitated the Gospel.

Ernest Best is curious of the internal evidences of occasion for the origin of the Gospel. "Strictly speaking the death of eye-witnesses in Rome could be regarded [as external occasion], ...what is in mind is rather something which was going on while Mark was actually writing: some pastoral need of the community or some threat to its unity, stability or orthodoxy coming from within it, or possibly indeed from without yet from within some other part of the church."[23] The Roman Church that has been suffering from the pain of persecution was guarded by the 'good news' of encouragement in securing its faith.[24] At the face of persecution, it tends to fall easily into false understanding of faith and even to give up the community. Hence, persecution as such is not the direct cause of the Gospel.[25] E. Best does not attribute any historical event as a direct cause

discipleship is valued. cf., H. KOESTER, *Ancient Christian Gospels: Their History and Development*, SCM - Trinity, London - Philadelphia, 1990, pp. 289-292. Richard L. Rohrbaugh includes Koester among those who support Syria or upper Galilee provenance.

[21] cf., C. A. EVANS, Review of the book of Peterson, *The Origin of Mark: The Markan Community in Current Debate*, in RBL 12/05/2001 in http://www.bookreviews.org.(accessed 02 March, 2006).

[22] cf., D. SENIOR, pp. 10-20.

[23] E. BEST, p. 34.

[24] A similar opinion comes from Kelber. The Gospel occasion was due to the failure of the oracular prophets (Mk. 7:1-23; 8:34-9:1; 9:35-50; 10:23-31.) to give a proper guidance to the community and thus it was a need for Mark to reconstitute the "stability and reliability" and restore "the authority of Jesus as one essentially belonging to the past." cf., W. H. KELBER, *The Kingdom in Mark: A New Place and a New Time*, Fortress Press, Philadelphia, 1974, pp. 129-144.

[25] Best responds to Van Iersel's proposal of persecution as direct motif in Mark (4:17; 10.29; 13:9-13; the two storm stories (4:35-41; 6:45-52) metaphorically assure the rescue of the

of the Gospel as above said factors like death of eyewitnesses, fall of Jerusalem and persecutions, or threat to the divine man Christology; they are only a few contributory factors.

According to the Letter to Romans we see that the situation seems so peaceful and 'Christian', then what occasioned to have a Gospel, a different genre than epistle, for this community?[26] V. Iersel reckons with T. Radcliffe's[27] position to answer this question. The Neronian persecution caused crisis in the community; they had remorse and shame in the world because Christians betrayed their fellow Christians to their authorities. Those who survived persecution felt guilty and agony of frustrations. "They needed figures with whom they could identify themselves and who could help them come to terms with their failure."[28] It was in this context Mark wrote his Gospel, which deals with betrayal by relatives, persecutions, theme of failure, and examples of following as well as the followers who failed. This situation made Incigneri to view Mark's Gospel as "pathetic", for it engaged in meeting the emotional needs of the Christians that faced persecution as well as their readmission of those who had given up the community.[29] He makes a difference in his view, by explaining the cause of stress as the destruction of temple

community by Jesus at the storm of persecution. For Best, persecution was "endemic" to the life of early Christians so the discourse on discipleship (8:34-38) should be put at the center of the Gospel. With this analogy, Best affirms that it would be unwise to consider Markan community as a fishing community since he used a simile of fishing for discipleship or an agrarian community since he used the parable of sower and seed. Mark primarily used the tradition that was available to him and his purpose was to be distinct from the literary nature of the used traditional materials. cf., E. BEST, pp. 3-8.

[26] Iersel relies on the account of Paul in Romans to outline the image of the Markan community in Rome. Claudius' edict against Roman Jews actually spared the non-Jewish Christians undisturbed. Later the expelled Christians Jews with the other Jews returned to the city in 54 CE and they found a gentile Christian community that was fairly large and structured (Rom 16, 1:8). Ever since this, the community became household (Rom 16:4,5 ; 14; 15) constituted of noble citizens, slaves, freed persons - a household communities of diverse cultural and social background (Rom 16). Their household gatherings were not open to outsiders; they were gathered at unusual and nocturnal hours, prayed, given instructions, sung together, had breaking of bread ritual and initiation rite with water, called one another brothers and sisters characterized by the praxis of common sharing, household code, solidarity, collection of money to help the poor ect. They did not participate in the public life, visit theatres and circus, sporting events. Some refrained from buying and eating sacrificial food. The keeping aloof from public life implied a disapproval of life style of an average roman citizen so that they were accused of being godless with no temples, despised and unworldly. cf., B. M. F. VAN IERSEL, pp. 23-30.

[27] cf., B. M. F. VAN IERSEL, "Failed Followers in Mark: Mark 13.12 as Key for the Identification of the Intended Readers", *CBQ* 58(1996), pp. 244-263. In this article, Iersel search for more convincing evidences of Radcliffe's argument.

[28] B. M. F. VAN IERSEL, *Mark*, p. 52.

[29] cf., B. J. INCIGNERI, p. 247; cf., K. D. Dyer, ABR, Vol. 54, 2006, in www.fbs.org; D.N.Peterson, RBL, 01/2005 in www.bookreviews.org.; M. F. Bird, RBL, 11/2005, in www.bookreviews.org. (accessed 09, June 2006).

during the Vespian period by Titus and his return to Rome disseminated fear among the Christians, especially of betrayal by their relatives before authorities.[30] Incigneri decodes many Markan cryptic codes written for the feared community, which was under the political pressing of Rome.

Unlike above authors, B. Witherington tries to explain the ethnic nature of the Roman community. As regard to the ethnic make up of the Markan audience, (Rom 16:13 = Mk 15:21) "it would appear that, at the end of 40s, Jewish Christians had to leave Rome for a period of time (Acts 18). By the late 50s, when Paul writes to Rome, it appears, the audience is mixed, but gentiles appear to be dominant (cf. Rom.11 and 16). If we move forward another decade and examine Mark's Gospel, we find him having to explain not only Aramaic words but also Jewish customs. This surely suggests that he assumes the majority of his audience is gentile Christians. These Christians were facing not merely marginalization in their own culture but possibly even execution."[31] Witherington sees the interconnection between those two poles, that is, the Jesus tradition of Galilee and the situation set up by Mark to define the crisis and articulate the response of his community in Rome. In the above said situation, "Mark must explain to them the way of the Cross that Jesus took, and the way the first disciples failed to follow his example. The message seems clear – follow the example of Jesus and avoid the mistakes of the first disciples."[32]

A Siro-Palestinian Audience to Mark

In the above section of the Roman audience, we were following a thematic order in evincing out the scholars' opinions and arguments, while in this section, we would follow an authorial order, because in the former it was preoccupied with the location and date preferably with the persecution elements, but for the latter, the concern is more on the social nature of the community and its corresponding historical situations. The arguments for the Roman provenance are homogeneous but, here authors have their own hermeneutical approaches, even sometimes for the same issues of the community. Here analyze the views of important authors namely H. C. Kee, B. L. Mack, G. Theissen, R. L. Rohrbaugh and J. Marcus.

Sectarian Approach

Howard Clark Kee viewed the Markan community in sectarian colours. He perceives the disciples in the Markan Gospel as portrayal of the Markan Community. Markan community is an eschatological one marked by a radical way of life. The disciples who abandoned family and means of livelihood to follow Jesus, had a prophetic and charismatic mission continuing the pattern of old covenant prophets of Elijah, Elisha and John the Baptist. They are bound to gather

---

30 cf., *Ibid.*

31 B. WITHERINGTON III, pp. 35-36.

32 cf., *Ibid.*

the community in preparation for the eschatological judgment.[33] Mark does not initiate any discontinuity with then existing eschatological hope but emphasizes the redefining of the continuity between the prophetic and charismatic mission of Jesus and of his disciples amidst the transitional phase of generations.

For Kee, the Markan community was a group advocated for a social transformation. This is evident from the Markan radicalism expressed in the discipleship, consists of breaking of family ties in view of an eschatological family. Mark hosts even antagonistic factors[34] to project this existence of a new eschatological family inaugurated by Jesus' movement. To what they have detached is being replaced with the 'new family' at large. The disciples, who follow Jesus foregoing their possessions, intrinsically foresee this promised reward of an extended communal family and their generosity.

Tracing the call narratives, Kee assesses the economic status, though uncertain, of the Markan community, to suggest that those of the community were not at the bottom of the economic scale, as some of the disciples owed boats of their own and even hired men, some were tax collectors. Moreover, the topographic references in the text indicate an urban village life of the Markan community. Most surprising elements of communal transformation reflected in the attitude, as observed by Kee, of openness to the children and women even to accept gentile women to the communion of the community. The earliest concern of the narrative, the ministration of women, is sustained even until the concluding parts of his narration that pre-shadows the women's status in the community.

Kee assesses the community of Mark as esoteric in nature. "Like Hasidim of two centuries earlier, Markan community was convinced that God had granted to it special revelation so that it could understand the goal and the intervening stages in the fulfillment of his purpose for the creation."[35] For Kee, not all the clandestine and secretive passages could be considered as messianic secret. Therefore, secret motif is not that Jesus heals and performs exorcism, because they are very public and well known. The messianic secret is the suffering of the Son of Man (8:30) who is to be vindicated by God (9:9) and his resurrection. The messianic secrecy has exclusively been revealed to the community of disciples who are privileged to bear basic information of the identity of Jesus. Mark is not inventing this for the community but reflects what owned already by his community from Jesus

---

[33] For these disciples, Jesus is a rabbi, not the one who interprets the Torah but who resembles the Qumran teacher of Righteousness who redefines the People of God and its future eschatological fate. cf., H. C. KEE, pp. 77-173.

[34] The traditional families and cultural religious traditions are antagonistic factors. cf., *Ibid.* For a detailed exposition of this theme, see S. GUIJARRO OPORTO, *Fidelidades en Conflict: La Rupture con la Familia por causa del Discipulado y de la Misión en la Tradición Sinóptica*, UPSA, Salamanca, 1998; Idem, "La Familia en el Moviemiento de Jesus", *EstBib*, 61 (2003), pp. 65-83.

[35] H. C. KEE, pp. 93-94. *Parabole* (4:11) for Mark is enigma, not metaphor or allegory (4:34). This view is extended throughout Mark (*kat' idian* 7:33, 9:18, 10:10, 23; 8:30; 9:2; 13:5). Most remarkable among them are the reference to 11:1-10; 14:12-16; 6:52; 8:14-21. cf. *Ibid.*

tradition. The secrecy is central and pervasive understanding of the community itself and of Jesus, that has been revealed to those ought to be "little ones" - believers- and not to the powerful (9:33 – 10:16).

From the literal reading of the apocalyptic chapter 13, it is normally considered that Markan community is exclusive that had been waiting an imminent end of the age. To its contrary, Kee, considering the hyperbolic language of the apocalyptic theme, sense a call for an awareness of a profound potency of the community to continue the mission of Jesus even to an extent of gentile lands like Jesus traveled to Sidon and Decapolis (3:8). He sees this inclusive feature on the far side of usual exclusivism. "The gentile mission of the Markan church has precedence and assurance of success in the ministry of Jesus as Mark portrays it. The important space devoted to setting aside the ritual laws of Jewish separateness (7:1-30) both in precept and in action shows that this was an issue for Mark's community, but one on which a firm position had been taken: the community was open across social economic, sexual and ethnic barriers."[36]

Howard Kee speaks about the historical context of the Markan community placing it among the prominent Jewish sects of the first century CE. The above-mentioned important features of the community conferred an identity to be different from other sects. It brought them troubles too. In the context prior to the first Jewish revolt (66-70 CE), there have been various modes of responses from the Jewish sects to the socio-political situation. One of them comprised of collaborating with the existing roman political dominion and its allies consequently to be conformed to the Greco-roman way of life, as the herodians did. The other has been a mode of collaboration, being aversive to the foreign rule by way of passive acquiescence, as the Pharisees did.[37] However, the Markan community was different from these "leavens of herodians and Pharisees" (8:15), but in no way was passive or indifferent to the situation. As Kee observes, the striking distinctiveness of the Markan community was its positive attitude on defilement, inclusiveness, belief in forgiveness and in its Christological belief, albeit its resemblances to the Essenes groups. Moreover, never could it be compared in view of identity, with the insurrectionist groups who represented a nationalist reaction of the first century Palestine. The Palestine land was insecure by sudden and frequent uprising and major revolts ensuing bloodshed suppressions. It was even extended to the Hellenized Jewish costal cities as Josephus mentioned.[38] As a result, a contagion of fear and suspicion was prevalent. At this situation, the Markan community, being repugnant and unacceptable to all other sects, had a claim of prophetic promise concerning the new covenant (14:24). It found itself to be defined as a radically alienated social group that could expect suspicion and hostility from

[36] *Ibid.*, p. 97.

[37] They were withdrawn themselves to their own business of personal and group piety and purity, being unaffected of any political and eschatological concerns. It was a lukewarm attitude.

[38] cf. H. C. KEE, p. 99.

fellow Jews and gentiles. "It was in such an era and in this sort of climate that the Gospel of Mark is most likely to have been written, to offer understanding and encouragement to this segment of primitive Christianity. Mark selected from the tradition available to him, formulating on his own the sequence of material with the emphases that set out the disciples in their perplexity and misunderstanding, in their favored position as recipients of divine mysteries and revelations, and as the paradigms of his own community in its critical situation."[39]

In respect to the geographical setting of the Markan community, "the linguistic character as a whole, points to a locale where Greek is the common language, although its cultural level is quite low and traces of a Semitic influence are evident."[40] Irrespective of its origin of the tradition, it shows that Mark "is writing from within a circle for whom Aramaic expression would serve neither scholarly interest in historical precision nor antiquarian curiosity but would enable the reader to identify more fully with the poignant and powerful narrative than a purely Greek account could accomplish."[41] From these characteristics of the text, Kee believes in a rural agrarian Syrian-Palestinian community.[42] Therefore, "Markan community from its base in rural and small town southern Syria held out the hope of a covenant people whose fidelity would be rewarded by God in the very near future."[43]

Philosophizing the Markan Situation

The magnificent work of Burton L. Mack[44] on the origins of Christian communities establishes the concern of origins of Mark at the background of general questions on the origins of Christian congregations and characteristic of Christian followers. We have an obvious picture of his view on the Markan

---

[39] *Ibid.*, p. 100.

[40] *Ibid.* Mk 9:1; 10:29; 13:30; 14:25; 3:28; 9:41; 10:15; 11:23, 9:14; 8:12; 12:23; 14:9; 14:18.

[41] *Ibid.*, p. 102.

[42] He partially supports the reasons of Lohmeyer, Lightfoot and Marxsen, in this regard, who further specify immediate setting as Galilee to the Markan community. The rural properties of the Markan text and certain archeological evidences on Galilee support their views. But, the geographical inconsistencies of Mark consider the author to be unknown of the Galilean typography accurately but only place names. Therefore, Kee has scholarly inhibition to point out Galilee as precise locale, but ascertain that a "Syrian provenance could be accounted." He is careful to rule out another possible hypothesis of Antioch. cf., H. C. KEE, pp.103. Moreover, the "anti-city stance" of Mark is much consonant with the portrayal of Jesus and disciples as itinerant preachers and missionaries in villages, accepting the hospitality that is provided by the habitants (Mk.1:35; 6:46; 14:32, 35, 38, 39). This factor of argument is well supported by the analogy of cynic-stoic charismatic leaders model of Gerd Theissen (At the time when Kee adapted the argument of Theissen, this stand was applicable only to Q community; later Theissen applied it to the Markan community). cf., G. THEISSEN, *Colorido Local y Contexto Historico en Los Evangelios*, Sigueme, Salamanca, 1997, p. 104.

[43] H. C. KEE, p. 103.

[44] cf., B. L. MACK, *A Myth of Innocence*, Fortress Press, Philadelphia, 1991.

community in the final part of his work where he approaches the Gospel as myth, apocalypse, parable and paradigm. Mark is an "intellectual" author who does a rationalization of the great catastrophe of his time that affects also his community.

B. L. Mack illustrates the crucial historical situation of the Markan community. The Jewish war was a decisive event to introspect the identity and the future strategy of the then existing groups and sects of Judea and Palestine. It had painfully embedded a long lasting memory to be philosophized for each group, especially the Christian sect. According to Mack, Jesus' apocalyptic instruction on Mk 13 coincides with the history that is drawn by Josephus.[45] An exception seen in Mark is that there is a mention of expulsion from the synagogue, which would take place before the coming of the Son of Man in power. Thus, Mack hypothesizes that Jesus' people, inherent in the Markan Gospel, might have been "well abuzz of a Jewish war and temor" in the general ambience. But, how this situation is to get connected with the Jesus movement? Have had anything of this crisis of Jerusalem to do with the Jesus' movement? At the back of their mind, there was a painful memory of Diaspora synagogue hostility experienced by the Jesus people, which aroused these presentiments of a Jewish war.

Mack by reading the external social crisis of the time, infers idea about location of the Markan community. Southern Syria in post 70 C.E., would be a place from where could view the happenings of the Jewish war and a community to which it was of great worry. Mack has another reason to claim on to southern Syria than Galilee as the location of Markan community. That is the error in the topographical description of Galilee and the reflected importance of synagogue reform movement in Mark. "Having thought of themselves as sons and daughters of Israel, the failure to find an acceptable arrangement with the Diaspora synagogue meant that the kingdom they talked about hardly represented the sect they had become."[46] This situation occasioned the Jesus-movement to which Mark belonged, to figure out the things in some other ways.[47] Mark's purpose was to tackle the problem of Jesus movement to stand independent of Synagogue.

---

[45] cf., *JW* 5: 21-26,371,424-38,446-52; 6: 288-300,310-315,420-434; 7: 26-36, 153-157. Four categories of apocalyptic predictions in Mark: early signs with warnings vv.5-8, sufferings in the Diaspora with advice vv. 9-13, desolation in Jerusalem with advice vv. 14-23, desolation in creation with advice vv. 24-37.

[46] Antioch is also in question for Mack because of Mark's unappreciative attitude to the "spiritual enthusiasm of the Hellenistic Christianity", though Antioch remained a place of origin of a vibrant Cristic cult. cf., B. L. MACK, pp. 316, 315-323.

[47] Regarding the location, Mack agrees with the Howard Kee, who accepts the Syria Palestine by distancing from the position of Galilee of Lohmeyer and Wrede. But in dating the Gospel, he goes contrary to that of Kee (pre 70 CE Jewish war) who presumes a Markan imagination of the Jewish war even before the end of it and destruction of the temple. It is as if Mark had an inkling of the imminent happenings. Mack prefers to hold Kelber's view of dating Mark to post 70s C.E. as more convincing. However, Kelber looses this perspective in his later work. cf., W. H. KELBER, *The Oral and the Written Gospel*, Fortress Press, Philadelphia, 1983, in B. L. MACK, pp. 315-333.

This is present dramatically through the couched terms of tradition, purity and ritual laws of purity, the code of Jewish identity and their violation by the Jesus' people. Mark has in turn opportune to confirm the legitimacy of the act of Jesus' people. It was to redefine for an alternative time at which the traditionalism was being overtaken by a new independent movement (of Jesus). A new authority (of Jesus) is an overwhelming and supreme to that of the Pharisees and the traditional identifiers, who have mistaken of this new 'covenant'. Mark tries to show that "the epic history would have to be channeled in such a way as to come to fulfillment in Jesus and the Jesus movement. The Jesus movement would have to be distinguished heir of the promise of the epic history."[48] This was the inter-group crisis and challenge of the Jesus movement of Mark.

The intra-group crisis addressed by Mark, according to Mack, seems to be a difficult task to be tackled. Mark was aware of numerous problems[49] in bearing the view on Jesus but in spite of all those, much mind-boggling problem was the internal confusions, regarding time, messianic understanding and excitements, betrayals, denials and apostasies - in a single term, crisis of discipleship. It means the wavering existence of the community, set free to an unsympathetic world of pluralities with its own internal weaknesses. In this situation, Mark was concerned of proposing a conceptual foundation for the continuing existence of his community. It was the crucial time at which he defined the concrete social place and practices of the movement in this world.[50]

Have they had a need for the Markan group of going back to the original charisma? As normal to any social institution in their march on to future, Jesus-group of Mark also was returned to their beginning, in the process of redefinition of their social identity amidst the changing pluralistic world of crisis; "what it was they intended to be and do". 'It was a necessary for Mark to go back to Jesus' authority and his image as leadership by underscoring his distinctiveness.'[51] At the historical background of temor and destruction of the Jerusalem, Mark brought the Jesus-material together, to create the image of Jesus as the King of the Kingdom of God, predicted by the prophets and acknowledge by his Father as the

---

[48] B. L. MACK, pp. 315-333.

[49] Mark was aware of many Christian groups who had claim on Jesus' name and who had different views of community and 'Christology', different sets of community leadership, and inter and intra problems of the growing communities of Jesus of his time.

[50] The table fellowship in the 'new family' system is a place of equality and humility directed by the egalitarian principles of the group. The ethics of service as the rule of behaviour is maintained, even without dispensing the normal codes (of Jewish sensibilities) of fasting, keeping the commandments, doing good and staying married.

[51] The dynamic process of transmission and development of traditional materials of Jesus is referred to by Mack as "logic of the creation of myths of origin of Jesus movements". From what Mark has received from this process of logic, he carved an image of authority in Jesus, which is necessary for the universal effect of the identity and message he suggests for the Christian community. cf., *Ibid.*, pp. 319-323.

legitimate heir of all the promises ever made for Israel among the nations. This image is authorized with an attestation of Mark's rhetorical presentation of Jesus' image as sovereign authority, through the miracle and pronouncement stories before passion narration. This would justify the place and scheme of a small group of Jesus, confused (with in the community) and rejected in the combative world. For fulfilling this purpose, Mark adopts two factors from the mythic tradition: the "logic of martyrdom" and "the logic of martyrdom as a vicarious effective event" which is a pattern of ethics for the Markan community.[52]

Syrian Community

One of the prominent arguments for Syro-Palestine comes from Gerd Theissen.[53] The synchronous closeness to as well as distancing of Palestine in Mark lead him for a profound search of the localization of the community of Mark in Syro-Palestine. His proposition is based on three arguments: 1.) textual indications of socio-topographical milieu, 2.) various original traditions and, 3.) statements of places (geographical errors).

Firstly, the use of the term 'sea' (2:13; 3:7; 1:16; 7:31) which belongs to the tradition is constructed with genitive form (*tēn thalassan tēs Galilaias* = he passed the sea along the Galilee / Sea of Galilee, 1:16) is a typical usage other than Greek and Latin.[54] The ancient Greek and Latin authors qualify sea and lake with adjectives. Moreover, a formation of name with a genitive case of the region is also rare.[55] Therefore, this Markan usage leads us to think of a milieu, where the use of names is determined by Aramaic idioms. Adding weigh to it, the story is fond of rural places in contrast to city, as well as the parabolic expressions are pregnant with the agrarian metaphors and rural set ups, which shows that the author and the immediate readers of the Gospel were familiar with the context characterized by the rural features because 'the world of the narrator is the world of narratee.'[56] Therefore, Syria is more probable than Rome.[57] Secondly, Theissen explains that Mark was indebted to the "pre-and para-Pauline" tradition derived from the Hellenistic Christianity (1:1; 13:10; 14:22-25 *euangéliōn* and tradition

---

[52] cf., *Ibid.*

[53] cf., G. THEISSEN, pp. 263-267, 259-316; Ídem, *Estudios de Sociología del Cristianismo Primitivo*, (trans. F. Ruiz - S. Vidal), Sígueme, Salamanca, 1985, pp. 11-79; Ídem, *El Movimiento de Jesús*, Sígueme, Salamanca, 2005, pp. 35-92.

[54] cf., G. THEISSEN, *Colorido Local y Contexto Histórico en Los Evangelios*, p. 262.

[55] The usage of *lacus Iudaeae* by Pliny is an exception. cf., *Ibid.*, p. 262.

[56] "Si el mundo narrado refleja algo del mundo de los narradores, es difícil imaginar al autor del evangelio de Marcos en la gran urbe de la época". *Ibid.*, p. 263.

[57] Iersel responds to it as "compelling but not convincing." Theissen has not noted the Septuagint usage of 'sea' for both sea and inland lakes. (Num 34:6, Ezek 47-48, also with adjective Ex 10:19, 2 Chr 2:16; 2 Esd 3:7; Num 34:11, Josh 12:3,7;13:27; 8:9; 3:16). Also neither can the frequency of mention about rural regions be accepted as the evidence for the Syrian countryside. cf., B. M. F. VAN IERSEL, *Mark*, pp. 37-38.

of the last supper), traditions of Judea (apocalyptic narration) and Jerusalem (passion narrative) and some popular and discipular traditions. These popular and disciples-traditions of charismatic itinerants had its origin within the limits of rural Palestine than afar at Rome.[58] Paul recollected his traditions from the ambience of Syria where he had been evangelizing for a long period. Hence, these communitarian traditions used by Mark were the original materials of a region other than Rome and so he proposes Syria – Hellenistic Christian ambience - as the origin of the Markan Gospel.[59] Thirdly, the geographical incongruence, especially two among them - position of Gerasa (5:1ff) and traveling "from the region of Tyre,...by way of Sidon towards the Sea of Galilee through the region of Decapolis" (7:31)[60] – in contrary to the common consideration that Mark was ignorant of Palestine, are compatible with the realities. Citing F. G. Lang, Theissen points out that Damascus was part of Decapolis with a common territorial boundary in the thirties of the first century of C.E.[61] and it was permitted to cross Decapolis from Sidon through the Galilean sea.[62] Regarding the dispute of Gerasa, it was part of the city of Decapolis beside the lake with a variant name of Gadara which is an "easy reading" than the Gerasa as "*lectio difficilior.*"[63] Even if they are real, these geographical inexactitudes in narratives were common to a time without map and similar as well to errors commonly found even in the secular narratives of antiquity.[64] The geographical errors and inexactitudes are not accidental out of ignorance but, to Theissen, seem to be intentional and meaningful in relevance to Syria-Palestine, to suit with the Markan ideology of the involvement of the 'Gospel' in the gentile territories. For this, Mark even breaks the geographical logic to make the evangelist's community involved in the narration.[65] With detailed extra referents to the text, the explanation of Theissen

---

[58] In Pauline letters, *euangéliōn* is a frequent term which comes to Paul from the pre-Pauline tradition (1Cor 15:1ff); also the Pauline terminologies are found influencing in the Markan last supper episode (1 Cor 11:23-26 // Mk 14:22-25). cf., G. THEISSEN, *Colorido Local y Contexto Histórico en Los Evangelios,* p. 263.

[59] "Probably the author of Mark was still in contact with these circulating traditions about Jesus and the Baptizer. But such contacts are more likely in Palestine and the neighboring regions of Syria than in distant Rome, especially since some of these popular traditions were formed in the Palestine region (e.g., Mk 5:1-21)." G. THEISSEN, *The Gospels in Context: Social and Political History in the Synoptic Tradition,* (trans. Linda. M. Maloney), T & T Clark, Edinburgh, 1992, p. 240.

[60] This "...makes about as much sense as traveling from Madrid by way of Paris and Vienna to Rome." *Ibid.*, p. 243.

[61] *Nat. Hist.* 5:16.74; *Ant.* 18.153.

[62] cf., G. THEISSEN, *Colorido Local y Contexto Histórico en Los Evangelios* p. 267.

[63] *Ibid.*, 267.

[64] Theissen gives detailed examples for this. cf., *Ibid.*, pp. 267-268.

[65] More textual explanations on geographical, climatic and linguistic factors concerning the text are given by Theissen, among which on' Syrophoenician' is eye-opening information. cf., *Ibid.*, pp. 269-282.

concludes that 'the Gospel of Mark appeared probably in the proximate Syrian regions of Palestine.'[66]

Agrarian Community

Richard L. Rohrbaugh (1995) presumes,[67] following Kee and Theissen that Mark was written in a village or rural context of either Southern Syria, Transjordan, or upper Galilee at a date very close to the events of 70 C.E. He assumes a "contravention" and "correspondence" between the real world of the author/audience and the story world created by the author to locate the social audience of Mark. He uses tools of agrarian model of the social science and stratifies the classes of people in the Herodian period of the first century as to locate Markan audience, through the corresponding internal features of the text and its characters.

Jesus' defense of the disciples subsequent to the Galilean controversies between Jesus-group and Jewish-groups (2:1 – 3: 1-6, 20-35) are texual evidence that reflects the social constrain of the Markan community to identify its social boundaries and identities in the context of war between Jews and Romans.[68] The conflict in the Markan Gospel is a conflict between the elite class and the agrarian group. As Saldarini says, Pharisees were opponents of Jesus movement in acquiring influence among that non-elite group.[69] The communities in the upper Galilee and at the border of southern Syria were forced to make clear of their stand. The apocalyptic chapter (Mk 13) shows the situation that stood prior to the war when Christians might be handed over to the councils and beaten in synagogues in an attempt to force them declare for one side or the other. The reconciliation of Jews and gentiles was opposed by Pharisees on purity grounds and encouraged the same by Romans on the imperialistic grounds. It was the occasion when the Markan community, an agrarian in nature, took its own stand making clear of its identity. The purity tradition was almost a difficult thing for the poor peasants of Jesus' time and they were not following them, to be different from the elite-religious Jews. "Jesus' lifestyle would have thus been familiar to them in every respect (through tradition). His defense of an internal purity that

---

[66] "Mark's Gospel was probably written in Syria near Palestine. It may view Galilee and Jerusalem from the north." G. THEISSEN, *The Gospels in Context,* p. 257-258.

[67] If the Markan Gospel has been written for the urban Rome, then the Markan audience would have been non-elite of the pre-industrial city. If it was written for the places of southern Syria, Transjordan or upper Galilee, then the Markan audience must then be located among largely non-literate peasants in a village or small town context. This is the basis of his presupposition. cf. R. L. ROHRBAUGH, "The Social Location of the Marcan Audience", *BTB* 23(1995), pp. 114-127.

[68] For, purity rules are boundary-setting mechanism in Mark, see, J. NEYREY, "The Idea of Purity in Mark's Gospel", *Semeia* 35(1986), pp. 91-128, in A. J. SALDARINI, *Pharisees, Scribes and Sadducees in Palestinian Society: A Sociological Approach*, Eerdmans – Dove, Michigan – Cambridge, p. 150.

[69] cf., *Ibid.*, pp. 150-151.

could be maintained without heavy expense or the disruption of necessary peasant farming practices would have surprised them indeed...Thus if Mark's Jesus is also defending Mark's community, what is really being provided is a statement that purity before God is possible within the limits of peasant way of life."[70] Hence, the Markan audience is constituted of marginal rural peasants (upper and lower level small free holders, tenants, day laborers, slaves) and, unclean and degraded appalling groups. So little Mark speaks of or has the role for urban non-elite groups.

Jewish-revolt Theory

The author of the Markan Gospel, for Joel Marcus, is likely the one well known to his community,[71] who might preferably have been associated with Pauline tradition. His community was a persecuted community (*thlipsis* 4:16-17, *diōgmōs* 10:30; 13:9-13). Mark appears to have added this notion of persecution later to the tradition he received, for reasons that, the middle section of the Gospel occupies the passion predictions and discourses of discipleship are closely linked with the notion of persecution (8:34-38; 9:42-48; 10:17-31, 38-39). After all, Jesus is the paradigm for the endurance of disciples' suffering. This notion is presented, not just to jolt the complacent situation of the community, rather the text is redolent of the actual situation of persecution (10:30 *nyn en tō kairō*; 13:19 *heōs tou nyn*).[72]

Where this particular persecuted community is to be located? It might have probably been composed at late sixties or early seventies of CE, because many of the elements of persecutions, wars and earthquakes are unique to this period of the Jewish and Roman history and coincide with the secular accounts of the history.[73] However, in contrary to the tendency as we have so far observed that the persecution and Latinism were seen at first sight in the Roman background of Neronian reign (Tacitus's *Annals* 15:44), Marcus veers in explaining them differently. The persecution was neither a unique phenomenon at the time of Markan community or during which Mark wrote his Gospel, nor does that

---

[70] R. L. ROHRBAUGH, p. 124.

[71] cf., J. MARCUS, *Mark 1-8*, (AB) Double day, N.Y. – London – Sydney – Auckland, 2000. The title of the authorship 'The Gospel according to Mark' is a later scribal addition whereas the original title of the author to the Gospel was *archē tou euangeliou Iēsou Christou* [*huiou theou*]. The absence of the author's name in the original text is a sign that the author was personally known to the community and had not necessitated his reference in title.

[72] The raging sea experience, fear of disciples and consoling presence of Jesus are echoes of actual fear and temor of the persecuted community. The change from the "until **that day**" (LXX, Dan 12:1) to "until **now**" (Mk 13) is probably a reflection of the Markan situation. "The "that day" of eschatological tribulation, the like of which the world will never again see, has now become a terrifying reality." cf., J. MARCUS, *Mark 1-8,* p. 29.

[73] cf., I Clement 5:4-7; Ignatius, *Romans* 4:2-3; Irenaeus, *Against Heresies* 3: 3-2; *Eccl.Hist.*2:25-27; *Ant* 20: 200; Tacitus, *Annals* 15: 44,13-17; Mk13:7-13.

mentioned in 13:9-13 necessarily indicate events under Nero. Even before that, there are sources that mention the sporadic persecutions of Christians from the mob.[74] To say precisely, in chapter 13 there is an admonition and advice to the Judeans, after the desolation of the temple, to flee to the mountains and more over this implied reader's note brings to our attention that the first readers could be the Markan readers identified as Judeans.

Unlike the 'Roman hypothesis' which concentrated mainly on the chapter of apocalypses (Mk.13), the Syrian provenance would be supported by the high coherence of both the chapter 13 and the Gospel in general, along with the point of the date of first Jewish revolt in 66-73 C.E. Regarding the war data, Markan account corresponds with the secular history of Jewish war, but regarding the related persecution of Christians, the direct evidence to link it with the Jewish revolt is scarce. Marcus' contention is that, since there is evidence for the persecution of Christians during the second Jewish revolt (2nd cent. or 132-135 C.E.) it is also plausible that Jewish Christians were disturbed due to the gentile–Jewish factors during the first Jewish revolt in Palestine.[75] At the proximity of the first Jewish revolt, Mark uses the past experience of Jewish revolt in the winter of 67-68 C.E., to admonish the impending war and abomination of desolation (Mk 13).[76] So, Mark was composed in a "geographical and temporal proximity" to the Jewish war, i.e., somewhere in the vicinity of Palestine, in the shadow of the destruction of war (either during the war or shortly thereafter). Though it is scarce, Marcus finds some evidence for this thesis in the prophecies of Mk 13, in the contrast in 11:17 between "house of prayer for all nations", and "den of brigands," in the Jew-Gentile theme throughout the Gospel, and in the ambivalent attitude

---

[74] In Judea (Gal 1:13,22); particularly in Jerusalem (Acts 12:1-5; 21:27-36; 23.12-15, *Ant* 20:200) ; in Damascus - Syria (2 Cor 11:32-22, Acts 9:1-2,23); in Asia minor (Acts 13:50; 14:19; 19:24-34) ; in Greece (Acts 16:19-24; 17:5-9,13; 18:12-13). 'hated by all' (Mk 13:13) refers to mob violence. The *Acts of the Apostles* speaks in full length the picture of persecution. For detailed reference, cf. J. MARCUS, *Mark 1-8,* pp. 32-33.

[75] "It is not implausible that they were similarly harassed in the first revolt, which also seems to have been catalyzed by messianic hope. Such persecution would have been especially likely if the church in Jerusalem included some Gentiles, a possibility that gains credence from the apparent reference to Christian evangelism of Judean Gentiles in 1 Thess 2:14-16 ... and from the account of the Apostolic conference in Acts 15, which suggests the openness of the Jerusalem church to Gentiles who observed certain conditions. Such mixed group of Jewish and Gentile Christians would have come under the fire of revolutionaries, since the revolt seems to have been inspired by a theology that was not only anti-roman but also anti-gentile." J. MARCUS, *Mark 1-8,* p. 34.

[76] cf., J. MARCUS, p. 35. The story of zealots rushing into Jerusalem under the leadership of Eleazer claiming over davidic messiahship and thus it became 'the den of brigands or robbers' (*lēstai*). cf., *JW* 4, 5, 6. Mark, is ambivalent to affirm as well as reject the davidic messiahship to Jesus in the story discourse (affirmative 10:47-48; 11:9-11; denial 12:35-37). Mark wants to tell that Jesus is Davidic Messiah, but fulfills that role in a different way through dominion over the satanic power.

toward Davidic messianism.[77] Marcus says that Galilee could be important to Mark and get it prominence in mention, not because it became the site of the community, but it was the historical locus of Jesus' ministry.[78] Therefore, we come to Roman province of Syria, which is contiguous to Palestine. Syria was close enough that the contact with many traditions about Jesus was likely and it was a predominantly Gentile region and an area of Pauline influence.[79] The Gospel might have been written for the Markan community after the flight from Jerusalem, for its re-formation perhaps through the incorporation into an already established, predominantly Gentile church in Syria and probably for the eschatological excitement to remain intense during the temple destruction and the end of the war.

A Galilean Audience to Mark

The arguments for the Galilean audience cohere with those for Siro-Palestinian audience. Here, the scholars are more specific to spot out the immediate context of the Markan community and that seems more adventurous and academic. The given below are the views of eminent scholars namely W. Marxsen, W. H. Kelber and H. N. Roskam, who reserved Galilee as Markan location for modern readers.

Willi Marxsen is one of the pioneers among scholars who locate the Markan community in Galilee, following the legacy of Lohmeyer. His mode of finding the unique place of Galilee in Mark, especially in the three consecutive areas; Jesus activities (Mk 1-9), his transitional phase of Journey to Jerusalem (Mk 10) and passion (Mk 11-16), attest the Markan favoritism for the toponomy of Galilee. All the verses that carry references to Galilee are redactional.[80] His ultimate contention regarding the geographical priority after his study of Markan redaction could be resumed as follows that there is no place mentioned as much important as Galilee and there is no place as frequently mentioned as Galilee in the Gospel. Even when Jesus gets out (1:39) of Galilee (could be the traditional materials), Mark tends to brings him back to Galilee as if he does not want him go out of Galilee for his proclamation. In this motif, the author breaks the topographical logic.[81] For another instance, Marxsen observes that, in 3:7, Mark speaks of people gathered around Jesus from numerous places like Idumea, Jerusalem and beyond Jordan but by presenting Galilee as isolated and primary with a great focus. Other places are subordinate to it. According to Marxsen, following the thought of Lohmeyer, 'there is a place in which those Christians have been gathering and it was more

[77] cf., J. MARCUS, "The Jewish War and the 'Sitz im Leben' of Mark", *JBL* 111 (1992, 3), p. 460.

[78] cf., *Ibid.*, p. 461.

[79] It corresponds with the Theissen's argument. See elsewhere in this chapter.

[80] W. MARXSEN, *El Evangelista Marcos: Estudios sobre la Historia de la Redacción del Evangelio*, Sigueme, Salamanca, 1981, pp. 49-109.

[81] cf., *Ibid.*, p. 57.

probable in Galilee and concretely Mark likes to make that congregation in Galilee. This place is "paradigmatic" or a place that is valid for the Christian believers.'[82]

Marxsen sees in the importance given to Galilee, a theological and eschatological value than any historical, geographical and biographical one. It is a place of imminent parousia. He explains three phases through which one could reach to Galilee. Primarily, the phase of historical Jesus and his activities which were inaugurated in Galilee as the tradition knows it well, yet Marxsen admits the difficulty to decide it with certainty from the tradition and as he presumes that, Galilee had only a very light significance in the tradition. Secondly, the phase of primitive Christian communities for which we need to turn to Pauline accounts. From him, however, the Jerusalem community is known much more than anything about a Galilean primitive community. Lohmeyer holds on to the opinion of a displacement of the Jerusalem community in the later time of the first century to a certain premise of Galilee as for him there were two groups of primitive Christians in Jerusalem and Galilee.[83] The third phase is the stage of Markan community. The orientation of Mark to Galilee is something real and actual which was existing to the time of Mark when he was writing this Gospel. He was the witness to the orientation of the primitive community from Jerusalem to Galilee. The Markan exposition of the importance of Galilee as the centre of Jesus' activities, has some geographical significance in the sense that this region was important in the contemporary epoch of Mark. His interest is, not to express what Jesus has actuated in Galilee, but inversely, where Jesus actuates, there is Galilee. Therefore, Galilee is the place where Christ has actuated and where the parousia will take place. The evangelist's intelligence is clear that for his motif of transmitting the traditional kerygma, he was less careful in the geographical accuracies and data. His only interest was Galilee.

Marxsen's thrust of thought based on the use of the concept "Galilee" and its imposed question is such as, is there behind it a community of Galilee or is it only intended to give an orientation towards Galilee for any community supposedly of Jerusalem?[84] The history of Passion reveals this orientation. Is the motif of the story is on the inhabitation of a community already in Galilee or it would be practically the same march of the community to Galilee that could be waiting in fact for parousia? Marxsen treats the tradition of a community's escape from Jerusalem to Pella in 66 C.E with due skepticism. In this set up of idea, he says that

---

[82] "Hay lugar en el que estos cristianos se congregan el mas de Galilee y concretamente Maracos es quien hace que se congreguen aquí. Entre las comunidades aparece en primer lugar Galilee. Se puede llamar, con Lohmeyer, a ese lugar del evangelio de Marcos "Pragmático" o "lugar valido para la Cristiandad creyente". *Ibid.*, p. 59.

[83] cf., S. GUIJARRO, *Los Primeros Discípulos de Jesús en Galilea*, in *Los Comienzos del Cristianismo* (Coord. S. GUIJARRO), UPSA, Salamanca, 2006, p. 71.

[84] cf., *Ibid.*, p.100.

the Gospel of Mark presupposes an already a community in Galilee or precisely it is constructed one at the time of Mark. From 14:70, that speaks about Galileans and Peter as Galilean, Lohmeyer deduce that 'the Galileans were immediately a *populus Christianus*" and Galilee was a *terra Christiana*."[85] Marxsen tries to be comprehensive in his view to say that the community in Galilee that was waiting for parousia, and the community that was journeying to Galilee for the parousia transform this land to a "terra Cristiana". That's in Mark.[86] Therefore, Marxsen speaks of a Markan community in Galilee and he initiated the thought of an already existent community as well as orientation to the Galilean community. This polarity of thought is further elaborated in a theoretical manner by Kelber.

Werner H. Kelber notices the special configuration of Galilee with its surroundings and the polarity between Galilee and Jerusalem that are keenly conspicuous within the literary context, in which Markan drama is culminated and a new body of ideology is produced.[87] He tends to override any metaphorical and symbolic attribution to the space dimensions of Mark. Galilee is the locus of the Kingdom of God from where its history began and wherein Mark's generation will be consummated. As Mark is so sensibly sympathetic to the Galilee and that he argues for it from the perspective of a Jewish Christian community, it is possible that Markan Gospel had addressed to the Galilean Christians of the north with an aftermath militates of 70 C.E., against a southern tradition. In this respect, Kelber's argument goes like this. Mark redefines the identity of his community of the north (Galilee) in the light of the destruction of Jerusalem affected upon the southern Christianity and subsequently he discovers a Galilean centrality to his ideology. From the southern point of reference, Galilee is denoted as one already been inhabited by Christian existence and yet being prepared to lay an invitation to the southerners who live in the dispersion of Judea (13:14), to join the Galilee. The schema of the Gospel that leads the reader forward from Galilee to Jerusalem and redirects again to Galilee is, north- south - north order.

The destruction of the temple and Jewish war are the motivational and situational factors for this invitation to Galilee. The Jewish war was an "apocalyptic Armageddon" misguided by the oracles of false prophets and their apocalyptic hopes. As Christians who shared messianic hopes with their fellow Jews (but differed to the temple centered messianic hope of prophets against which Christians represent a temple that intimately bound to 'the body of Christ'), and apocalyptic similarities in their interest, Kelber thinks that Christians also were collaborative in this war of Armageddon and thus a total departure of Christians

[85] "Los Galileos son inmediatamente un *populus christainus* y Galilea una *terra christana.*" cf., *Ibid.*, p. 101.

[86] *Ibid.*

[87] cf., W. H. KELBER, *The Kingdom in Mark: A New Place and a New Time*, pp. 68-147.

from Jerusalem to Pella is disputable.[88] In contrast to it, for Leif E. Vaage[89] the frontier zone of Galilee is the location of the Markan audience who departed to Pella from Jerusalem to whom Mark proposes a radicalized movement of life, which is contra-positioned to the existing temple and tradition. He is differed from Kelber's view by holding that Galilee is a symbolic theology paused against the system of Jerusalem in the ambience of destruction and war.

Kelber's argument is also agreeable to that of Vaage's in affirming the Galilean position over the Jerusalem mother church that had an upper hand in traditions and an affection to the root traditions of Jewish life (Sabbath, purity, fasting and traditions). Among them developed the faith in eschatological Parousia in a vulnerable manner even to an extend of not having had due importance of Cross and resurrection of Jesus. They became exclusivists in mind leaving no room for gentiles in their ministry. For Kelber, the 'fallible disciples' of the Markan story are the representatives of what came to be the Jerusalem Church.

Here, the Jewish war and the false prophetic hope was the occasion; the crisis was that the Kingdom did not come at its appointed time and in the promised place. In other words, there was a false notion of time and wrong choice for place of the Kingdom. Mark's purpose was to show the new place and a new time of the Kingdom. Galilee is the real and new place, a center of life designated by Christ. It has become a reality that had been longed for an ardent hope and messianic focus on Jerusalem by which Mark rejects the traditional localization of the Parousia in Jerusalem, for, the New Jerusalem is Galilee. The empty tomb is a sign of Markan disinclination to show the Resurrected in Jerusalem; *the city of absence* (16:6, 7b evkei/) of the Resurrected is *now* oriented to Galilee. There is a diffidence of Mark, evident to present the Resurrected in Jerusalem. Mark also suggests the temporal dimension of the community that survived the aftermath of the destruction of Jerusalem at 70 C.E. Kelber has his flowery expression regarding the time of the community as "a middle time". The community is in the midst of time, 'not out of or without time'. It is a time that concurs with the eclipse of the kingdom. It is a time of crisis in which persecution is 'not an end but an opening door to the world'; dislocation is not "the sign of Christian bankrupt but a chance to reach the new place of life." In sum, "[Mark's] Gospel furnishes the new spacio-temporal universe in which one can breathe again, relate and orient oneself, find identity, and undertake new action."[90]

---

[88] Mark has mentioned of Christian prophets involved in the Jerusalem fall offers the reader some clue about the Christian involvement in the event. The negative characterization and repudiation of false prophets in Mark indicates their prominence and authority at *that* time and indirectly the necessity of the redefining and reinterpretation of the history misguided by false prophets. There could have some of the Christians who had allegiance to those prophets.

[89] cf. L. E. VAAGE, "El evangelio de Marcos: una interpretación ideológica particular dentro de los cristianismos originarios de Siria-Palestina", *RIBLA* 29 (1998), pp. 10-30.

[90] W. H. KELBER, *The Kingdom in Mark*, pp. 140-144.

When Marxsen finds importance of Galilee and Kelber gives more a theoretical facade to the Galilean position, Roskam, by benign and secure arguments,[91] focuses on the situation of the Galilean community that paved the way for a "Galilean Gospel"[92] From the key understanding of 13:9, Roskam argues for a suffering community of Galilee in the aftermath of the Jewish War. Jesus' restoration of the disciples in Galilee as well as the poor geographical accounts except Galilee is another nodal point of the Gospel for the argument of a Galilean community. In her words, it is clear that "Jewish leadership after Jewish war was concerned to keep the peace themselves and would hand over troublemakers in order to avoid violent Roman intervention." Markan purpose was to suppress the Jewish suspicion over Christians instead of going against Rome and Jewishness. Her important observation that supports her thesis is that, the community seemed to be a threat not to the Romans, but Jews, and therefore the depiction of Jesus' death as result of Jewish ill-will and not anti-roman political ambition backs this fact. Hence, Markan purpose was not to instigate enmity to any group but to avoid ire to both Jews and Romans. Therefore, it becomes an apologetic writing to the Galilean community in a biographical form to defend the faith and Jesus' innocence to these followers to block apostasy and external hostile factors.

It is appropriate to treat, before concluding this section, the view of Mary Ann Beavis[93] about the Markan audience. From the literary analysis of Mk 4:11-12 and considering its rhetoric features that are amenable for a public performance, Mary Ann reaches to an approximate conclusion that Markan audience was a Greco-Roman community and Mark, the skillful scribe and teacher of the community, made this compendium of Jesus' tradition for his missionary preaching.[94] She leaves her study unspecified of the *Sitz im Leben* of the Gospel. Her conclusion seems to be at the verge of considering an open audience for the Gospel of Mark.

For Mary Ann, one of the features of the Markan community is that, it is an open sect as much to think of it as exclusive. In parallel to the contemporary esoteric, exclusive sects (like Qumran), it had to bear features of sectarianism, but in spite of that, it had to remain open to outsiders; it had to bear open witness of their life to the outside world (13:9, 10-13). Like Pauline churches, it remained eschatological with a strong sense of group boundaries and open to all with its own attractions of the new message simultaneously. Secondly, the Gospel was supposed to address even non-converts, the potential Christians, since the radical

---

[91] cf., H. N. ROSKAM, The *Purpose of the Gospel of Mark in its Historical and Social Context*, Brill, Leiden, 2004, in the review of Z. A. Crook in RBL, 08/2006, in http://www.bookreviews.org. (accessed 25 November, 2006)

[92] cf., W. MARXSEN, pp. 85-89.

[93] cf., M. A. BEAVIS, *Mark's Audience: The Literary and Social Setting of Mark 4:11-12* (JSNTsup._33), Sheffield Academic Press, Sheffield, 1989, pp. 167-172.

[94] cf., S. GUIJARRO, "Los Primeros Discípulos de Jesús en Galilea", in *Los Comienzos del Cristianismo* (Coord. S. Guijarro), UPSA, Salamanca, 2006, p. 73.

life of Jesus movement had created certain diffidence in non-converts as it was necessary to assure them of a fact that Christians are 'insiders' in God's design. Markan references (1:4,14-15; 2:13-14; 3.13-19; 14.15-20; 6:7-13,30; 938-41; 13:10) suggest that the Gospel originally functioned as propaganda and for this purpose, Mark use the esoteric element as a 'propaganda value' to attract the 'outsiders', inviting them to know, see, hear and understand the new life in Jesus.

Conclusion

We have seen above a brief outline of the scholarly views on the Markan community from which we understand their main twist and trend. Martin Hengel defended for the traditional view of Roman setting, arguing that Mark was written during the turbulent time after the murder of Nero, and this proposition has been backed by Donald Seniors and Ernest Best. The attempt of Incigneri to argue for the Roman provenance of the Markan Gospel stands unique in the field of biblical scholarship by dating it a post 70 C.E. But, Marxsen came to refute this dominant traditional argument by his proposal of Galilean setting. In association with his view, Howard Kee and Theissen came up with a major body of studies advocating the pre-fall social setting for Markan community in Galilee or in an adjacent area such as southern Syria. When above authors all were for the pre-fall period of Jerusalem, Joel Marcus and the recent study of Roskam advocate for a post-fall Galilean/Syrian provenance. Besides these scholars, there are writers who either universalize the community boundaries of Mark or become pessimistic for a true Markan community. For instance, while Bauckham speaks of a circular Gospel for communities, (recently Hengel also joins him), Peterson concludes with pessimism, hoping any community/ies possible for Mark.

Regarding the date and occasion, among them, some were dating the Gospel before 70 C.E. while others 70 C.E.; some speak of a tensed time that was leading to the destruction of the temple, while others point out a time after it. As we have seen, some locate it in Rome while a few in Galilee and yet others for Syria Palestine. There is also no consensus among scholars over the nature of the community, for while some advocate for Jewish community, others for gentile and yet others for mixture of Jewish and gentile one. Regarding the purpose of the Gospel origin, arguments are rich in variety, that it was either for establishing a community against the Jerusalem power (Kelber) or as some view it as a struggling apocalyptic community (Kee); also arguments are there like Myer's who says that it was "to steer a mediating political path between Roman imperialism and Jerusalem hegemony;"[95] for Mack, it was for forging a new myth of Christian origin out of a variety of disparate tradition; for Joel Marcus, it was to define as a new Israel according to God's plan in the Christian community of Mark after the destruction of temple and Jewish war. Therefore, to say in short, there is "...

[95] cf., D. N. PETERSON, pp. 152-153.

no consensus on the setting of Mark, nor is there a method agreed upon for describing the social makeup of a given community on the basis of a text."[96]

Regarding the method and approach, we cannot analyze them completely from the scope of this short and brief study. This survey is only an outline and inexhaustive because some of the authors have been referred to from the secondary sources. In short, Martin Hengel and associates mostly follow the historical-critical method; Kee and Theissen follow sociological approach; Kelber uses redaction criticism and Myers', socio-political approach. From the textual viewpoint, the authors who hold the position of roman audience rely preferably on the diachronic analysis of the text often focusing on the structural and generic elements (like Latinism, Aramaism) and the apocalyptic chapter. On the other hand, those who hold the view other than roman audience follow a synchronic method of study from the literary and ideological point of view. The former seems imposing the historical situation of war and trials upon the text while the latter attempts to situate the text in a historical context. Moreover, the concern for the social identity of the community as such is much pertained to the study of the latter. The variety in their looking into the theme motivates this study to look at the social features of Markan community anew from a different ideological perspective.

As we go through the versions of different authors, on some points the scholars come to a common agreement. Primarily, it is evident from this survey that the majority of the authors agree to an assumption that there should be an indisputable existence of a Markan community and any reliable construction of the same is inevitable to read and interpret the text rightly. In addition, that historical situation of the community is reflected in the very text. The community is an important control on reading Mark, so the context of the text is accepted as important with regard to its interpretation. But, regarding the method, approaches and the result to which they all arrived at, they differ to each other.

Secondly, Markan community had to face a severe social identity crisis due to the social, historical, cultural and religious turbulence of the time. None of the authors overrules the possibility of persecution to the community in either manner of direct or indirect, but in turn only questioned of its integrity. As a result, the community was confronted by the need of the time to rediscover and reconsider its Christological, eschatological, ecclesiological and ethical base in their social world of the first century. This study will principally traces those bases which correspond to the three elements that constitute the social identity of community – the cognitive factor or logos, emotive factor or pathos and valorative factor or ethos of the community.

The scholars also discuss the problems of the community, as it is useful to extrapolate from their studies, the important challenges that the Markan community had responded to. They are as follows in short: a crisis of the community

[96] J. R. DONAHUE, p. 2.

in the transitional phase of first generations (I cent. C. E.) in transmitting the kerygmatic traditions (Best, Kee,); persecution and all varying types of trails against Christians in Judea Palestine and Rome (Best, Iersel, Witherington, Marcus); delay in the Parousia and a need of redefining the messianic and eschatological hope (Best, Mack, Kelber); conflict between Gentile and Jewish Christians, divisions, Synagogue reform (Iersel, Mack, Rohrbaugh, Marcus); Jewish War and destruction of the Temple (Kee, Mack, Kelber); a need of right Christology and its importance in the Christian life (Best, Mack, Kelber); a need of communal transformation and identity in the pluralistic Jewish world (Kee,); the question of discipleship and failure in following Jesus (Best, Iersel, Mack); the abuse of leadership within the community and dominance of Jerusalem community, false oracles and, misguiding prophets (Kelber); class segregation and conflict between agrarian and elite groups (Rohrbaugh).

Thirdly, in spite of varying opinions on the crisis and situations, the scholars are unanimous on telling that the historical Jewish war and the destruction of the temple is the unique point of reference to situate the Gospel in a context even when a date is uncertain to be confirmed. Joel Marcus is discreet to put it in a better language that Mark and his community were *in the shadow* of the war and destruction of the temple.

When all the authors are preoccupied to articulate the date, place and situations, which necessitated a Gospel of the Mark, the social identity as such of its community is less underscored by the scholars. From the scholarly survey, we know that the search for the Markan community is yet remained as a passionate task. This is the point of our departure. As we go for a new look at the Markan community, we are really founded by the scholarly belief that the vital context is explored from the text and the text should be read from the vital context. This new look at the text and reading of it for reconstructing the social identity of the community is enhanced by the use of an effective model – the model of the Social Identity theory. Before applying this model, we must know what this model is. For this, we need to switch on to the next chapter.

Chapter 2

TEXT, IDENTITY AND HERMENEUTICAL METHODS

Memory is a dimension of our faith which we might call deuteronomic, not unlike the memory of Israel itself…the believer is essentially one who remembers.

(Pope Francis, *Evangelii Gaudium*, 13)

The written text is an archive of memory. In the ancient times, "it appears that writing develops first and primarily as an aid to memory, a repository of cultural information that might otherwise be forgotten."[1] Beyond this archive function of the writing, the text, especially the Gospel texts, witnesses further a rhetorical function, which the redactional hand of the author constructs meaning and perspectives to the transmitted tradition. As it was mentioned in the 'introduction', the exegetical method followed in this study is the redaction criticism. The social memory theory would offer to this exegetical criticism, valuable terms and approaches to realistically analyze the traditional and redactional elements of the text in order to understand both of its archival and rhetorical motives.

This chapter therefore deals with the perspectives and hermeneutical approaches, to speak mainly on two areas of interpretation; the Social Identity theory (hereafter referred as SIT) and the Social Memory theory (hereafter referred as SMT). The SIT will guide the interpretive task of this study while the SMT will give sense to our approach to the text in finding out its context. This

[1] T. THATCHER, "Why John Wrote a Gospel: Memory and History in an Early Christian Community", in A. KIRK, – T. THATCHER (eds.), *Memory, Tradition, and Text: Uses of the Past in Early Christianity* (Semeia Studies 52, SBL), Atlanta, 2005, p. 80.

is necessitated by the present acclaim that "all we have is the text"[2] and this text was formed due to a long process of communitarian oral tradition and redaction of an author.

Social Scientific Approaches to the Scripture

In the analytic method that pertains to the social scientific exegesis, the use of theories, models and analogies is inevitably presumed. In this sort of synchronic method, the model or theory[3] is an interpretive tool which draws social facts from the fragmented data of antique text. In order to have clarifications on ancient social properties and cultural systems embedded in the 'sacred text', we need the help of modern and systematic verified tools of interpretation without which alike interpretation would be possible by our "putative common sense" but would not be systematic, disciplined and thus scientific.[4] The model used would be a conceptual image kept in the mind of the researcher for the empirical and analytical social studies of the text.[5]

There are objections to the use of social scientific tools and models in the area of biblical studies, 'judging them as illicit, seeing them as impositions of alien concepts on unsuspecting biblical data. However, everyone uses models; some studies use them consciously while others, unconsciously. When they are used unconsciously, models remains unspoken, unrecognized as assumptions and prejudgments based on personal experiences in the study; if they are consciously used, the interpreted facts pass beyond any suppositions and they are verified by the acknowledged theory or model.'[6] Philip Esler's opinion is a better clarification to the above said 'misconception' on the use of models. "...the purpose of a model is essentially comparative. A model is not a set of pigeon-holes into which data is

---

[2] cf., M. MYLLYKOSKI, "Mark's Oral Practice and the Written Gospel of Mark", in J. MRÁZEK – J. ROSKOVEC (eds.), *Testimony and Interpretation: Early Christology in its Judeo-Hellenistic Milieu*, (JSNTsup.), T & T Clark , London-NY, 2004, p. 97.

[3] cf., J. H. ELLIOT, *What is Social Scientific Criticism?*, Fortress Press, Minneapolis, 1993, p. 41. Elliot has defined and distinguished the difference and similarity between 'theory and model'. Theory is based on "axiomatic laws and states of general principles." cf., T. F. CARNEY, *The Shape of the Past: Models and Antiquity*, Coronado Press, Lawrence – Kansas, 1975, p. 8. in J. H. ELLIOT, p. 41. Models are intrinsically welded to their correlative theories or to say, models constitute a part of high complex theories. The highly theoretical models are "consciously structured and systematically arranged in order to serve as speculative instrument for the purpose of organizing, profiling and interpreting a complex welter of raw materials.". cf., *Ibid.*

[4] cf., J. H. ELLIOT, p. 40.

[5] A model would prompt to look for coherence, regularity, correlations, and patterns among the textual materials. Models are like shapes and size of maps or "model mannequins". They have no "ontological status but are only cognitive representations of realities". Map is not a "real territory but simulated pattern of the selected land to give the traveler an overview of given territory". cf., *Ibid.*, p. 43.

[6] cf. P. F. ESLER, *The First Christians in their Social World: Social-Scientific Approaches to New Testament Interpretation*, Routledge, London – USA - Canada, 1974, p. 12.

slotted. It is a heuristic tool, allowing comparisons to be made with the texts for the purpose of posing new questions to them. The texts must supply the answers, not the model."[7] The question, herein therefore is not the validity or invalidity of its use but "...whether it is useful or not." On the whole, the sociological tool would prompt the 'researcher of the text' with a "sociological imagination."[8]

A model will have a dual function in a socially approached study of a text. Firstly, the empirical function that helps the study to determine the materials to be examined, according to the relevant elements of the model/theory. It would dictate that the competing sets of social properties and materials should be examined and regarded as data for the succeeding analysis of the social features of the text. Like a cognitive map, a model/theory would assist in "observing", "categorizing", "comparing", and "synthesizing" elements of social data and drawing generalization and conclusion about their salient social features in the text. Secondly, a model/theory will function as a driving force of interpretation in the whole project of the study. In this analytical phase, it plays a role as criteria of evaluation and guides the very process of analysis of the text according to the theme and aim of the study.[9] They would provide means for "analyzing and explaining repeated behaviors", "social roles", "institutions", "patterns of stratification", "modes of social interaction and conflicts", "correlations between beliefs and behaviours", "social organization and world views."[10]

Models/theories are differing among themselves in scope and complexities, that they can have operation in both macro and micro levels regarding their application.[11] So, the selection of a model for the use is to be done discreetly. The utility of theories/models is counted with the similitude and correspondence lie between the textual material under examination and the elements of theories/ models. Moreover, acclaim of models predominantly attained by the use of scholars, would show their fitness for further application in an extended area of studies. Besides all, as canons, Bruce J. Malina has proposed six features of a model as requirement for its use in the area of biblical studies. 1) 'A model must facilitate cross cultural comparison between social situation of the present world and of the text; 2) its level of abstraction should be enough for a comparison basing similarities; 3) it should have a large socio-linguistic framework for interpretation

[7] *Ibid.*, pp. 12-13.

[8] cf., *Ibid.*, p. 12.

[9] cf., J. H. ELLIOT, pp. 60-61.

[10] cf., *Ibid.*, pp. 40-45.

[11] In macro level, a model/theory is applicable to explain the entire Mediterranean world, which enables to have a comparative study between the modern world and the Mediterranean and circum-Mediterranean world of the text. In micro level, it is used to explain various aspects of the Mediterranean world like specific regions (Jerusalem, Antioch, Ephesus, Rome, Syria, Galilee. ect.) and various social aspects of their life. Here, in this study, the immediate specific social context of the text is treated. Lower level of the social life like family, kinship, rituals, governance, values, personality, ect., could also be of greater concern in this level. cf., J. H. ELLIOT, p. 40.

(richness in concepts); 4) it should be designed from experiences; 5) its meaning should be culture-specific; 6) and its quality should conform to social scientific standard.'[12]

Why we demonstrate the model of the Social identity theory, here at the beginning of our study? The early elucidation of model/theory is methodologically important because it is the guiding principle and it should be clearly explained first. The guide moves first before the guided ones; selective tools are to be gotten ready before any planned operations. If it is set out at the outset, it will be easy that the relevant data are to be gathered and driven them for the analysis. The theory given ahead as well would make clear the researcher and the reader what is investigated.

The Social Identity Theory as Interpretative Model

This study chooses some basic principles of the SIT as models of explanation. The SIT is a verified model, which constitutes of the essential socio-psychological elements that explicate the salience of group identity. It will explain *what* and *how* of the group identity. However, we start this search for the social identity of Markan group with an assumption that the elements of the said SIT would testify its competence because of its correspondence to the social characters, properties and social interactions, which are found, though fragmented, in the Markan text. For instance, the out-group, in-group concept of SIT and the 'insider' and 'outsider' mentality in the Markan text coincides to have us a presumption that SIT will be feasible to assist us in interpreting the Markan reshaping of the social self. Above all, SIT deals with the group and its identity, whilst our search is also for the identity of a group – the Markan group.

We are not the ones who use this model for the first time, but a number of reputed biblical scholars have applied it in their social studies of ancient sacred texts. Philip Francis Esler[13] is prominent among them, who dedicated a

---

[12] cf., B. J. MALINA, "The Social Sciences and Biblical Interpretation", *Int.* 37(1982), pp. 229-242, in J. H. ELLIOT, p. 45.

[13] cf., P. F. ESLER, *Conflict and Identity in Romans: The Social Setting of Paul's Letter*, Fortress Press, Minneapolis, 2003. See also its translation in spanish: Idem., *Conflicto e Identidad en la Carta a los Romanos: el Contexto Social de la Carta de Pablo* (trans., J. P. Escobar), Verbo Divino (Estella), Navarra, 2006. The rest of his works include some essays: cf., Idem., "Jesus and the Reduction of Intergroup Conflict: The Parable of the Good Samaritan in the light of Social Identity Theory", *BibInt* 8 (2004, 4), pp. 325-357; Idem., "Social Identity, the Virtues, and the Good Life: A New Approach to Romans 12:1-15;13", *BTB* 33 (2002, 2), pp. 51-63; Idem., "Collective Memory and Hebrews 11: Outlining a New Investigative Framework", in A. KIRK – T. THATCHER (eds.), *Memory, Tradition, and Text: Uses of the Past in Early Christianity*, (Semeia Studies 52), SBL, Atlanta, 2005, pp. 151-171; Idem., "Ezra-Nehemiah as a Narrative of (Re-invented) Israelite Identity", *BibInt* 11(2003, 2-4), pp. 413-426; Idem., "Ludic History in the Book of Judith: The Reinvention of Israelite Identity?", *BibInt* 10(2002, 2), pp. 107-143; Idem., "Making and Breaking an Agreement Mediterranean Style: A New Reading of Galatians 2:1-14", *BibInt* 3 (1995, 3), pp. 285-314. It has been useful a private rough draft of his paper delivered in the 'Construction of Christian Identity'

number of works and essays on the subject of identity conflicts and the early Christian movements. His works have been simultaneously contributive to the area of scholarship on identity issues of the early Christian movements as well to the introduction of 'social identity model' as an appropriate tool for better interpretation of the early group formation and reformation. Much known among his work is *Conflict and Identity in Romans* in which he evidently uses the theory to monitor the inter-group conflict among Roman Christians and consequent Pauline strategy of resolving it by suggesting a super-ordinate identity to subgroups within the Jesus group. It is remarkable the application of the re-categorization principle by which Esler argues that Paul, rather denying proper identities of Jewish and gentile Christians, proposes an overarching identity which would satisfy the whole group. 'His is not a newly found fact but a new way of looking at the same fact through the lens of SIT.' In a revised seminar paper, *Jesus and the Reduction of Intergroup Conflict*, Esler's focus is on the use of decategorization process of SIT. In this paper, he assesses so distinctly the contextual background of the parable of good Samaritan (Lk 10:25-37) from internal and external evidences to the text in order to arrive at an overwhelming meaning of 'neighbour' and inclusive moral behaviour viewed by the narrator for pacifying the inter-ethnic tension (between 'Judeans and Samaritans' in the narrative). His another article, *Social Identity, the Virtues, and the Good Life: A New Approach to Romans 12:1-15;13,* articulates the role and function of norms in inculcating a social identity to any group members. In the essay, *Collective Memory and Hebrew 11*, with the backing of SMT, Esler argues how the author of Hebrew pervasively reconstructs the Israelite's past, which is even remote reaching up to Cain and Abel, in order to establish and maintain a particular identity for the Christ-movement in the present. Here, he demonstrates the possible intersection of the SIT and the SMT in the area of studies on the origin and identity of primitive Christianity.

Ann Faulkner in her essay *Jewish Identity and the Jerusalem Conference: Social Identity and Self-Categorization in the Early Church Communities,*[14] explicitly uses the Self Categorization Theory (hereafter referred as SCT) to understand the group dynamics and to answer the identity question raised at Jerusalem Conference (Acts 15). After over-viewing the SIT and SCT, she analyzes the background of group relations between Judean Christians and gentile Christians in the Mediterranean world, leading the essay to consider the proposition of an overarching identity for neutralizing the divisive identities of subgroups within the Jesus groups (Rom 10:12; 1:28-31, Gal 3:27-29, 5:19-23, 1 Cor 12:11-14; 6:19-11, 1 Thess 4:3-5). In *Los Primeros Discípulos de Jesús en Galilea*, Santiago Guijarro evidently uses the

Section, at SBL Meeting held at San Antonio, Texas, on 21st November 2004 titled, *Prototypes, Antitypes and Social Identity in First Clement: Outlining a New Interpretative Model.*

[14] cf., A. FAULKNER, *Jewish Identity and the Jerusalem Conference: Social Identity and Self Categorization in the Early Church Communities,* www.sharp.arts.gla.ac (an authentic electronic publication of the University of Glasgow), eSharp Issue 6: Identity and Marginality (Autumn 2005).

principles of prototypicality, in-group - out-group comparisons of SIT in order to identify and localize the primitive disciples of Jesus in Galilee.[15] Victor H. Mathews in his essay *The Determination of Social Identity in the Story of Ruth,*[16] elucidates with the use of SIT perspectives, but unspoken of the theory as such, the shift and redefinition of the then social identity replicated in the Book of Ruth. There are some more namely, Leif E. Vaage, John K. Riches and Antoinette Wire[17] who used different aspects of SIT to analyze identity formation, crisis and struggle for the perseverance of the social image of the early Jesus groups, which consequently conditioned for the emergence of variant early Christian writings.

For any type of application of SIT and SCT, it is necessary that the group under consideration must have an established identity pattern and an in-group/ out-group must be an existing reality in the atmosphere of competition because the SIT theory is interested in the area of 'group process' than 'group formation'. Here, the relevant question is that, is SIT be applicable to any group oriented study of the ancient Mediterranean world? The answer tends to be positive. As Bruce J. Malina proposes, group identity was more salient and important than the personal identity in the Mediterranean world and their personality concept was a group oriented one. The pivotal values like shame and honour acted as catalysts triggering off constant groups' conflicts and competitions.[18] Therefore, the selection of this model for our search for the social identity of the Markan community is motivated not because of its whatever theme of community or the title of it has something to do with the group, rather we need to deal with a first century Mediterranean group – the Markan group.

---

[15] cf., S. GUIJARRO, *Los primeros Discípulos de Jesús en Galilea*, pp.71-91. in S. GUIJARRO (ed.), *Los Comienzos del Cristianismo*, UPSA, 2006.

[16] cf., V. H. MATHEWS, "The Determination of Social Identity in the Story of Ruth", *BTB* 36 (2006, 2), pp. 1-6.

[17] cf., L. E. VAAGE, *Galilean Upstarts: Jesus' First Followers According to Q*, Trinity Press, Pennsylvania, 1994; J. K. RICHES, Conflicting *Mythologies: Identity Formation in the Gospels of Mark and Mathew*, T &T Clark, Edinburgh, 2000; A. WIRE, *Early Jewish Birth Prophecy Stories and Women's Social Memory*, in A. KIRK – T. THATCHER (eds.), pp. 173-189.

[18] cf., B. J. MALINA, *The New Testament World: Insights from Cultural Anthropology* (3rd ed.), Westminster John Knox Press, Louisville - Kentucky, 2001, pp. 27-106, 198-219.

Relevant Components of the Social Identity Theory

The SIT[19] was developed under the scholarship of British Social Psychologists in 1970's. The chief proponent of this theory is Henri Tajfel,[20] a Jew native of Poland but lived and developed his theory outskirt of Poland. The crux of his theoretical projection is that the identity of a concerned group (intra-group / in-group identity) is determined by the inter-group interaction, comparison and differentiation, in a given particular context. His proposition of inter-group conflict is based more on the methodical study of psychosocial and cognitive process of group.[21] The basic questions addressed by SIT are that, how a group attains its identity. When does a member of a group act in the name of the group and what are the conditions under which, the members are determined to be members of the group?

The *idea of group* is the fundamental element of the treatise that is to be understood descriptively in the light of social psychology than with a compact definition. According to Tajfel,[22] a group is a set of a whole of individuals with three basic features. They are cognitive, evaluative and emotional. These three factors that constitute the identity of the group are inter-dynamic in its operation

---

[19] I would like to present a set of basic works that has been generally referred to for the explanation of the theory. cf., H. TAJFEL, *Grupos Humanos y Categorias Sociales: Estudios de Psicologia Social* (trad. C. Huici), Herder, Barcelona, 1984; D. J. TERRY – M.A. HOGG (eds.), *Attitudes, Behaviour and Social Context: The Role of Norms and Group Membership*, Lawrence Erlbaum Associates, NJ, 2000; J. C. TURNER, *Redescrubrir el Grupo Social* (trad. P. MANZANO), Morata, Madrid, 1990; J. C. SÁNCHEZ, *Psicología de los Grupos: Teoria, Procesos y Aplicaciones*, McGraw – Hill, Madrid, 2002, pp. 271-285; A. BLANCO – A. CABALLERO – D. L. La CORTE, *Psicología de los Grupos*, Prentice Hall, Madrid, 2005; S. MOSCOVICI, *Influencia y Cambio de Actitudes: Individuos y Grupos* (1ª ed., trad. D. Rosenbaum), Paidós, Barcelona, 1985; W. DOISE, *Psicología Social y Relaciones entre Grupos: Estudio Experimental* (1ª ed.), Vol. 1 & 2, Rol, Barcelona, 1979; M. SHERIF, *Intergroup Relationship and Leadership: Approaches and Research in Industrial, Ethnic, Cultural and Political Areas*, John Wiley & Sons, NY, 1962; D. L. SILLS (ed.), EICS (V. C. Tomás, ed. española), Aguilar, Madrid, 1974-1977; CYPRIAN E. FERNANDEZ, *Identity in Conflict: A Socio-rhetorical Reading of the Markan Story of Jesus*, Asian Trading Corporation, Bangalore, 2016, pp. 5-13.

[20] H. Tajfel contributed his theory in collaboration with John C. Turner, constructor of the SCT. After the Second World War (during which he suffered a period of concentration camp) when he had been relieved of its ill effects, he took up his career in the University of Bristol. Having been chaired the Cathedra of Social Psychology in Bristol, he organized social psychology with its proper identity, founded 'the European Association of Social Psychology', and was to become the first Editor of the Journal. He is known for his outstanding work *Human Groups and Social Categories* (1981) in which he stipulated basics of his theory.

[21] cf., H. TAJFEL, *Grupos Humanos y Categorías Sociales*, pp. 293-310.

[22] The classic definition of Tajfel for SIT: "...entenderemos por identidad social aquella parte del autoconcepto de un individuo que deriva del conocimiento de su pertenencia a un grupo (o grupos) social junto con el significado valorativo y emocional asociado a dicha pertenencia. Resultará claro que ésta es una definición limitada de "identidad" o de la "identidad social"". cf., H. TAJFEL, p. 292.

and one of them would spontaneously draw to the involvement of the other in the identity formation of the group.[23] Therefore, what we mean by the social identity of a group really subsists in the very concept of the group. There will be no group exists that we could perceive without a proper identity.

The criteria of group identity consist in a collective conscience of the group members as a socially differentiated entity from the other groups. They perceive and define the shared common identity of their group, which consists in the process of establishment, organization, regulation of the group, through the mediation of a system of categories, norms and values. This system prescribes for adequate beliefs, attitudes, conducts (behavior) of the group that are expected to be generated as positive responses of the same group members. The membership of the group members is acceptable and enjoyable to themselves when the group serves them with a satisfactory social identity and offers a self-esteem through which they attain a social self-identity. The individuals view themselves esteemed in the group as group members rather than mere individuals where "I" become "we"; "me" versus "you" become "us" versus "them."[24] On the contrary, the individuals may abandon the group when the group does not contribute a positive social identity to the group members in order to be configured with the group. It happens when the members loose the self-esteem as members of their group and it is considered as the crisis.

The whole process of group formation, operation and enhancement is called, by Turner,[25] as Self-categorization. The cognitive act of *classification*, as in our ordinary tongue, is the basic principle of *categorization*. The categorization involves in a process of merging of a self-identity into a group category and thus attain a social identity; a movement from the auto self-perception to the social self-perception within a social frame and the given situation. In this process of depersonalization, 'the importance of the personal identity of the individual is decreased and the importance of his social identity is augmented in which the individual takes the properties and the attitudes that are characteristics of the group.'[26] Hence, as consequences of the depersonalization of members, group

---

[23] cf., J. C. SANCHEZ, *Psicología de los Grupos: Teoría, Procesos y Aplicaciones,* pp. 271-285.

[24] cf., DUCK - HOGG - TERRY, *Perceived Impact of Persuasive Messages*, pp. 269-291, in D. J. TERRY- M. A. HOGG (eds.), *Attitudes, Behaviour and Social Context: The Role of Norms and Group Membership*, Lawrence Erlbaum Associates, NJ, 2000.

[25] Turner says that, "las teorías de la identidad social y auto categorización…son aliadas y ampliamente complementarías, haciendo tareas diferentes desde la misma perspectiva psicosocial. Es por esta razón por la que el termino teoría de la identidad social se utiliza algunas veces (a un nivel mas inclusivo) para referirse a ambas teorías" cf., J. C. TURNER, *Redescubrir el Grupo Social,* pp. 6-7.

[26] 'The depersonalization does not mean that the individual by his belongingness to a group loses his identity as a person or individual, nor consist in the loss or submersion of 'I' in the group ("de-individualization"), nor a type of regression to a form of identity more primitive and inconsciente.' It is rather a change from the level of personal identity to that of social, a change in the

produce an accentuation of the *perceived similarities* between the self and other in-group members and an accentuation of the *perceived differences* between the self and out-group members.

From the above preview of the theory, one can understand that the SIT is based on three important components such as values, emotion and cognition of the group. We now analyze in detail these three elements and how they function in shaping the identity of a group.

Norms, Attitudes, Prototype: Valorative Factors of the Group Identity

Norms:[27] Norm is a defining and distinguishing factor of a group. Generally, it is "in any given culture, the established mode of behaviour to which *conformity* is expected."[28] As Philip Esler explains, norm as "a scale of values defines a range of acceptable (and unacceptable) attitudes and behaviours for members of a social unit."[29] For Rupert Brown, norms are "certain rules for how group members should behave and thus are the basis for mutual expectations among group members."[30] For Tajfel, they are "collective construction", which are essential in connecting members to the group.[31] In whatever form they may be, they are certainly meant to play an important role in the group to bring an order and predictability to its environment. The group would prompt to each members as follows; "if you wish to share in this group identity, to tell yourself who you are in relation to your belonging to this group, these are the values you should hold and this is how you must conduct yourself."[32] The norms are subjectified as values and personified as group prototypes (discuss it in detail later) that represent beliefs, attitudes, feelings and behaviors.[33] When individuals are assimilated into the group norms,

---

nature and in the content of auto-conception corresponding to the functioning of the perception of 'I' in a level more inclusive of a social abstraction. cf., H. TAJFEL, *Grupos Humanos y Categorías Sociales*, pp. 293-304.

[27] The Oxford dictionary defines the literal meaning of norm as "standard", "model", "pattern", "type" (regarding groups it is a "shared patterns of behaving, feeling and thinking"). Values, as Oxford defines, are "the principles or standards of a person or society, the personal or societal judgment of what is valuable and important in life." Norms are in sense universal like 'a scale of measurement' while values are in sense 'particulars' and relational. cf., J. A. SIMPSON – E. S. C. WEINER (eds.), *The Oxford English Dictionary* (2nd ed.), Clarendon Press, Oxford, 1989, Vol. 10, p. 515, Vol. 19, p. 416.

[28] A. BARNARD – J. SPENCER (eds.), ESCA, Routledge, London – NY, 2002, p. 615. (Italics in the citation is mine).

[29] P. F. ESLER, *Social Identity, the Virtues, and the Good Life*, pp. 51-63.

[30] cf., M. SHERIF, - C. W. SHERIF, *Social Psychology*, Harper and Row, NY, 1969, p. 56.

[31] cf., *Ibid.*

[32] H. TAJFEL, *Human Groups and Social Categories: Studies in Social Psychology*, Cambridge University Press, Cambridge, 1981, p. 36, in P. F. ESLER, *Social Identity, the Virtues and the Good Life*, pp. 51-63.

[33] cf., D. J. TERRY - M. A. HOGG - K. M. WHITE, *Attitude-Behaviour Relations: Social Identity and Group Membership*, in D. J. TERRY - M. A. HOGG (eds.), *Attitudes, Behaviour and*

their self-perceptions are hitherto defined according to the beliefs, attitudes and feelings generated by the group prototypes. The genuine group membership makes them to think, feel, behave and act according to the group norms that prescribe the context - specific attitudes and behaviors appropriate to the group members.[34] The above description on what do the norms mean to a group, illumines us that they are factors which bring uniformity, unity and cohesiveness to the *group-in-action.*

We need to understand that norms are preferably abstract values but the group members are called to concretize them in action than simply leaving them as "disembodied construct". A social identity and self-categorization approach assumes that the impact of activating a group prototype goes beyond making an attitude merely accessible; it makes an attitude normative, providing the prescriptive power for cognition to be reflected in action.[35] Hence, norms lead the members to create a positive attitude that would in turn make them to behave consistently in the group for their self-esteem.

Norms function by regulating the social existence and by coordinating the attitudes and activities of the group members. They assist the group in achieving its goal of the vision, which is realized through the acceptance of the norms, because they reveal the *point of view* of the group. According to Esler, 'the norms are broader than ethical principles, a broader concept of goodness, life and virtues that are to be installed in the minds of the members. They have positive and negative functioning in the group of installing distinctive identity on individual members. The *positive dimension* of installing the group identity is by generation and inculcation of norms, as he calls them "*identity descriptors.*"[36] They tell that what pattern of behavior, feeling and thinking they should adopt for their shared identity of the group. The *negative dimension* of installing the identity is telling the members who they are not by the differentiation of the in-group from the out-group. For in-group, the values, norms, social dispositions of the out-group are distinct and opposite to those of them.'[37] Norms are normally embedded to group and the group members need not always be conscious of them unless the group faces certain identity crisis wanting of revitalization.[38]

Social Context: The Role of Norms and Group Membership, Lawrence Erlbaum Associates, NJ, 2000, pp. 72-74.

[34] cf., *Ibid.*, pp. 72-74.

[35] cf., *Ibid.*, p. 78.

[36] cf., P. F. ESLER, *Conflict and Identity in Romans,* pp. 20-24.

[37] *Ibid.*

[38] The social science encyclopedia implicitly says that norms are originated as a response to the social conflicts or crisis. "Muchas de las reglas de comportamiento parecen ser consecuencia directa de unos problemas que se presentan una y otra vez y que entrañan un elevado coste social." cf., R. M. WILLIAMS, JR., *Norms*, in D. L. SILLS (ed.), EICS (V. C. Tomás, ed. española), Vol. 7, pp. 348-351.

Attitudes: Attitudes can be different from the group norms. They are personal, idiosyncratic[39] and unrelated to norms, but in the group categorization, attitudes can be widely shared by the group members as they may be considered as part of the group prototypes.[40] 'Though the attitudes are seen as personal, the group often conveys them to the members. So, the group membership influences the attitudes of the members and the members in the group behave accordingly to their group-built attitudes. The behavioral pattern of the group members should attitudinally congruent. It is important to note that the norm congruency of the group will be independent of the attitude accessibility and behavioral decision making of the group members.'[41]

The attitudinal congruency in the area of norms, the behavioral decisions and uniform accessibility to the attitudes by the group members are engendered through the means of the group communicative processes, especially through the in-group information by literatures, which pertains to the attitudinal change, maintenance, and enhancing. For instance, the group members are exposed to persuasive in-group messages produced by the communicative information of the literatures like the Markan text of Gospel, aimed at persuading the readers to take up a particular attitude. The persuasive messages (through literature) on group-relevant-issues should increase people's capacity, as well as their motivation, to process the message wherein the group norms are suggested to become the appropriate guide for action in that context.[42]

Prototype: Literally speaking, a prototype is a "primary type", "form", or instance of something serving as a typical "exemplar", "pattern", "model", "representation" or "standard" for other things of the same category.[43] In semantics, prototypes or prototypical instances combine the most representative attributes of a category. They are the *best examples* among the members of a category that serve as benchmarks against the surrounding of weaker instances. The prototype theory holds that not all members of a category have equal status.[44] According

---

[39] Literal definition of 'attitude' shows its idiosyncratic nature. Oxford mean it as "fitness", "adaptation", "disposedness", "disposition", "posture", "settled behaviour or manner of acting as representative of feeling or opinion." cf., J. A. SIMPSON- E. S. C. WEINER (eds.), *The Oxford English Dictionary,* Vol. 1, p. 771. To define it sociologically: "an attitude is a relatively enduring organization of beliefs around an object or situation predisposing one to respond in some preferential manner." cf., M. ROKEACH, *The Nature of Attitudes,* in D. L. SILLS (ed.), *IESS,* The Macmillan Company & The Free Press, NY – London, Vol. 1&2, pp. 449-457.

[40] cf., D. J. TERRY - M. A. HOGG - K. M. WHITE, *Attitude-Behaviour Relations: Social Identity and Group Membership*, pp. 72-74.

[41] cf., *Ibid.*

[42] cf., *Ibid.*, pp. 92-93.

[43] cf., J. A. SIMPSON- E. S. C. WEINER (eds.), *The Oxford English Dictionary,* Vol. 12, pp. 701-702.

[44] For example, chair is more prototypical of the concept furniture, than, say, lamp; a robin is more prototypical of a bird than, say a penguin.

to this theory, "...humans classify their world, not in terms of criteria which must apply to all items in a particular category, but through the recognition of best-cases, or prototypes, which become the model to which other items in the category approximate."[45]

In the milieu of SIT, the group will accredit certain individuals as actualizing highest degree of values and behaviors. Philip Esler defines better the terms of modalities of the group representations and its norms. An *exemplar*[46] is an actual person *who is thought to typify* the identity of the in-group. He/she is the most representative of the shared social identity and consensual position of the group as a whole. A *prototype* of a group will be a *representation of a person thought to typify* the group. It is a cognitive representation of the social category containing the meanings and norms that the person associates with the social category. As theoretically evinced by Tajfel, within whatever group *some persons* would be perceived to be more prototypes than others and that those groups would be structured internally based on the prototype. The individual takes the image of prototype of the group to be depersonalized by becoming a member of the group. Such prototype need not necessarily be current or actual members of the group but rather the image of an ideal person who embodies its character. Prototypes are the "possible selves" for the in-group members. Antitypes are opposite to prototypes, who tell the members what to shun, reject, or distance from.[47] The reason for the existence of prototypes in a group has a strong motivational basis, that is, to *behave* consistently with a group prototype, as a consequence of people's need for both positive self-evaluation (self-esteem) and the reduction of uncertainty. A group prototype is a broader construct that embodies how one should *behave* as well as how one should *think* in the group.

Hence, we conclude that the norms, values and prototypes are 'marks of reference' of a group to identify itself in difference to out-groups. In the Markan narrative, for example, the norm of self-sacrifice and Cross-bearing is exemplified in action by the example of Jesus while this attitude is inculcated in the Markan

[45] cf., A. BARNARD – J. SPENCER (eds.), ESCA, p. 619. The Prototype theory originated in Berlin by Kay's work on colour category, but has been developed into other areas of cognitive sciences. Eleanor Rosch has defined the term 'prototype' in her study *Natural Categories* (1973).

[46] Literally speaking, 'exemplar' and 'prototype' have no much difference in meaning, but 'exemplar' is descriptive in the dictionary. Oxford means it as "a person or thing which serves as a model for imitation; an example ...the model, pattern or original after which something is made; an archetype whether real or ideal." cf., J. A. SIMPSON- E. S. C. WEINER (eds.), *The Oxford English Dictionary*, Vol. 5, p. 524.

[47] cf., P. F. ESLER, *Prototypes, Antitypes and Social Identity in First Clement: Outlining a New Interpretative Model.* The notion of possible selves would help the social identity theory to address past social identities and the manner in which past, present and future may be reconstituted to create meaningful 'stories' at both the individual and group levels. Prototypes represent those desired possible selves and the group members are urged to manifest in their own lives. This will be dealt with elsewhere hereunder 'memory theory and text'.

community through the prototypes, for instance, the poor widow's offering of 'all' and Simon of Cyrene's Cross-bearing image.

Cognitive Factors of the Group Identity

The cognitive factor of the group identity implies in group's perception over the unity and similarity enjoyed by it. It is something about the awareness of the sense of belonging of the group members. There are two important characteristics of the belongingness to a social category: the grade of interiorization or of identification of 'I' with an in-group /out-group, and the evaluative importance of the belongingness to a group in the definition of the 'I'. The cognition of the similarity between the members in respect of values, attitudes, proximity and social contact, common destiny shared (or to be in the same boat), shared successes and failures, threats, enemies common and also the shares styles, is the fundamental determinant for the cohesion of a group. The differences between the in-group and out-group and the subsequent conflict and competition, would provoke a great meta-contrast and produce a great positive impact in solidarity, moral and mutual acceptance between the members of the proper group.

In a group where the identity is well defined, which confer upon the members a self-esteemed social identity, at the times of failures, that group would be more responsible for their proper actions and members will have to identify more with their group to explain and justify their actions. This is only possible in such a group where the members are comfortable with the social self to which they are identified. In such a critical situation, the responsibility of the group is reaffirmed by the cost than the reward. The studies shows that the members of the group are more united (cohesive) after the failures and defeat of the group members than in those moments of victory, while members and even out-group members get attracted to the group when the group or members have victory than those moments of defeat or failures. Therefore, identification of the members with the group would provoke better cohesiveness of the group.

Emotive Factors of the Group Identity

Emotions are assumed to play a significant role in the inter-group relations. According to inter-group emotions theory proposed by Smith, prejudice or bias is a group-based emotional reaction and it can involve a whole range of specific emotions (eg., fear, anger, contempt, resentment, etc.) where the target is an out-group appraised to have some implication for the in-group. This presupposes the intra-group emotional bias, that members have a strong affinity and intimate favouritism for the group, or to say in clear terms that, they will have love and affection for their group. Due to this, there will be a uniformity of the appraisal of the group events. It is likely that group members react or respond to the group-events in consequent to the appraisals conveyed by their fellow in-group members. In the same way, when there arise the situations of inter-group conflict, group members tend to have the same emotional reactions towards events. This phenomenon has been called emotional contagion; the tendency of individuals to experience and express emotions similar to people around them. One major function of emotional contagion is affiliation or bonding: the joint experience and expression of emotions is assumed to strengthen the social bonds between individuals.'[48] In short, the emotional factors are the animating force of the group that is invisibly active to make the group united and vibrant in the relational level.

Social Comparison

How does a group get its identity? The SIT mainly addresses this question explaining that a group gets its identity through an inter-group process. This inter-group interactive process is a cognitive mechanism. No group is isolated in respect to the other. The identity of a group is determined in respect to the interaction of a concerned forum with the other groups, through the medium of social comparison and differentiation. The criteria by which this process of comparison and differentiation is made through three above-mentioned basic elements of the group identity, particularly among which values and norms play a very important role.

The group conduct is important to monitor identity and its significance. The uniformity of the conduct of group members make their group in-group and subsequent differentiation of the conduct make the others out-group for them. The identity is relational in terms of its differentiation and identification. The stronger the social identification, the more pronounced the tendencies toward perception of similarity or equivalence between self and in-group members (in-group assimilation) and towards perception of difference between in-group and out-group members.[49] Here, it is observable that we speak of the social identity of a group only in a particular given context or a situation, which means, only in a given social framework of a category the identity is considered due to their sense of uniform conduct and belongingness, while the same members could also currently be included in a numerous other social groups in another different contexts and situations.

Inter-group conflict and Intra-group 'storming'

When does a group search for its identity? When does the 'group' or any representative of the group, speak or describe or treat its social identity? A group

---

[48] cf., V. YZERBYT (Coord.) *Emotions and Social Identity: Toward an Integrated view of Intergroup Conflict:* An outline of a Research Project of the Department of Psychology under European Science foundation; European collaborative Research Network, Catholic University of Louvain, Belgium, 2004, Doc. A1-10, Electronic resource: www.esf.org/generic. (accessed 08 April, 2007).

[49] cf., DUCK – HOGG - TERRY, *Perceived Impact of Persuasive Messages*, in D. J. TERRY - M. A. HOGG (eds.), *Attitudes, Behaviour and Social Context: The Role of Norms and Group Membership,* pp. 269-291.

is subconscious of their social identity and alertly introspective of it when it is in time of crisis. The possible situations could be that social identity is badly defined or marginally viewed that would bring difficulty for the members and in turn signaling them for a time to redefine their identity. It could also be due to the challenges and threats from the other superiorly accepted groups due to the conflict of norms and values. In short, because of social comparison, an in-group tries to confirm and cognitively establish their identity as superior, higher and positive to the other groups. If they come to have about themselves a negative, lower social identity image when comparing themselves to others, it can result in social mobility or a social change.[50] The social identity theorists have proposed systematically some ways of reducing this kind of group tensions.

There are mainly three ways of reducing the inter and intra-group conflicts[51] and crisis of identity. They are Re-categorization, De-categorization and Cross-categorization. De-categorization is a social response to a tensed situation by "dissolving the problematic group (subgroup) boundaries altogether"[52] by which the interest of the group or subgroup is channelized to a type of "idiosyncratic" features of each individual. It is made possible by frequent interacts between the opposing group's individual members. Cross-Categorization involves in using one category membership that people share to cancel out another categorization where they differ.[53] Due to the relevance in this Markan study, we go for a little detailed description of the next mode of reducing group tension.

Re-categorization is a 'common in-group identity model' that redefines "a situation of conflict so that the members of rival groups (subgroups or antagonistic group) are subsumed into a larger single, super-ordinate category."[54] It proposes a study of the best condition where the members are brought together into

---

[50] Social mobility means, as outcome of the negative image of social identity, members may abandon the group to have better satisfaction of their social self. Social change means it implies that they may change their perspective of looking their existing status as impermeable or do positive reevaluation or redefining the group status satisfactorily; or they may compare themselves with another out-group for better social identity image.

[51] The subject of intra-group conflict is less concerned to SIT. When a situation which leads a group to the verge of schism or conflict is so intense, in the eyes of SIT, those 'subgroups' about to be divided are viewed as two separate entities with their own distinct categories. As Philip Esler says, "some times it is difficult to decide whether we are dealing with two subgroups of one group or whether schismatic pressures have become so pronounced that it is preferable to speak of two separate groups." cf., P. F. ESLER, *Conflict and Identity in Romans*, p. 27. When the opposing positions become incompatible within a group such that to accept it would be to subvert the very nature of the group where compromise becomes impossible and negotiation is blocked. This brings 'storm effect' in the group and may lead it to schism because the nature of identity is contested. Argument, negotiation and persuasion are the three levels of approach needed by leaders to solve the in-group contest of the identity crisis. cf., *Ibid.*

[52] P. F. ESLER, *Conflict and Identity in Romans*, p. 27.

[53] cf., P. F. ESLER, *Jesus and Reduction of Intergroup Conflict*, pp. 325-357.

[54] *Ibid.*

one category that will often be accompanied by close personal contact. It is a suggesting of a new overarching identity for both so-called 'subgroups'. It is done by increasing the salience of existing common super-ordinate group membership. Most of the Pauline strategy interpreted in the letters of Romans and Galatians conform to this healthy mode of reductionism of group tension.[55]

This common in-group identity model is recently seen from a slight different point of view by recent version of SIT.[56] It is useful for the interpretation of Markan strategy in solving his group crisis. According to Brewer, inter-group bias is to be seen primarily as representing a "pro-in-group orientation" rather than an "anti-out-group orientation". In-group members could perceive and treat out-group members positively but in-group members even more positively. Group formation brings in-group members closer to the self without changing the distance between the self and the out-group (or non-group) members much. "If members of different groups focus their attention on a super-ordinate category that encompasses both the in-group and the out-group in a single social group, in-group attitudes toward former out-group members will become more positive. This type of re-categorization is not designed to reduce or eliminate categorization. The aim is rather to structure a definition of group categorization to reduce inter-group bias and conflict."[57] This happens without even denying the subgroup distinction or subgroups abandoning their earlier categorization. Rather, it relies on the basic common salience of those subgroups identity over the differentiated subcategories.

Memory Aspect of the Social Identity

We are in search of the group identity of Mark, wherein the social identity theory will provide us scientific language to explain systematically the proposed identity of the Markan group. But, like any contemporary groups or like any community (group) evidently marked in the Epistles and other early Christian writings except the Gospels, we are not presented directly of any social image or crisis, problems and conflicts of the community that the Markan Gospel addressed to. It is not less easy to make direct connections between narratives about Jesus and the way such narratives may have shaped the identity of his later followers, as it is easier to do so with the Pauline and other pastoral letters. They directly dealt with controversies within of the primitive Christian communities.[58] However, we

[55] In this regard, I adapt more to the clarification of Philip Esler who explains the innards of this process that are supplementary for our understanding. For more, see, P. F. ESLER, *Conflict and Identity in Romans*, p. 27; also P. F. ESLER, *Jesus and Reduction of Intergroup Conflict*, pp. 325-357.

[56] Gaertner and his colleagues are interpreters of this new version of the SIT. cf., J. LIPPONEN – J. LESKINEN, "Condition of Contact, Common In-group identity, and In-group Bias toward Contingent Workers", *JSP* 146 (2006, 6), pp. 671-684.

[57] *Ibid.* p. 680.

[58] The inner problems and confusions in the early churches were related to the table fellowship, admission of gentiles, circumcision and non-circumcised members, food eaten that have been

proceed with reasonable presumptions that Gospels are the evidence of Christian sense of identity, given in the form of Gospel genre, story-modeled narratives similar to a biographical sketch of Jesus' life and death. Now the question so crucial is that, what is the role of the text that makes us to peep into the concrete immediate context of the community of Mark, and how the text acts as a window for us to look into the reality of the community and its identity formation?[59] What is the role of the text, author and the content/message in forming or reforming the identity of a community which conditioned the text? What kind of orientation did the collective memory have for the sense of identity of those participants in the *Sitz im Leben?* The memory theory will elucidate how the text presents the selected past tradition for the identity reconstruction for the 'present' of the group. It is a new way of understanding the process of tradition and the diachronic aspect involved in the formation of its textual fabric.

The Social Identity and its Temporal Dimension

The social identity theorists have shown little interest on temporal dimension of SIT, but anthropologists and sociologists did. This existential link between the time and the social identity persuades us to view the social realities as an ongoing process rather than a static one. Social life is "composed of discrete moments and contexts" which could be described as "temporal trajectories."[60] In this sense, the intimate link of the present with the past defines the temporal dimension, not in a very narrow sense but in a broad sense: the social time is macro as well as micro; the social group has an extended time from the present to the past and has a targeted time extended to the future. The "fragmentary experiences of a group are related across the temporal boundaries. Even the momentary social self-image involves an awareness of the present, past and anticipated future."[61] A group level social time includes elements like the foundation of the group, important early successes or reverses, internal or external threats posed to it at particular points in the past, the destiny its members envisage for themselves. The social identity necessitates a retroactive and proactive memory: a historical phenomenon of stretching the social memory backward and forward in time like a pendulum of a clock. As to the past, the collective memory nourishes the collective identities (encompassing events and treasured ancestors), invention of tradition and history writing. As to the present-future, the collective memory forms precautionary measures, strategies, measures and plans as anticipatory behaviors to sustain and

---

offered to idols, whether they are allowed to participate in the meals in temple, etc. The central factor of all those crisis and conflicts among them was 'jewishness'.

[59] cf., J. R. DONAHUE, "Windows and Mirrors: The Setting of Mark's Gospel", *CBQ* 57(1995), pp. 3-4.

[60] cf., P. F. ESLER, *Conflict and Identity in Romans*, pp. 22-24.

[61] *Ibid.* p. 23.

enhance the identity. Here it is necessary to investigate the notion of collective memory and its function in the formation of social identity.[62]

Social, Collective and Cultural Memory

Maurice Halbwachs (1877-1947), who is known as the father of the Memory theory[63] deals with the phenomena of memory as a social reality than as an individual neurological mechanism of a mental faculty. Nowadays, a century old memory theory gets its importance and attention in the area of biblical theology because of its potentiality to explain the origin and identity of the early Christian groups and the process of their tradition.[64] As a result of the far-ranging application of this theory in the biblical and cultural studies, there is a confusing variety of terminology to represent the social memory.[65] We herein trace in brief the different concepts of social memory in view of this short and simple study.

The Social memory comprises of communicative memory or collective memory.[66] The collective memory is the first-hand memory or remembrance of the past by the first generation of eyewitness. They are the living memory of the original generation, which exists, in the synchronic axis of the time (approximately 8-100 yrs.) and events. The cultural memory is the memory transmitted as tradition and the group constitutes the remembrance of the past generation. It involves the diachronic axis of the time and event. This shift from collective memory to a cultural memory is occurred by the memory crisis, which could be

---

[62] cf., *Ibid.*

[63] Maurice Halbwachs was a disciple of Henry Bergson, reputed French philosopher, proponent of the school of personalization. Halbwachs later left the individualistic theory of Bergson and joined the school of the French sociologist Emile Durkheim, to construct the thought of "operation of Memory" in social frame. cf., M. HALBWACHS, *Los Marcos Sociales de la Memoria* (trans. M.A. Baeza – M. Mujica), Anthropos, Barcelona, 2004; M. HALBWACHS, *La Mémoire Collective*, Presses Universitaires de France, Paris, 1950; M. HALBWACHS, *La Memoria Colectiva* (trans. I. Sancho – Arroyo), Prenas Universitarias de Zaragoza, Zaragoza, 2004; M. HALBWACHS, *Morphologie Sociales*, Armanda Colin, Paris, 1946.

[64] Among the authors who apply this theory in their study of the origin of Christianity. Gerhardsson, B. Mack, J. Crossan and Schroter are some who give new directions for the research. cf., A. KIRK – T. THATCHER, *Memory, Tradition, and Text*, pp. 34-42. Mack's *A Myth of Innocence* and Crossan's *The Birth of Christianity* are particularly referred to this regard.

[65] The literature uses distinct terms like, family memory, local memory, popular memory, public memory relational memory, cultural memory and so on. According to Vaage, the variety of expressions carries various connotations but often employs synonymously. Halbwachs distinguishes social memory between autobiographical or historical and collective. However, there are authors who distinguish the autobiographical or the collective as on the one hand and the cultural as the later development from the former one on the other hand. It is also said that, while the German school of scholars speaks of cultural memory, the English school speaks of the same in terms of collective or social memory. For James and Chris Wickham, social memory is distinct from collective memory, the view that is adapted by Leif Vaage. cf., L. VAAGE, *Galilean Upstarts*, p. 322.

[66] cf., CYPRIAN E. FERNANDEZ, "Memory and its Social Vitality; A Biblical Understanding", *LW* 121(2015), pp. 8-28.

observed as a disruption of the organic connection of the group with the past and the oral transmission. At this breakdown of the tradition, the community's scribal technology takes on its particular importance. For endurance of their memory from the loss of connection (crisis), they write them to stabilize the group memory. They work out the connection to the past in the midst of drastically altered circumstances. The writing of the memory in this case becomes an extraordinary efficient medium of symbolic objectification. Here, a question becomes relevant that what is the inner communicative mechanism of transmitting of the social memory before it is being written.

Telling and Re-telling Mechanism of the Memory-transmission

Here we try to understand the popular operation of memory. Remembering is the process by which people bring into awareness the past persons and events. They remember *what* and *who* that personally experienced (collective memory) or that they have learned from the others (of earlier generations–cultural memory). As Olick says, "genuine communities are the communities of memory that constantly tell and retell their constitutive memories."[67] Both *identity* and *continuity*, in fact the very survival of a community, depend upon its constant revitalization of memories.[68] These memories are preferably of its origin, the events that mark the group's emergence as an independent social entity and other landmark events in its history. In this mnemonic process, a mnemonic synchronization takes place where a community integrates different personal pasts into a single common past that all members jointly come to remember.[69] The commemorative practices of a group are represented by artifacts, commemorative narrative and ritual practices. In these practices, past is exemplary for the group that commemorates - an act of fixing the meaning and purposes of the group.[70]

The narratives, as to our concern in this study, pick up "bedrock events experienced with powerful immediacy and discern its meaning and significance through the act of commemoration. These meaning and significances are "distilled out and concentrated into a highly symbolic words, gestures and objects."[71] In this, the historical objects are receded for its symbolic objectification. Therefore, those past events and persons in the narrative are to be treated not as a "window onto

---

[67] J. K. OLICK, "Collective Memory: The Two Cultures", *ST* 17(1999), pp. 333-348, in A. KIRK – T. THATCHER, p. 4.

[68] cf., B. SCHWARTZ, "Postmodernity and Historical Reputation: Abraham Lincoln in Late Twentieth-century American Memory", *SF* 77(1998), pp. 63-103, in A. KIRK – T. THATCHER, pp. 1-24.

[69] cf., L. VAAGE, *Galilean Upstarts,* pp. 322-323.

[70] cf., CYPRIAN E. FERNANDEZ, *Memory and its Social Vitality*, pp. 14-17.

[71] A. KIRK, *Social and Cultural Memory,* in A. KIRK – T. THATCHER, *Memory, Tradition, and Text,* pp. 1-24.

the cognitive workings of their memory but only as a description for a specific pragmatic and rhetorical purpose."[72]

Now we have a theoretical base to presume that the Markan narrative was formed out of a long process of telling and retelling activity of community's past memory. It is time now to speak about the real author, text and its message conveyed, and what approach we need to have at them.

Text, Message, Author and Identity Formation

What is the text that we have now at hand? The text is a response to the crisis of the collective memory in the wake of the "breakdown in tradition" as Assmann says *Traditionsbruch*.[73] It attempts to articulate the memory in durable cultural artifacts and practices or to call text as commemorative artifacts. Memory gets a coherent shape in the text, being articulated in normatively typical social practices in an "aligned genre of discourses."[74] This articulation of the past is a "dynamic and unceasing" activity because "to remember is to place a part of the past in the service of the needs and conceptions for the present."[75] It is constructive. But Halbwachs clarifies that it is not an act of "*retrouver*" but "*reconstruire*"[76] that aligns the image of the past with present. So, it is reconstructive.

When memory of the past becomes the construction of the past for the reconstruction of the present, then the determining factors that help to select the past elements are the current needs and preoccupations of the community. They determine what kind of elements of community, memory or past are to be given prominence for the reconstruction of the present in the textual form for the community. As Leif Vaage reminds that, the reality of the past reconstructed would remain real only to the extend that it has been recalled and recreated "in a particular place by specific persons for particular purpose."[77] This act of construction and reconstruction is done by "moral entrepreneurs", shaping values and maintaining or achieving power, through "molding the past into certain types of symbolic texts", on behalf of the community; being selective to the parts of the past leaving others unmarked.[78]

---

[72] P. F. ESLER, *Conflict and Identity in Romans*, pp. 22-24.

[73] cf., J. ASSMANN, *Religion und Kulturelles Gedächtnis: Zehn Studien*, Beck, Munich, 2000, pp. 87-88, in A. KIRK - T. THATCHER, p. 6.

[74] cf., A. KIRK – T. THATCHER, pp. 1-24.

[75] B. SCHWARTZ, "The Social Context of Commemoration: A Study in Collective Memory", *SF* 61(1982), p. 374, in A. KIRK – T. THATCHER, pp. 1-24.

[76] M. HALBWACHS, *On Collective Memory* (ed. & trans. L. A. Coser), University of Chicago Press, Chicago, 1992, p. 40, in A. KIRK – T. THATCHER, *Memory, Tradition, and Text*, p. 10.

[77] L. VAAGE, *Galilean Upstarts*, p. 4.

[78] cf., *Ibid.*

Author of the Text and the Identity Formation

We have seen above that the collective memory becomes a reconstructed tradition. According to Botha, "tradition is interpretation", because "tradition should not be pictured as older, more pure; tradition is dynamic, developing aspect of human self-understanding and communication."[79] But how and why this social process is translated on to the narrative by its agent, that is, the author. To answer this from the social identity perspective, "leader and followers must define themselves in terms of a shared social identity,"[80] because the activities of both are collective than deriving from personal interests. A leader who stands as an in-group prototype (prototype group member) will epitomize better as a leader of the group. The ability of a leader is to influence (persuasiveness of the message activated through him) the members as a whole and to positively differentiate between in-group and out-group and to make their group "special". Leader is an "entrepreneur of identity, capable of turning "me" and "you" into "us" in relation to a particular project in a particular context that will bestow on the shared social identity meaning, purpose and value.[81] Philip Esler consolidates the overwhelming picture of leadership as follows; leader of a group is "someone who is highly adept through argument, negotiation, and persuasion at managing the debate, by neutralizing views antagonistic to his or her own and by stimulating a process of consensualization around a particular vision of group identity."[82] The leader is the one who is dynamic in creating, installing and maintaining a particular social identity in the minds and hearts of the people.

The role of a leader as identity definer could easily be equalized with the role of an author of a text that defines the identity for the group members to whom he belongs and shares the similar membership of them. There is a functional similarity between the role of an author and a leader in a group, irrespective of the designative status of the leader and absence of such status to the author in a group. Both endeavors to reconstruct the identity through their group-mediated persuasive messages and prototypical membership in the group.

Text is a 'Model of' and a 'Model for' the Group

Schwartz says, social memory is like *mirror* and *lamp*. The social memories as *mirror* reflect the group and social memories as *lamp* show it a way further, when they are told and retold in the community. As a *model of*, the collective memory reflects the past events in terms of the needs, interests, fears and aspirations of the present; as a *model for* the group, collective memory embodies a template that organizes and animates behavior and a frame within, which people locate and find

[79] P. J. J. BOTHA, "The Historical Setting of Mark's Gospel: Problems and Possibilities", *JSNT* 51 (1993), p. 40.

[80] cf., P. F. ESLER, *Conflict and Identity in Romans*, p. 84.

[81] cf., *Ibid.*, p. 88.

[82] cf., *Ibid.*, p. 39.

meaning for their present experience.[83] The text that contains the articulations of the memories of a group is really a *reflection of* and a *response to* the social and cultural setting of a group, simultaneously.[84]

The distinction between the *model of* and *model for* of the social memory is analytical and not empirical; both are realized in every remembrance. Memories must express current problems before they can pogrom ways to deal with them. We cannot be oriented by a past in which we fail to see ourselves. Memories as *model of* aspect are reflexive or expressive symbols, for articulating present predicaments. Memories, as *model for* aspect, are orienting symbols, like a 'map' that locates the group through the predicaments by rating *where we are to where we have been.* In the case of the Gospel of Mark, as Theissen says, "Mark's Gospel is shaped by community traditions. The most probable conclusion is that this entire Gospel is a record of Jesus traditions written for local communities, and that in this Gospel, popular tales and traditions from the disciples have been adopted and adapted in a new way for the use of these communities."[85] Hence, the Markan text is an encoded memory of the community and its study in understanding the memorial aspects of tradition is the very act of knowing what the community was. From the principle of the social memory theory, the Markan text and the author's persuasive message and the imposition of an identity to the community of Mark could be justified and explained.

As Frentress and Wickhans says, "when we remember we represent ourselves to ourselves and to those around us to the extent that our nature that which we truly are can be revealed in articulation, we are what we remember."[86] The study of the way we remember - the way we present ourselves in our memories, the way we order and structure our ideas in our memories, and the way we transmit these memories to others - is a study of the way we are.[87] Applying this to the encoded texts of memories of a community has the same output - understanding of the community of the text, its crisis, predicaments and reinterpretation of the identity. The decoding of memories and messages communicated by the text thereto becomes necessary to understand the Markan community.

---

[83] cf., B. SCHWARTZ, *Abraham Lincoln and the Forge of National Memory*, University of Chicago Press, Chicago, 2000, p. 18, in A. KIRK – T. THATCHER, p. 10.

[84] cf., J. H. ELLIOT, *What is Social Scientific Criticism?* pp. 7-8.

[85] G. THEISSEN, *The Gospels in Context: Social and Political History in the Synoptic Tradition*, (trans. Linda. M. Maloney), T & T Clark, Edinburgh, 1992, p. 282; also refered, G. THEISSEN, *Colorido Local y Contexto Histórico en Los Evangelios: Una Contribución a la Historia de la Tradicion Sinoptica* (trans. M. O. Gaztelumendi), Sigueme, Salamanca, 1997, p. 309.

[86] J. FRENTRESS – W. CHRIS, *Social Memory: New Perspectives on the Past*, Blackwell, Cambridge – Mass., 1992, p. 7, in P. F. ESLER, *Collective Memory and Hebrews 11*, in A. KIRK – T. THATCHER, p. 157.

[87] cf., *Ibid.*, p. 7.

Conclusion

The SIT has offered us with socio-linguistic frame and sufficient vocabularies to explain the group process. Moreover, the SIT and Memory theory have constructed for us a mental outline of what social identity consists of, in order to approach the ancient text and the messages and to construct the identity of the Markan group designed by the text. All that has been spoken of text above is applicable to the Markan text, all that has been said about the author is about Mark, the real author, and all that has been said about the memory and message is about the inherent tradition and message of the Markan Gospel. From this phase of theory and concepts, the study has to move further with a basic presupposition that, Mark is using the past collective memory of his group in a particular social context in which the group faces inward predicaments and outward conflicts [it is now a speculation] that quaked its group identity. Mark uses its memorial past with a motif to suggest or reaffirm the group identity (reconstruct the past for the 'present').

Our search questions now seem simple for the further phase of this study; how does the Markan story of Jesus project the in-group identity? What are the properties that should be gathered from the text in order to, primarily, articulate the suggested identity in Mark? What is the salient category and its, norms and values of categories, prototypical characters and their subsequent beliefs and attitudes, symbolically objectified in the narrative? The social identity model prompts us to have the observing, organizing, and categorizing activities over the given social data and the in-group, out-group behaviors shown in the narrative. The distinguished identity offered through the narrative to the respective first readers of Mark would lead further any to raise question on the intra-group predicaments and the inter-group conflicts that had paved way for this narrative discourse on Jesus-memory which had been directed to the historical community of Mark.

Chapter 3

DISCIPLESHIP AND IDENTITY DESCRIPTORS

Not the temple, not the tomb,
but the house is the center of Jesus' action.

(E. S. Malbon, *Narrative Space,* 117)

The previous chapter has recommended the model and methods of this study and advised for the essential textual properties, which are to be investigated here. The main concern in this chapter is to explore the text and find out what are the norms of discipleship that Mark suggests and how the characters are built up configuring to those norms, as models of discipleship. It is our presumption that Mark is using the past of the community to articulate the present. From this understanding, we investigate the textual elements to understand how he reconstructs the traditional collective memories to suggest a model of living in his community.

In order to categorize a group, one needs to find out the salient category to which the group is identified. Before we set out to define what the social identity Mark offers to his community through his text, we need primarily to know all the components that constitute the Markan image of his group identity. In the Gospel of Mark, it is doubtless that discipleship is the salient category in question. Hence, our primary task is to explore the norms and values of discipleship and how Mark creates prototypical role models being conformed to those values. To distinguish his in-group identity we also need how Mark constructs contrastingly the out-group characters.

This chapter deals with the first part of our task that consists of studying the meaning of discipleship and its constructive norms and attitudinal dimensions. It will find out what is the emphatic meaning that Mark suggests to the discipleship?

Here, we will have a redactional approach to understand the ideological tendencies of Mark that shaped the sayings of discipleship from the pre-existing tradition.[1] Most importantly, the Markan radactive materials will prompt us to see the nuances of his "otra visión"[2] or the 'social possible selves' of his community. As we proceed in this part, we will encounter leitmotifs among the ideas of discipleship; for example, the Christo-centric aspect of discipleship is a frequently reflected theme in the concerned pericopes. Those recurring ideas are presented in this chapter without omitting or amalgamating so that this study may not lose the Markan emphasis.

This part will deal with the discipleship as *vocation* and *disposition*. It would be a surprise that, first we analyze the norms and attitude of discipleship as disposition, then as vocation, by breaking the chronological order of the text, where Mark has all the principal call narratives in the first half of the story and the discipleship discourse appears after the middle section of the narrative. It is natural to the human behavior that the right disposition and attitude leads to right actions. The conviction precedes to any mission. The discipleship of Mark is a mission continued even out of the narrative world of the story, so that the same mission must be fulfilled out of conviction before anyone set out for that. The disciples are called to conform themselves to the convictions and attitudes of the discipleship.

The second part of our task treats the characterization of characters and the way Mark presents them as prototypes and antitypes as models or bad examples respectively. The prototypes will be the motivating characters of the community, telling them, what they ought to be and how they ought to behave, while the antitypes tell them that what they should not be. The author has a dream of his community categorized after the model of this prototype group. In this part, we use the method of narrative criticism to unpack the characterization of the characters.

Disposition to the Discipleship

The task of the Markan Gospel is preferably an attitude building. Mark proposes what a disciple of Jesus is to be in his/her given world that would naturally oblige one for a corresponding comportment. It is left up to the disciples to discern the praxis according to the given disposition of discipleship. It is noticeable that the content of the teaching of Markan Jesus is not evidently expressed in detail. Even the teaching content of the disciples who are sent out for mission, is concealed. It would be right to say that the Gospel of Mark is

---

[1] cf., R. LATOURELLE, *A Jesús El Christo por Los Evangelios*, Sígueme, Salamanca, 1992, pp. 188-200; "The Historical-critical Method", in *The Interpretation of the Bible in the Church*, The Pontifical Biblical Commission, 1993.

[2] cf., L. E. VAAGE, "El Evangelio de Marcos: Una Interpretación ideológica particular dentro de los Cristianismos Originarios de Siria-Palestina", *RIBLA* 29 (1998), pp. 10-30.

prioritized to project *a would-be world* of disciples - *a new way of being disciples in this world.* It is oriented to give a profound attitude and mental orientation than giving stipulated laws for the practice of discipleship.

The central teachings of Markan discipleship is concentrated on what his Jesus discourses to his disciples in three important blocks: **8:31-9:1**; **9:35-50**; **10:42-45**. In this section, Markan Jesus' interest of speech is on two sets of matters: 1. passion prediction 2. the discipleship. Mark structured this section of discipleship in a coaxial manner against the realities of passion prediction of Jesus and the 'failure' elements of the disciples.[3]

A. The first prediction of the Passion (8:31)
B. Peter's misunderstanding/disciples' failure (8:32-33)
C. Teaching about discipleship (8:34-9:1)

A. The second prediction of the Passion (9:30-31)
B. The disciples' misunderstanding/failure (9:32-34)
C. Teaching about discipleship (9:35-37)

A. The third prediction of Passion (10:32-34)
B. The disciples' misunderstanding/failure (10:35-40)
C. The teaching about discipleship (10:41-45)

This structure indicates the importance of the teaching given to the disciples on *the way to Jerusalem.* As it is set at the foreground of the Cross and resurrection of Christ, the clue of the Markan emphasis is very evident, that his understanding and reconstruction of the category of discipleship is mainly affiliated to the Christological event of Cross and resurrection. The episodes of the blind men cured, into which sandwiched these discourses of discipleship [(8:22-26) – (8:31-9:1; 9:30-37; 10:32-45) – (10:46-52)], are significant to the reader, that the understanding of the Christological events is a prerequisite for the right following, like the blind ones who see Jesus at first-sight than anything of this world (8:22-26; 10:46-52). As Mack says, "...Jesus' death is a model of discipleship to be imitated...[this section is] a charter document of discipleship...the constitution of the community ...[that includes] the community's ethics."[4] Lets' turn to analyze in detail these discursive blocks of discipleship.[5]

---

[3] B. L. MACK, *A Myth of Innocence*, Fortress Press, Philadelphia, 1988, p. 390.

[4] *Ibid.*, pp. 340-341.

[5] I use mainly the following secondary resources to analyze the pericopes to distinguish the redactive Markan material. E. BEST, *Following Jesus: Discipleship in the Gospel of Mark*, (JSNTsup.), Sheffield, England, 1981; R. BULTMANN, *The History of the Synoptic Tradition* (tran. J. Marsh), Basil Blackwell, Oxford, 1963; J. GNILKA, *El Evangelio Segun San Marcos* (tran. V. A. Martinez), Vol. 1&2, Sigueme, Salamanca,1996 ; J. MARCUS, *Mark 1-8*, (AB 27), Doubleday, N.Y- London – Toronto – Sydney – Auckland, 1999 ; J. SCHMID, *El Evangelio Segun San Marcos*, Herder, Barcelona, 1967; R. A. GUELICH, *Mark 1-8:26*, Vol. 34ª, WBC, Word Books Publisher, Dallas–

Greatness of Bearing Cross and Following Jesus (Mk 8:34-9:1)

As we have seen in the above structure, this set of logia is originally linked to the previous unit of sayings (Mk 8:27-30; 8:31-33) but are distinguished because of the presence of 'crowd' along with the disciples in v. 34, which is a Markan addition. The crowd is a collective character in Mark who receives teachings from Jesus, but not the Messianic secret. Mark makes the crowd recipient of discipleship discourse from Jesus in order to hint the reader that the mandate of discipleship is universalistic to bind all who wish to follow him.

Mk 8:34-38 is a pre-markan unit used by the author from the available tradition.[6] The v. 34 contains the important elements of the discourse (*aparnēsasthō* = "let him deny"; *stauron* = Cross; *akoloutheitō* = "let him follow"). These important elements belong to the tradition including 'self denial', which is placed with a reformulation.[7] The introductory part of this verse (v. 34a) is Markan as it echoes the Markan idea of Jesus in movement 'on the way' (1:16,19; 2:14; 10:17).[8] This authorial work is efficacious because, the traditional awareness in one being a member of Jesus-group is being illumined by his emphasis on *self-denial* and *Cross-bearing*. The v. 35 is given another focus to this meaning by the Markan addition of *euangelion* (Gospel, 1:1,14,15; 10:29,1310;14:9) to emphasis the personal commitment of the faithful to the crucified Christ who is 'yet to come'. The expression *heneken emou* ("on account of me" 8:35) is as well a Markan addition, as it is omitted by other Gospels that followed Markan sequence more closely, probably for the reason that it hadn't been from the tradition (Lk 17:33; Jn

---

Texas, 1998 ; J. MATEOS, *Comentario al Evangelio de Marcos*, Comisión General de la HOAC, Madrid, 1976 ; G. THEISSEN, *Colorido Local y Contexto Histórico en Los Evangelios* (tran. M.O. Gaztelumendi), Sigueme, Salamanca, 1997.

[6] It is a traditional material. The reasons are: Markan style of using *gar* to conjunct the separate logia together; absence of evidence elsewhere that Mark use to compile long sequence of sayings like this; if he has the same elsewhere he draws that from the tradition irrespective of the logical connection with his argumental part of the same unit of sayings. For example, v.38 has no connection with the theme of 'suffering' of v.34; vv. 36-37, instead the secular proverb is connected with v.35ff with a catch word *psychēn* (life). Again, Mk. 9:1 is an introduction by nature joined a pre-markan tradition by *kai elegen autois* ("and he said to them" 2:27; 4:2,11,21,24). There are parallels of Mk 8:34, 35, 38; Lk 14:27; Mt:10:38; Lk 17:33; Mt 10:39; Lk12:9; Mt 10:33. Gerd Theissen suggests that the idea "following" is a part of the tradition of Markan community. cf., G. THEISSEN, pp. 313-314. Bultmann says that this part has originally been separated and it is "a secondary combination conditioned by slight association circulated separately." cf., R. BULTMANN, pp. 82-83; E. BEST, pp. 29-54. Gnilka finds sequence of Q with it. cf., J. GNILKA, Vol. 2, pp. 182-183.

[7] See the parallels to this tradition: Mk 4:23; 7:16; 9:35, Rev 13:9; 2 Thess 3:10; 1 Tim 3:1; 1 Cor 16:22; Rom 8:9; 1 Cor 7:12-13.

[8] cf., J. GNILKA, Vol. 2, pp. 23-30.

12:25).[9] The vv. 36, 37 are traditional.[10] In the v. 38 *me kai tous emous logous* ("me and my words"), as we have seen in the previous verses, is a Markan attribution while the 38b will be a material from the Jewish religious memory, remembered from the prophetic verse of Daniel 7:13.[11] We can see another Markan accent on the memorial element he received by the addition of his pronoun *autou* to the noun 'father' (*his father*) to show that the Son of man is identified with the Son of God in the realm of his supreme authority.[12] For Gnilka, the full phrase *en tē doxē tou Patros autou* ("in the glory of his father", 8:38) is Markan, as mentioned above it is Mark's favorite act of linking Christological importance to the teaching of the discipleship.[13]

The 9:1 is linked with the previous logia (8:38, *doxa*) through the catch word *dynamis* (power). As the concept of *doxa* owe to the primitive tradition, the word *dynamis* too has its provenance from the same.[14] While W. G. Kümmel and A. Vögtle advocate for a traditional character of this verse, Perrin speaks of it as Markan product for several reasons.[15] *heōs* (until) is a usual Markan word (6:10,23,45; 9:19;12.36); the phrase "some standing here will not taste death" is a Markan variant of the apocalyptic saying (IV Ezra 6:25ff) of 13:30, "this generation will not pass away"; "kingdom of God" is a Markan style of expression (1:15); the verbal form of *erchomai* in 3:38 and 9:1 is similar in echo.

Now we move for an overview of Markan redactive hand in this pericope in order to analyze his accentuation in proposing the norms of discipleship and

---

[9] Bultmann considers it as addition with a Christological motif (losing the life of Christ). So it is secondary. He says: "reference to the person of Jesus is frequently a secondary introduction into the sayings...often done without change or new formulations..." cf., R. BULTMANN, pp. 93, 111, 150.

[10] They are wisdom sayings with an interrogative character directed to the disciples. cf., J. GNILKA, Vol. 2, p. 25.

[11] The plural form of *logos* is purposely used to get the attention of the audience who cared least for the Cross aspects of Christ and also to indicate that disciples had to fulfill the demands of discipleship that are not only so much have been expressed by Jesus and received through the tradition in the text or in this section of discourse, but also all that of extended in the tradition unwritten regarding the discipleship. cf., E. BEST, pp. 52-53.

[12] In v.38, there is no room to suppose that Mark added *epaischynomai* (ashamed of) under the presumption of Neronian persecution, for it is a pre-markan material (used only in v.38), normally connotes a general public witness (missionary aspect) and does not necessarily need any prejudice of a persecution (13:9) while reading it. cf., E. BEST, pp. 52-53.

[13] cf., Mark is only emphasizing the identity between the Son of God and Jesus that was existing before him. The apocalyptic event related to the Son of Man is a Christological event. J. GNILKA, Vol. 2, pp. 25-27.

[14] cf., *Ibid.*, pp. 23-30.

[15] cf., N. PERRIN, "The Composition of Mark ix 1", *NovT* 11(1969), pp. 67-70; E. HAENCHEN, "Die Komposition von Mk viii 27.ix 1", *NovT* 6 (1963), pp. 81-109.

thereafter to describe identity descriptors. Mark's redactional emphasis is as follows:

> **8:34** and having called together the crowd along with his disciples/let him deny himself and let him take up his cross. **8:35** for the sake of me and the good news. **8:38** in the glory of his father. **9:1** And he was saying to them / that there are some here of the ones having stood who will by no means taste death until they see the kingdom of God having come in power.

The whole meaning of discipleship that was developed in the vocation narratives is now become permeated beyond the twelve. Its meaning is given through clear-cut teachings that *anyone* who follows Jesus must deny him/herself and take up his/her Cross. Whatever is done on account of discipleship should not be out of any other motives but ultimately for the sake of Christ and his Gospel preached in the given circumstances. Whoever is ashamed of the same Christ and his Gospel will be judged and charged when the Son of Man comes in the glory of his Father. The Parousia is the certain time at which the discipleship becomes decisive.

Discipleship is inclusive in its nature. The teaching of discipleship binds to whoever wishes to follow Jesus. The reader can experience a Markan shift in his narrative from the esoteric teaching of Jesus (8:31-33) directed to his disciples to a teaching directed to a mass community included of crowd and disciples. Here, it is seemed to be a corrective approach in this Markan shift where discipleship is viewed in effect without any apartheid, Jews as wells as gentiles, leaders as well as the 'little ones'. The Markan inclusion of disciples and the crowd implies that the matter of following Jesus is an open option. Theissen views that Mark is giving new colors to the traditional dimensions of discipleship in his community. The traditional itinerant mode of discipleship is now being visualized universally as hereafter the new Markan colors of service, suffering and sharing the table fellowship are applicable to both itinerant and non-itinerant members of the community. In short, the horizon of the community of disciples is extensive and inclusive, as Mark has a fictive image of future disciples too, viewed at the present organism of his community.[16]

Discipleship implies following Christ by self-denial and Cross bearing. The self-denial is not something that is denied to self, but for Mark, it is the denial of him/herself because the direct object of the verb *aparnēsasthō* ("let him deny" v. 34) is 'himself' (*heauton*). The self-denial is opposite to self-affirmation, which means putting value on oneself before man or God. The self is defined as, all the statements a person makes that include the word *I*, *me*, *mine* and *myself*. All aspects of social motivation is included in it, so the Markan idea of self-denial

---

[16] cf., G. THEISSEN, p. 314.

involves also the denial of the kinship ties.[17] Best explains that "self-denial ... obviously involves the willingness not to affirm any right to life when faced by the persecutor, though it cannot be confined to this, since by itself it does not contain any idea of literal death."[18] The term *psychē,* (vv. 35, 36, 37) is a two part mashal[19] with the double sense of both, life preserved from the death and life lost through the death.[20] The man who embraces totally for the natural, earthly life risks the eschatological essential life. In the second rhetorical question (v. 37) with an allusion to Ps 49:8, Mark develops his idea of discipleship with the question of losing life that "nothing is as valuable as the human existence that is realized in the discipleship."[21] In the words of Best, "the man who denies himself (34b) is the same as the man who loses [destroys] himself for the sake of Christ (35b) and the Gospel; he saves himself. The man who refuses to deny himself [for the sake of Gospel and Christ] but rather affirms himself is the same as the man who wishes to save his whole being [to preserve it for himself]; he loses or destroys himself."[22] The radical renunciation of the desire for life is itself the way of attaining the essential life. Not that the very renunciation precedes to its reward rather the very act of detachment subsists in the reward. This deepest level of denying is enabled only through the personal adherence and allegiance to Jesus ("for my sake and my Gospel").

The Cross bearing has a metaphorical sense, being different to the Lukan expression of "daily Cross" (Lk 9:23-27). As the teaching is directed to the crowd as well as disciples, it does not bear any presentiments of bearing death, as the only way of being disciples. The 9:1 speaks about someone who would survive until Parousia and hence Mark does not expect all to be martyred. It implies an outward willingness to make any sacrifice. Jesus' Cross-bearing is the very continuum of all that of his life meant to him; Cross is coherent of all that brings uneasiness, challenge and risks over the radicalism of discipleship demanded by Jesus.

Mark is focal on underscoring two conditions of discipleship: denying oneself and Cross-bearing. No one can follow Jesus unless follows the way of the Cross. The disciples following Jesus implies not only understanding his way of the Cross but also following it essentially in act through self-denial and Cross-bearing. Bearing of the Cross was indigestible and indemonstrable to Jews for two reasons: firstly, it was a pagan mode of execution; secondly, Deut 2:22-33 speaks of the one dying on the tree defiles the land given as the possession of God. However, Markan community is now conferred upon a self-image of a *new Israel* with a new meaning of life. For them, the Cross-bearing becomes a symbol of their

[17] cf., B. MALINA, "Let him deny himself Mk 8:34", *BTB* 24 (1994), pp. 106-119.

[18] E. BEST, p. 53.

[19] It agrees with all the tradition of Q and par. (Mt and Lk, Jn 12:25, Gos.Thom.)

[20] cf. EDNT, pp. 501-502.

[21] *Ibid.*

[22] E. BEST, pp. 52-53.

self-awareness and hallmark of their identity. This unique feature of discipleship is conformed with the divine viewpoint evaluated at the background of the OT reality that God's self-revelation is accompanied always by a demand to whom that is revealed (Ex 20:2, Rom 12:1, 2). It is a biblical pattern that is insistently used by Mark to dissociate meaningfully the concept of following Jesus from that of Hellenistic-rabbinic mode of relation between teacher and disciples.[23]

Discipleship implies personal allegiance to Christ. In the contemporary period of Jesus, it was customary that leaders of various sects used the model of discipleship after the image of Prophets (Elijah and Elisha). For instance, the rabbinic mode interested in inculcating law; Hellenistic philosophers had disciples to generate sense of truth in them. In these models, pupil could change their teacher for another as, they choose their teacher, nor vice versa.[24] To its contrary, Mark advice a discipleship that demands an indispensable alliance with Jesus (8:34 *opisō mou, akoloutheitō moi*). There are two complimentary ways of being allegiant to the person of Christ: "for the sake of me and the for the sake of the good news". This Markan phrase signals a transitional phase of Markan generation, during which (*genea* 8:38) he affirms the need of a personal commitment to Jesus. This personal commitment is denoted with the Markan addition of "for my sake" and "good news" – a missionary terminology. In this shift from collective memory of the first generation to the cultural memory of the second generation, there had been perhaps a tendency to replace the personal commitment to Jesus by the sufficiency of the Good news verbally communicated. To its correction, Mark intervenes to confirm both the person of Christ and his message as double faces of the same reality. The personal adherence of disciples to the person of Christ as well to his message makes realize the presence of Christ. Gospel preached is as authentic as the tradition came down from Jesus.

The discipleship takes precedence to Parousia. The diverse Christological implications are presented by Mark to teach his community that *the way* has been traced and contrived by Jesus. The way of Christ is tested and proved by him. The *middle time*[25] that falls between the death and the return of Christ is the time of and in which his disciples are with the same pattern of his mission of preaching, living and dying for the Gospel. This link lies between v.38 and 9:1; "Who is ashamed of him and his word, the Son of man also will be ashamed of him when he comes in glory / someone will not taste death until see the kingdom come in glory." Moreover, since v.38 ends the sequence of the discipleship discourse with a tone of threat, Mark ascertain in his antithetical promise of 9:1, the coming of the Kingdom by reinterpreting the Parousia and establishment of the kingdom as one

---

[23] cf., *Ibid.*, p. 35.

[24] cf., M. HENGEL, *Seguimiento y Carisma: La Radicalidad de la Llamada de Jesús* (tran. J. A. Jáuregui), Sal Terrae, Santander, 1981, pp. 31-54.

[25] W. H. KELBER, *The Kingdom in Mark: A New Place and a New Time*, Fortress Press, Philadelphia, 1974, p. 140.

and the same entity to be fulfilled in Christ.[26] The witness to the establishment of the kingdom is a promise to a limited and specific member of the group who will remain steadfast under the threat of persecution. This is the Markan emphasis in 9:1. He does not intend to make an ideological transition on the delay of Parousia but reassures it. His reinterpretation of Parousia is further clear in chapter 13 when he speaks about the certainty of it but uncertainty of its time, igniting his community to continue Jesus' mission on this world with vigilance on the establishment of the Kingdom. After all the eschatological act of vindication is ultimately of God's act in His time and Christ is the assurance of it. Markan hope is that the disciples in spite of any trial and persecutions are set ultimately to witness and participate in the establishment of the Kingdom and to be constantly vigilant. Mark affirms the eschatological hope bound to a time meanwhile the community of disciples is that the one constantly engaged at the cause of Gospel being oriented permanently to the coming of Christ.

Greatness of Serving in Humility (Mk 9:33b – 50)

This passage of discourse contains a bulk of themes that are allied to the subject of discipleship, like servanthood, becoming least, avoiding segregations and scandals (9:33b-35). Though it finds little logical sequence and lack of a unified purpose, the parts of this section are linked through catchwords like *onoma* (vv.37,38,39,41) *dexētai* (vv. 36,37) *paidiōn*, *mikrōn* (vv.36,37,42) *ballō*, *kalon*, *estin* (vv.42,43,45,47) *skandalisō* (42,43,45,47) *pyr* (43,48,49). This section can be subdivided into three parts according to its ideological importance: vv.33-37 (greatness of discipleship); 38-41 (inclusiveness of discipleship); 42-50 (avoiding scandal to the little ones).

In vv.33-37, vv.33, 34 are completely Markan construct.[27] Probably Mark had added these verses to heighten the dramatic irony - Jesus on the way to humiliation and disciples in debate on 'greatness'. The vv. 35,36,37 are generally from the communitarian tradition[28] but v. 37b is a Markan construct;[29] v.36 is a

---

[26] cf., E. BEST, p. 45.

[27] Reasons: there are two fold introductory settings (vv.33 & 35); a confusing setting with disciples and the twelve; Markan creativity to symbolize geographic space like Capernaum; his own *en tē hodō* motif; it has signs of traditional material in the immediate verse (*ephōnēsen*) to which Mark prefers *proskaleō* (3:13,23; 6:7; 7:14; 8:1,34; 10:42; 12:43; 15:44). cf., E. BEST, pp. 75-77; R. BULTMANN, pp. 61-62.

[28] Bultmann categorizes v.36 as traditional material as Mark has taken over it to introduce a complex sayings. The v. 36 might have been taken from the tradition of 10:16. cf., R. BULTMANN, pp. 61-62.

[29] For Gnilka 35a is a Markan construct for setting a base for Jesus' teaching and for the mention of the twelve but it is a counter evidence to Best's argument as it is unconvincing that Mark himself construct two introductory settings for the same pericope. Gnilka provokes us to consider the first introduction v.33 as traditional, which is unconvincing, for, it contains more Markan

Markan adaptation from the primitive Christian memory about Jesus in parallel to 10:16.

The verses 38-41, especially vv.38-40 are encrusted here from the Markan traditional source, which had been in sequence as it is now but made available to us through catchword *onoma.*[30]

The vv. 42-50 is attached to the previous part of the pericope with the catchword *mikros* (little ones), *skandalisō*. These believing [ones] (*toutōn tōn pisteuontōn* 9:42) is explanatory to the preceding word (*tōn mikrōn*) that seems to be a latter addition.[31] Regarding vv. 43-48, Mark uses them in a metaphorical sense because they have an Aramaic touch (*geenna*) and mutilation (*apokopto*) is against Jewish moralism.[32] They cannot be a literal advice because there is no need to jettison the organic part of the body as they are hardly harmful in themselves, but are so when they lead a person to evil. The verses 49-50 does not show any logical progression from the previous sayings but appears to be pre-markan, incorporated with catchword pu/r, to highlight the theme of discipleship. It finds difficult to articulate the motifs and meanings of this complex and varied implication of catchwords. The final invitation to peace is Markan for the reason that his résumé grant a solution to the internal crisis of the community; the ultimate hope is for peace.

Let us see the Markan redactional hand in this pericope.

> **9:33** and they came into Capernaum. And being in the house, he was questioning them, what on the way were you arguing about? **9:34** but they were being silent for with one another they argued on the way, who [was] greater. **9:37b** and whoever receives me not [only] receives me but

---

favorite themes of *on the way* and significance of passion sense, and reference of Markan mythical space (Capernaum). cf., J. GNILKA, Vol. 2, pp. 64-65.

[30] Bultmann considers it as 'I' saying. The 'I' sayings are predominantly polemic against Hellenistic Churches with a beginning in the Palestinian Churches. The vv. 38-40 can probably be a formulation by the Church under the spirit of Jesus. cf., R. BULTMANN, pp. 25, 54. Also cf., J. GNILKA, Vol.2, pp. 67-69. Best believes that this sequence had been of pre-markan as the compilers of the tradition found catchwords to form in a unit. Reasons: if Mark had formed and inserted, he would not have broken the sequence of vv.37&42 that both speaks of child and little ones. If one makes this insertion, he could do it better after v.42 so fittingly. Moreover, vv.38-40 are seemed to be more natural than 38-41 sequence. This block contains many early Church vocabularies that confirm the traditional value than any of the redactional (eg. *your name ; my name; speak evil of me; because you are Christ's* ; Acts 19:13; 1 Cor 12:3; 1Jn 4:2; Did. 11:8-12). cf., E. BEST, pp. 75-77; H. FLEDDERMANN, "The Discipleship Discourse (Mk 9:33-50)", *CBQ* 43 (1981, 1), pp. 57-75.

[31] The verses 44, 46 do not appear in the ancient text authorities that are identical to the vv.48. The original author had limited the repetition. cf., B. M. METZGER, *A Textual Commentary on the New Testament* (2nd ed.), UBS, 2005, p.86-87. The v. 48 has allusion to Isa 66:24 as it is radactive because fire is repeated like salt in vv.49 and 50. cf., J. GNILKA, pp. 64-65.

[32] According to the Jewish concept, concupiscence or human instincts are located in the human organs. cf., Sir 6:17; 27:20; 6:18; J. GNILKA, Vol. 2, p. 75; E. BEST, pp. 75-77.

[also] the one having sent me. **9:42** the ones believing. **9:50** and be at peace at one another

The norm of discipleship is groundbreaking and radical to trespasses the cultural system of values by accepting children and little ones after the model of Jesus, who received children and became as 'insignificant' as child on the Cross. The inversion of the value system in the 'new community of Israel', the Jesus-movement, is definitive; greatness is to serve the little ones of the community in all means. Greatness involves in becoming servant to all. To receive the little ones therefore is to receive Jesus and to receive Jesus is to receive who sent Jesus - God. Now, we will focus on the central and new aspect of discipleship that Mark brings to the limelight.

Discipleship is service to the little ones. Jesus use child metaphor as means to teach the value of discipleship. It does have both symbolic as well as literal meaning. Markan Jesus' mandate, "do not prevent him" in the case of anonymous exorcist corresponds with his mandate to the disciples who hindered children (10:14) saying, "do not hinder them". If we read them together, the expression of "little ones" is reciprocal in its use as literal and metaphorical. Primarily the child (*paidiōn*) is physically termed by the verbal qualification *enankalisamenos* ("having taken in arms" v. 36) which to mean literally as child. In the Mediterranean culture, a child was insignificant, weak and non-ideal. There was a lack of emotional sympathy for them.[33] One was not mature until he became – *bar mitzwa*.[34] In contrary to this, disciples are called on concretely to have a rupture with the cultural values that are detrimental to the human dignity, irrespective of age and status. They are ought to be ready to accept, welcome and recognize such unimportant ones in the community (10:13-16). Disciples, who are culturally inspired to be first or to crave for power and status, must become least and last like children of their culture, in the *new family* of disciples. They should give attention to the children the insignificant and the least, in the name of Jesus who became the least, the last and insignificant on the Cross.

Secondly, Mark added "the little ones" (*mikros autōs*) to define metaphorically, "ones believing" (*tōn pisteuontōn*) because the whole section is a warning, which pricks the conscious of bad exemplars of the community. The simple insignificant believers are encouraged not to abandon their faith because of the exclusive mentality of the members of the community and amazing wealthy ones. The term "little ones" is technical. Believers in the primitive Christian tradition were who turned to the community in faith seeing the wonders and who confessed their faith and disclosed their old sinful ways (Eph 1:12; 2 Thess 1:10; Acts 19:18). They were who believed the testimony of the Apostles and hoped for the second

---

[33] W.A. STRANGE, *Children in the Early Church*, Wipf & Stock, Oregon, 2004, pp. 1-37.

[34] cf., J. GNILKA, Vol. 2, p. 65; J. S. JEFFERS, *The Greco-Roman World of the New Testament Era*, InterVarsity Press, Illinois, 1999, pp. 247-249.

coming of Christ. It is evident throughout the Markan story, how Mark treats those 'minor-believers' (minor characters) as exemplars and prototypes than the privileged disciples. Hence, those believers (little ones) in this context could be; 1. "whoever gives to drink a cup of water" 2. "whoever is not against us". The one who cares and gives attention to the little ones in his name is rewarded. To restrict the community by exclusive hard and fast lines and to ignore the little ones (anonymous and simple believers) will be a great offence and it will lead one to destruction in *geenna*. In gist, we can abridge the whole idea like this; the greatness of a disciple in the community lies in accepting those who are physically weak, spiritually ingenious and psychologically simple.

Discipleship has interest in the sanctity and integrity of the community. This Markan understanding preserves the unity of thought in this complex pericope. The disciples of Jesus must be in a disposition to fight decisively against evil, to refrain from giving scandals and to accept renunciation and personal sacrifices. All these are intended not only for personal virtues but also to enrich and strengthen the communion of the disciples. All those evils such as craving for to be first and great, giving scandals, ignoring little ones, will threaten the communion and unity of the disciples. The Markan metaphor of amputation of bodily organs (vv.43-47) to avoid scandal could be read as communitarian in the light of Quintilian sayings.[35] Then it will be seen that it is implicitly applicable to the health of the community; members of the community of believers who gives offense should be 'amputated' (1 Cor 5:1-13; 1 Cor 12:12-27). The choice of the members in the community for the eternal life or loosing ones life hence becomes not a personal affair alone, but rather a demand for the preservation of socio-religious health of the community of believers.

Greatness of being Servant and Slave of all (Mk 10:35-45)

This section of the discourse consists of two parts: first, the conversation between two disciples and Jesus and its pattern is petition (vv.35-37) and response (vv.38-40); second, the doctrination of discipleship. Mark joins these two parts with literary patterns of parallelisms and repetitions.[36] Bultmann is skeptic about the historicity of the persons of John and James in this pericope. According to him, the traditional materials of the primitive Christian community have no interests in the response of the persons rather than Jesus.[37] Therefore, the focus of

---

[35] "Ut medici abalienta morbis membra praecidant, ita turpes ac perniciosos etiam sin obis sanguine cohaerant, amputandos" in *Institutio Oratoria* 8.3.75. cf., H. KOESTER, "Mark 9:43-47 and Quintilian 8.3.75", *HTR* 71(1978), pp. 151-153.

[36] Repetition: v. 38, to drink, to baptize; Parallelism: right and left (vv.37,40), synthetic parallelism of vv. 42-43, "you know" (v. 42) and "you do not know" (v. 38); Dialogue and Monologue: first part of the section is dialogue and second part is monologue; in the first part Mark use the conjunction *de* and in the second part it is *kai*.

[37] Were the sons of Zebedee the original questioners or questioners in the tradition? Are the names of them are secondary or later addition as representatives? cf. R. BULTMANN, p. 63. Some

this section, as to our concern, is not on the characters, but the doctrinal sayings of Jesus on discipleship.

The unit of vv. 35-40 is a creative contribution of Mark[38] because of its eschatological reference, but with a slight exception to v.35. Particularly, Mark would not have reintroduced James and John as sons of Zebedee as he had them already in 1:19; 3:17. Therefore, v.35 is believed to be from the tradition.

The vv. 41-45 will be a theme of criticism against those who are held of power. The vv.42-45 are seemed to be pre-markan without the setting of the pair disciples (but *hoi deka* vv 41-42), but brought them into the text by Mark. Bultmann suggests that, vv.43-44, the central teachings of discipleship would be the older dominical sayings of the earliest community created independently and in the Markan text this is the replica of the original sayings of Mk 9:35 (similar terms are *prōtos, pantōn doulos, hymōn diakonos*). *hymōn* (v.43) is a later formulation of tradition comparing to 9:35 and the saying is originally referred to the service and its greatness in the Christian community and now the author links it to his context in the light of Jesus' ultimate service on the Cross.[39] Best argues that v.45 proceeds from the tradition but 45b (to give life as a ransom) is an older article of faith which interprets the death of Jesus as salvific, transmitted independently in the semitic ambience of Palestine and Mark added it to the v. 45a. It is because v. 45b (1 Tim 2:6) is absent in the Lukan parallel tradition but shares the tradition regarding v. 45a (the Son of man) which apparently breaks itself from v.44.

We see here the editorial emphasis of this pericope.

> **10:36** and he said to them what do you wish me [that] I may do for you? **10:37** and they said to him grant to us that one on your right and one on [your] left we may sit in the glory of you. **10:38** but Jesus said to them, you do not know you ask, are you able to drink the cup which I drink or the baptism which I am baptized to be baptized [with]? **10:39** and they said to them, we are able and Jesus said to them the cup which I drink

take the reference to James as historical, supposing his martyrdom.

[38] Reasons for that vv.38-39 are addition of the author: the sequence of the question of dual brothers (v. 35ff) and the answer of Jesus (v.40) is broken by vv. 38, 39 as it seems to be Markan interpolation to link the new dimension of discipleship with martyrdom of disciples especially of James. cf., J. GNILKA, Vol. 2, pp. 110-123. Best agrees with Bultmann ruling out the martyrdom element of James. Reasons are as follows: Mark always links the matter of discipleship with the theme of Christ's death and resurrection and here the service is after the model of the sacrifice of Jesus. Secondly, these two sons of Zebedee are not heroes to make them great figures. Thirdly, these verses implies that power, authority, position and even heavenly places are dearer for disciples but following Jesus, which involves suffering like Jesus, for his name and Gospel is reminded crucially important. Finally, the 'sacramental act' of community is stressed since discipleship is associated with community as well as the cause of its celebration – the power, death and Jesus' memory. cf., E. BEST, pp. 123-133.

[39] cf., R. BULTMANN, pp. 145-146; J. GNILKA, Vol. 2, pp. 114-123; E. BEST, pp. 123-133.

> you will drink and the baptism which I am baptized [with] you will be baptized [with]. **10:40** but to sit on my right or [my] left is not [for] me to grant, but for the ones it has been prepared. **10:41** and having heard the ten became angry with James and John.

Markan endeavor is on setting more a context for reinterpreting the meaning of service and authority for his community. He makes use of the community's teaching of service to give a new emphasis against the internal crisis of the community regarding the same. To have a share in the authority of Jesus is to have a share in his way of service because his authority consists in fulfilling the mission in total service as ransom for many. Mission of disciples after the example of Christ is the mission of total service. The greatness of the discipleship consists in being slave and servant to all rather than domineering over the little ones.

Discipleship demands a disposition to serve all than imposing authority. This teaching offers us an impression that Mark tries to address an internal problem of his community regarding power and discipleship. We may presume from his emphasis on the making of a context of vv 35-40 that, in the initial period, the sense of authority and ruling in the community could have been conceived as primary position, than seeing them as ruler and ruled in the literal sense (1 Cor14). It is psychologically observed that anyone who works within a community or organization would be wished to have his work acknowledged by his fellow-colleagues. Before the tendency to craze for recognition and dominant position turns to become a 'ruler-ruled' relation among the believers, Mark interferes with a radical caution. He presents two contrasting ways of exercising authority – civic way and the way in the community of believers (42b, 43a), but these verses (vv.42, 43) do not focus on exercising the authority, but contrast between authority and service (vv.43b, 44). These two contrasting concepts are denoted by the words, *diakonos* and *doulos*.[40] The civic way of exercising the authority is negated to describe the meaning of service in the community. Mark makes an inversion of priorities in the value system. The more he negates the civic style of authority, the more he uses the civic concepts (servant and slave) of service to indicate the modality of his communitarian service. When the more one desires to be owner and master of others in the civic society, the more one should become slaves and servants in the new eschatological community of Mark. The discipleship is a call to become 'servant' and 'slave' in the community reigned by

[40] *diakonos* is unimportant subordinate service for work while *doulos* is a status of a person who sustain a permanent servile relation to the another in the Mediterranean Greco-Roman world (1 Cor 7:20-23). A slave is a bondman. cf., J. S. JEFFERS, pp. 221-236. These two words are conceptually different and distinct – synonymous in certain aspects of service but not the same. These two concepts of service could be appropriate for the discipleship in the Markan community. The concept of *diakonos* is a secular word which was widely used by Paul; Mark use this concept to indicate the service of women (Rom 11:13; 2 Cor 3:3,6; Rom 15:25,31; 2 Cor.8:4; Mk.1:31; 15:41; Lk.8:3; 10:40; Mt. 25:44). It had no biblical background prior to NT usage. cf., J. H. THAYER (ed.), *Thayer Greek-English Lexicon of the New Testament* (electronic edition), IBT, 2000.

God, not by human masters. In the secular field, preeminence is associated with public honour and position (v.42) while in the Markan group it should emerge in humble, unrewarded service (vv.43f). Best is in opinion that disciples are not called to imitate the service of Jesus by giving their life as ransom. It is unique to Jesus and efficacious to men. Rather Mark alludes the service of disciples to the table fellowship, which commemorated the perfect service of Jesus' death. This table fellowship is the foundation to the community's concept of all other services in their way of discipleship.[41] Hence, any one 'called' to the community of believers is to be profoundly 'baptized' (10:30) to this mentality of Jesus' service. The disciples are called to follow the spirit of Jesus' service in the community. The vocation to discipleship is the vocation fundamentally to serve and not to be served. For this, Jesus calls and gathers disciples so that they may configure their mentality with that of Jesus.

Vocation to Discipleship

We will see that Markan call narratives are basically constructed in a similar pattern. For this reason, we will not deal all the respective pericopes as meticulously as did above in order to distinguish redactional materials of Mark but certainly seek for the essential Markan intonation of discipleship informed in the following call narratives. We would analyze 1:16-20; 2:13-17; 3:13-19; 6:6b-13; 10:17-31. These sections contain the factors of Jesus' call and disciples' response, which are elementary to the discipleship.

Follow me (Mk. 1:16-20)

The discipleship is the prominent category to which Mark dedicates an enormous part of his intelligent story. From the outset, Markan Jesus gathers his followers to campaign the radical change that he is going to launch on earth. As part of the Markan task in rediscovering the Christological significance of discipleship, he formulated this call narrative with a combination of traditional materials and his editorial contributions.[42] For Bultmann this call narrative only seems to be a "description of an ideal scene" of the discipleship than constituting any historical record. By ideal, Bultmann means that they embody a truth in some metaphorical sort of situation, which, because of its wider reference, gives the apothegms their symbolic character. The "fishermen" in this call narrative is an already circulated pre-markan metaphor and all the elements of this pericope like, time, place and details of the narrative situation, are associated with this single

[41] cf., E. BEST, p. 127.

[42] Reasons to show the Markan creative use of tradition: Markan conjunction *kai* and Markan parenthetical clause *gar* ; 'fishers of men' usage is from tradition for he has not used it anywhere else in his work; Andrew with Peter is mentioned so it is presumed that it comes from the tradition for Andrew is not a prominent person in the Markan narrative elsewhere; he does not give any preferential option for James and John than Peter and Andrew although the early church had a 'James and John' faction which led the creation of this tradition. cf., E. BEST, pp. 165-169.

metaphor, 'fishermen'.[43] The Markan priority is clear[44] when he constructs this pericope with a geographical scene of Galilee, which is an important site for the meaning of discipleship in Mark (16:7).

Discipleship is to follow Jesus who is its author and origin. This pericope lies between the initial picture of Jesus' identity as a person (the Son of God of prologue and baptism) and his identity of mission (Galilean ministry). This Christological emphasis in 1:1–15 serves as thematic tone which sirens a relationship between Christology and discipleship.[45] In this call narrative, we have four fishermen who receive Jesus' call and leave behind their material possessions and kinship to follow him. This act of foregoing has an apparent *symbolic value* of *metanoia*, the demand of Jesus' inaugural preaching which implies a total turning away, a reorientation or a departure from the former life. All these implications of conversion are shown realized now in the four fishermen. Their following becomes an apparent model of following the Gospel. In an indirect manner, the discipleship becomes a true response to Jesus' arrival, mission and his preaching of God's dominion.

In this episode, the followers are called in an incidental way and the lack of explanation on what happens to their psychological world indicates that Jesus is the absolute author of their call. The vision of Jesus (*eiden*) is fixed on them and his perception of mission is addressed to them - "fishers of men". The call is inspired not by the choice of disciples but purely of Jesus' initiative. This idea is reechoed in the other call narratives also (3:13-19); "he went up the mountain and called to him those whom he wanted and they came to him." The discipleship is a privilege conferred on the disciples not out of their merits but out of the powerful choice of Jesus. In another angle, Suzanne views this call as intentional, to mean that the disciples were not in a strayed position rather occupied with

---

[43] cf., R. BULTMANN, p. 28.

[44] For Joel Marcus, this story is a mixture of tradition and redaction of Mark. Reasons: an evident trace of it is seen in the Markan style of conjoining the two similar materials together like rising of Jairus' daughter and healing of hemorrhaged woman, unknown growth of seed and mustard seed; paralleled with Levi's call, in it shown Markan hand of creation as v.16 *Kai paragón para tēn thalassan tēs Galilaias* is his own redaction for the idea of Jesus' movement and significance of Galilee in the theology of Mark is important; some of the phrases like *eiden, ēsan gar halieis, kai euthys* (2:14; 3.34; 6:34; 8:33; 9:25; 10:21ff) are frequent in Markan usage. This call narrative use the typology of O T call of Elisha and Elijah (2 Kings 19:19-21). However, observes some uniqueness in the call of disciples from that of Elijah and Elisha. cf. E. BEST, p. 168. There is no room to say that Markan call narrative had been formulated after the model of those prophets but they might have left some impressions on its process of shaping. The twin call instances of Peter and Andrew as one set and the call of James and John as another set were coupled by Mark, because the primer group was casting the net while the second group is mending the net, which are usually done at separate times. These calls could be presumed as occurred traditionally at different times of the day; casting net at nighttime and mending at daytime. cf., J. MARCUS, pp. 179-186.

[45] cf., R. A. GUELICH, *Mk 1.16-20*, WBC; S. W. HENDERSON, *Christology and Discipleship in the Gospel of Mark*, Cambridge University Press, N.Y., 2006, pp. 48-65.

their livelihood and their call is intentional according to the viewpoint of Jesus.[46] Another point regarding the centrality of Jesus in discipleship is that their call sets them in motion after Jesus, paying heed to his invitation "come after me". Discipleship is a movement after Jesus, though the missionary aspect of 'sending out' is also vitally implied in the call.

Discipleship demands leaving of material possessions and cultural system of kinship tie. Mark introduces the fore-status of the disciples; "for they were fishermen." This explanatory parenthesis informs of the disciples' occupation and sets the stage for Jesus' call of disciples to become "fishers of men" (1:17).[47] They seem, especially James and John, to be more like the managers than the laborers in the fishing business. Culturally speaking, they are people having subjects under their proprietorship. The leaving behind of 'all' for the sake of discipleship has more significance because they are leaving not merely material possessions or kinship ties but managerial position of ownership and honour in order to follow the authorial position of Jesus.

The wholeness of their life is in question for the sake of discipleship. It is well developed in 10:28-31 that not only forgoing of the material possession but also the kinship and household ties are under the demand of discipleship. This kind of renunciation of self-oriented ties would bring persecution and pain along with membership to a communion-oriented families on the basis of spiritual ties (10:30,31). This teaching points towards a solidarity of a *new family* system in virtue of the discipleship. In another word, discipleship does not gratify anyone with a sole renunciation rather it is in making of a community – "a new covenant community" sought to live the will of God.[48]

Discipleship constitutes a family of a new house of God. We have seen that the call ultimately presupposes a making of a new community, and that is through a profound detachment to the patriarchal family system and its kinship. It is a prerequisite, which is further developed while the Markan story progresses (10:28-31). Here, in order to understand the discipleship as a making of a new

---

[46] The commentators opine that Mark is careful to convince the credibility of the call of disciples and the authority of Jesus with a prophetic allusion hired from the prophetic tradition of Elijah-Elisha call (1 Kings 19:19-21). This shows that the community of Mark has a Jewish background of knowledge to be convinced of the divine origin and credibility of their status as disciples at the background of the call narratives of the past. cf., J. MARCUS, pp. 179-186; S. W. HENDERSON, p. 57.

[47] Wuellner's study has demonstrated the fallacy of the prevalent caricature of "fishermen" in Jesus' day as being simple, illiterate, lower class laborers. Providing one of the staples of the Palestinian diet, fishing was a very profitable business in the Greco-Roman world, including Palestine. While the common image of the biblical "fisherman" had its validity for the "hired hands" in the fishing business (Mk 1:19–20), these four disciples most likely belonged to another class who owned and operated the boats and fishing equipment. cf., R. A. GUELICH, *Mk 1.16-20.*

[48] cf., S. C. BARTON, *Discipleship and Family ties in Mark and Mathew*, Cambridge University Press, N.Y., 1994, pp. 96-107.

community, we need to understand a bit about the historical situation of Markan time, a time of radical movements in pursuit of freedom; a time of wars and upsurges in pursuit of liberation from political dominion. But, Mark wants to present a different pursuit of liberation for the Jesus-movement which is presented as radical and rebel in a new way, where the hope is to have a dominion of God than of the worldly powers and possessions. The call to discipleship is preparatory, forming a new battalion of the said new mode of war, for a new world. The war is fared against the demonic power than human powers because at the root level, the former influences the latter. The means of violence is substituted by the culture of service even unto the persecution. The discipleship is the way of discovering the authentic human identity amidst the corrupted cultural institutions and values. Its norms restore the authentic human identity in two ways; by being with Jesus as disciples and by exercising the mission that pertains to him.

This warfare starts from the very nuclei of the society, the family. A rupture of family is apparently called on. Barton's study on the discipleship and family ties in Mark concludes on this as follows; "there is no sign, however, of antipathy toward familial and occupational ties *per se*. The motivation for leaving is presented, not in negative terms, but in terms of the prophetic call to a mission to people of all kinds (2:15-17)...The leaving of familial and occupational ties for the sake of Jesus and the Gospel (8:35b) dramatizes powerfully the movement's sense of new priorities, while intimating, at the same time, what those new priorities might cost in personal and social terms."[49] It is obvious from the literary context of the text that, Mark is silent of leaving wife when the list of forgoing is stated even for twice (10:28-31). Moreover, Markan Jesus is in favour of securing the integrity and dignity of marriage by prohibiting divorce in categorical terms (10:1-12). Here, the subject of giving up is the one who possesses family as object, i.e., father – the one's family origin. Virtually the demand of renunciation is pointed towards the 'father' of the family. In the patriarchal system,[50] father was the 'owner' and family members were wealth and possessions to his honour; even female members were taken for as possessions of *paterfamilias* than relations.[51] "The distinctive features of kinship in first-century Israelite society include...emphasis on the male line of descent, patrilocal marriage,...the family as unit of production, emphasis on family traditions,...ties of affection between brothers and sisters and mother and children rather than between husband and wife, and the wife as a blood relation who often remained a stranger in the house."[52] Mark, through discipleship, brings in a rupture in this cultural system of household domination substituting with a fictive kinship or a *new family of families* where God is the Father and Owner;

---

[49] *Ibid.*, pp. 66-67.

[50] cf., B. J. MALINA, *The New Testament World: Insights from Cultural Anthropology* (3rd ed.), Westminster John Knox Press, Louisville – Kentucky, 2001, pp. 134-159.

[51] cf., J. JEREMIAS, *Jerusalén en tiempos de Jesús*, Cristiandad, Madrid, 2000, pp. 449-469.

[52] B. J. MALINA, p. 158.

the community of disciples, *the new Israel* owned by Christ, are 'the possession' of God.[53]

And he got up and followed him (Mk 2:13-17)

We have another story of call and response in Levi's episode that transpires with minimal details set against a controversial dialogue. Verbally and structurally, 2:14 parallels **1:16,18.**[54] This stereotyped structure of both call scenes reflects that either Mark found this short call narrative in the tradition or he adapted it from the tradition in order to conform it to the vocation scene in 1:16–18.[55] A daisy-chain pattern of the structure will shows follows what the distinctive norm of discipleship, Mark wants to display to his community.[56]

A	2:14	sitting at the tax [A] booth
AB	2:15	tax collectors and sinners [B] were reclined
BA	2:16a	he was eating with sinners and tax collectors
AB	2:16b	why does he eat with tax collectors and sinners?
B	2:17	I did not come to call righteous people but sinners

Discipleship is potentially open to all kind of people. The call of Levi would mean that the circle of Jesus' disciples includes more than the Twelve. Levi has a prototypical role to provide a positive example of responding positively to the invitation of Jesus. Here the called is pictured as a sinner, who holds a different and indignant social status from that of those who were called before him in the story (1:16-20). Mark tries to show by this that the discipleship is open to all kind of people, even to the morally outcast. The kernel idea is that as Marcus says, "our story, then, is not intended to trace a great missionary career back to its inception; its interest, rather, lies in the questionable nature of the person called, the surprising fact of his choice, and what this choice reveals about the caller."[57] Jesus has been shown as a person of authority for forgiving sins in the preceding pericope of healing (2:1-12) and now his same authority is extended to show that Jesus is the important in the matter of discipleship and he has the authority not only over the non-polemic persons but also over the polemic outcaste of the

---

[53] cf., S. GUIJARRO, *Fidelidades en Conflicto: La ruptura con la familia por causa del discipulado y de la misión en la tradicion sinoptica*, Plenitudo Temporis, UPSA, Salamanca, pp.197-224; L. E. VAAGE, "En otra Casa: el discipulado en Marcos como ascetismo doméstico", *EstBib* 63 (2005, 1), pp. 21-42. Vaage's suggestion is that discipleship in Mark is demanding and anti-familial or a project of the socially marginal. At the same time, it is not a call to homelessness but, rather, to inhabit "an other home", whereby one enters into the kingdom of God. cf., T. E. SCHMIDT, "Mark 10:29-30; Mathew 19:29: 'Leave House...and Region'?", *NTS* 38(1992), pp. 617-620.

[54] *paragōn... eiden leuin* [***Simōna kai Andrean***]... *kai legei* [***eipen***] *auto...akolouthei moi* [***deute opisō mou***] *kai anastas* [***aphentes ta diktya***] *ēkolouthēsan autō.*

[55] cf., E. BEST, pp. 176-177.

[56] cf., J. MARCUS, p. 229.

[57] *Ibid.*, p. 230.

society. His authority is not only to forgive sins but also to call the sinners to follow him. Therefore, the discipleship is a personal adherence of the disciples to the one who has authority over sins and sinners.

And he appointed Twelve (Mk 3:13-19)

There are textual difficulties to ascertain the Markan radactive hand and the traditional materials in this passage. In spite of uncertainties, it is certain that in vv.16-19, name of the twelve is a traditional element of the primitive Christian community (1 Cor 15:3-5; Mt 19:28; Lk 22:30). For Mark, the twelve functions as "an initial point of departure for his own community's missionary activity rather than an exhaustive or even privileged designation of Jesus' followers."[58] The thematic connection found between the call and the commissioning of the disciples (13a and vv14, 15) suggests that they are traditional as it is found also in the first instance of call narratives (1:16-18).[59] To this traditional material, Mark adds *echein exousian* (3:15 to have authority) for he is concerned with the authority of Jesus, which is relevant equally for the disciples who are authorized by Jesus in mission (3:15) and for the opponents who are challenged by his authority (2:1-3:6).

Mark is a good redactor to plainly tell us the purpose of the discipleship. 'To be with Jesus' and 'to be sent out' with 'authority' are two central purposes of their gathering around Jesus. We shall now see the meaning of the first element; the latter will be explained together with the following section of the missionary journey.

Discipleship is to be with Jesus wherein a personal allegiance to Jesus is required. What does the presence of the disciples with Jesus meant by Mark? Is it

---

[58] S. W. HENDERSON, p. 87. This pericope creates certain confusions in the reader. Does Mark create a special group of disciples in the twelve? Does Mark mean to have two types of discipleship? For me, many of the answers including telling of the identification of both twelve and disciples are not much convincing. Mark has a direct telling of a separation but no direct telling of identification of the both. Here, we sideline these questions since our aim is to outline the norms of discipleship rather than to clear out such textual confusions. The choice of Jesus in choosing disciples and appointing the twelve is made vague due to the word *hous* (3:14) leaving the doubt that whether he is appointing the twelve from an already called group of disciples or whether the calling and appointing is of the same twelve. Best speaks of two phases of calling and appointing. He explains that the intrinsic meaning between the two stages as Mark intents to teach his readers; "every disciple may 'fish' for men but not every disciple is necessarily chosen to preach and exorcise." E. BEST, p. 183. Joel Marcus holds to this view. cf., J. MARCUS, p. 266. All the disciples are called to be with Jesus or have personal relation with him, being adherent to his Gospel in his name proclaimed and to bear witness through their identity in the world as Christian or disciples of Jesus. Among them, some are appointed to exercise the very mission of Jesus preaching and exorcising. They do not form any organization or having special operation as a single body except this power of authority of Jesus. This unit of twelve is seemingly with the disciples and not apart. cf., E. BEST, p. 180; J. MARCUS, p. 265.

[59] cf., E. BEST, pp. 180-181.

a physical presence or a spiritualized one normally explained by religions? To be with Jesus and to be sent out for missions are not separate concepts to be imagined quantitatively by the temporal gaps, but rather they are actualized concurrently to each other. The narrator tells us that they are called and appointed for the missionary activities of exorcism and preaching (3:15; 6:6b-13). Later we will see that they fail to exorcise (9:18) and at that juncture, Markan Jesus reveals the key for their success and at the same time the clue of their failure, that is, *prayer* (9:29). If disciples' presence with Jesus and their mission goes together, it could be logical that their failure of misión also must go together with their 'absence with' Jesus. The prayer (*proseuchē*) is "being with Jesus" (3:14 *met' autou*). It is the personal adherence to the Lord and living in his memory. The communities of believers that live in the memory of Jesus experience the same presence of Christ among them when they are in communion. The Markan portrayal of Jesus who is almost constantly surrounded by a circle of disciples[60] is a rhetorical invitation to his community to live in a constant presence of Jesus-memory in words and action. "Mark involves the group as witness to Jesus' activity even if they remain otherwise in the backdrop; though the effect is a subtle one, Jesus' mission in Mark emerges not as a strictly individual enterprise but as one enacted alongside his followers, since they remain "with him" throughout his Galilean ministry."[61] Therefore, in the thought of Mark, it is right to say that, not Jesus present where the community is, but inversely, the disciples are present where Jesus is.

Send them out two by two (Mk 6:6b-13)

Until now, the role of the disciples has been to "be with Jesus" (3:14). Here, for the first time Mark portrays them sharing actively in Jesus' ministry. Mark implicates a definite significance in relation to disciples when he places this pericope in the middle of two rejection stories; Jesus rejected at Nazareth and John the Baptist rejected to death by Herod.

Mark has adapted the missionary elements from the tradition of the primitive Christian communities and molded his model of discipleship. Its vocabulary, style and content, point to Mark's own redaction, based largely on the call account of the Twelve in 3:13–19. The repeated vocabularies are *apostellein* (3:14; 6:7); *kēryssō* (3:14; 6:12); *echein exousian* (3:15; 6:7, 12); *proskaleitai* (3:13; 6:7). For Mark, disciples' ministry is obviously an extension of Jesus' ministry, as the summary of the pericope (6:30) refers to all that they *did* (*epoiēsan*) and *taught* (*edidaxan*).[62]

---

[60] Mk 1:29; 2:19; 3:7; 4:36; 5:37,40; 6:50; 8:10; 9:8; 11:11; 14:7,17,18,20,33,67. These are redactional.

[61] S. W. HENDERSON, p. 70.

[62] To say that Mark has created this scene, however, does not mean that Jesus never sent his disciples in mission during his ministry. The multiple attestations of instructions for such mission activity in the Gospel tradition (Q, Mk, Mt and Lk par.) requires such mission activity. In other words, Mark's account did not create *de novo* the idea of such a sending. Nor did the evangelist

This pericope can be divided into four parts: 6:6b, 7 (mandate); 6:8-9 (instructions related to the journey on the way); 6:10-11 (instructions related to conduct while in the house); 6:12-13 (summary of the mission being realized). The vv. 6b-7[63] is an introduction that speaks about the twelve who are sent 'two by two' as 'official representatives' of Jesus with the allusion to OT witnessing (Deut 17:6 ; 19:15).[64] The v.7 contains Markan verb *archō* compels to consider it as a rewritten tradition. The vv. 8-9 bear parallelism with Q, cynic traditions and allusion to the Exodus story. The vv. 12, 13 are purely from tradition. In this summary of report (vv.12,13), Mark did not miss to indicate repentance as a content of their preaching. Markan mind of disciples' mission is not so different from that of their master who launched his misión with call of repentance (1:15).

Discipleship is to share the same mission of Jesus as ambulants. The first disciples were called to be "fishers of men" (1:17) and appointed to be sent out to preach and to have authority over the demons (3:14–15). All these aspects of the call are realized in disciples as they have gone out and preached the message of repentance and cast out demons and healed the sick. They go out for mission not voluntarily rather by a mandate of Jesus, who remains always the primary figure throughout the call narrative scenes, where he calls together, begins to send them out giving authority. His prominence is underscored while he is shown as the one who commands (6:8) and who speaks throughout (v.10). Through the Markan showing of Jesus as the supreme commander of the mission, Mark wants to instruct that disciples' mission covers the whole spectrum of Jesus' ministry by participating in and carrying out Jesus' project of the Kingdom of God. In this way, disciples become the instrument of God by the very participation in the in-breaking power of the new age initiated through Jesus. When disciples do their mission, the very mission and authority of Jesus is perpetuated concretely and tangibly, irrespective of time and space.

It is not an imitation but participation in the very mission of Jesus in view of an eschatological in-break of God's rule. Jesus is intrinsically and fundamentally the author and origin of disciples' mission. Instead of leaving disciples as mere bystanders or onlookers, waiting for the full disclosure of God's dominance, Mark enlists them as agents in the showdown, which will usher in the *new age*. Hengel

---

create the materials from which he constructed this scene. He used a traditional motif whose roots doubtless lay in Jesus' own ministry. cf., R. A. GUELICH, *Mk 6:6b-13.*

[63] V.6b is appeared to be an isolated clause. If it is considered to be the part of this missionary narrative, then it adds a meaning to the mission of the disciples that their mission is connected to the mission of Jesus who circuited around the village. Moreover the term *ērxato* indicates a new beginning of the phase of his mission. After being rejected by his hometown, he turns to entrust his misión to his disciples. The more he is rejected, the more he turns to his disciples with the demands and mandate of following him and his mission. E. BEST, p. 190.

[64] cf., J. MARCUS, p. 383.

gives an explanation that the role of Markan disciples is not to repeat the tradition of mission but to prepare for the service of the approaching rule of God.[65]

The disciples who are delegated by Jesus for mission would also represent the rejection that Jesus experienced from the same generation. They must respond to it with a prophetic sign, 'shaking of dusts, completely leaving of the place' so that 'not even the tiniest reminder of the place that has rejected the missionaries is to remain with them; they must assiduously purge themselves of every trace of it and depart, not giving their persecutors another thought.' They, so that, leave the judgment completely to God.[66]

Missionary disciples are under the providence of God. Though we call this pericope as of a missionary journey, actually it is a report by the narrator on what Jesus instructs his disciples who are about to set for mission. The vv.8-9 comprises the instruction on the road. The provisions that are described in the mandate are more paralleled with the allusion to Exodus story than to cynics. Joel Marcus compares it with the table of parallels between such instruction of cynics and Exodus:[67]

Mk 6:8-9	Q	Cynics	Exodus Story
staff	*no staff*	*staff*	*staff (of Moses & of Israelites, Ex 12:11)*
no bread		*bread*	*no bread (but manna from heaven)*
no bag	*no bag*	*bag*	
no money in belt		*no money*	*loins girded (Ex 12:11)*
sandals	*no sandals*	*no sandals*	*sandals (Ex 12:11; Deut 29:5)*
single tunic		*double cloak*	*single garment (Deut 8:4;29:5)*

From the above table we can understand that the missionary behaviour of the Markan group is unique to itself. The Markan set of demands for the missionaries is less austere than the Q version and more rigorous than the way of cynic itinerants. Staff and sandals are allowed after the typology of Exodus while the rejection motif on the way (6:11) is typically a Markan situation (this motif is absent in Q). The Markan community needs to be aware of, as this instructions reveals, that disciples have to witness not only the resurrected Christ and the kerygma but also to perpetuate the mission which the earthly Jesus realized as his own eschatologically charged earthly mission.[68]

---

[65] cf., M. HENGEL, pp. 108-121.

[66] cf., J. MARCUS, pp. 389-390; S.W. HENDERSON, pp. 161-164.

[67] cf., J. MARCUS, pp. 389-390.

[68] cf., S. W. HENDERSON, p. 144.

The instructions demand the disciples to travel light, unencumbered by provisions for their journey. The central idea of minimal provision is that disciples are by the authority of Jesus and under the providence of God and so, they need not depend on the human material provisions, instead they are taken care of by God and guided under the impulse of the Spirit (13:11). Mark sees in these missionaries, a *new people of Israel* inaugurated by the new Exodus. The community that follows Jesus will be entering into this divine act of eschatological liberation and the God of the Exodus and of Jesus Christ will sustain them along the way. Eschewing even the characteristic "beggar's bag" and bread of the itinerant cynic preachers, the missionaries were to receive their provisions solely from those who heard and received them by way of hospitality. God is the father and owner of the new family, the insiders of the Kingdom of God where the disciples as apostles are heeded and have the right to be fed and sustained.

Then come, follow me (Mk 10:17-31)

Here, we have a Markan assemblage of rich man's story composed of three sets of sayings in narration (Mk 10:17-22; 10:23-27; 10:28-30). These sayings are situated at the setting of a dialogue between Jesus and the rich man that comprises sayings about riches and then about reward. Mark formulated this episode to show that discipleship is an exigency at amazement, to be fulfilled after the model of Jesus for his sake with the power of God, and the journey of disciples on the way is not futile but rewarding in both this age and the eternal. Let us turn to see what Mark wants to say about the meaning of discipleship through this story.[69]

The radical discipleship is possible only with the power of God. In the radical call of the rich man and his abandoning of Jesus' invitation because of his richness, the Markan frame of reference is clear that the property and richness are not an immediate reference but the discipleship. The failure of the rich man to respond positively to Jesus' call is something adumbrative to any kind of failures of disciples detrimental to the following Jesus. The call need not be always responded positively; it can be rejected by the human will.[70] Those who have initiatively accepted the call and responded positively can fail in the long run to persevere in fidelity. So, in this doctrination of discipleship, Mark presents a new dimension of following Christ. Those opted for Jesus may be conferred upon the power in order to make possible this difficult task of following Christ in this world. In short, the material resources or worldly efforts are not that make possible but the power outside of them that make possible the humans to follow the 'eternal life'. The faith matters much more than anything else to the believers that would neutralize

[69] cf., E. BEST, pp. 110-119; cf., J. GNILKA, Vol. 2, pp. 96-102.

[70] Levi is obedient to the call while this rich man is reluctant to the call. Mark is least bothered of the psychological factors of human choice in Levi's case but here human will is given its space of importance. The Levi configures to the call exemplarily while the rich man disfigure his image turning down the call.

fear and amazement 'on the way' of following Jesus. The grace of God above all could start eliminating the human debility and impossibility at the juncture where human intelligence and strength has a finishing point.

Discipleship is a transformation from the law to the personal allegiance to Christ. The two demands of Jesus, selling and giving to the poor and following Jesus, exceed the Decalogue. Jewish beliefs are not against the charity, almsgiving, and good works; they are rewarding for heaven (4 Esd. 7:77). What more demanded of is the following of Jesus. Jesus, being the perfection of charity, is the ultimate goal to be followed; but foregoing the richness is only a radical preordination to follow him. The judeo-hellenistic culture knew very well the renunciation of the fortunes[71] but renunciation gets its meaning and motivation in ultimately following the person of Christ, because that is made possible and becomes a reality to whom one is united with him who had given up everything voluntarily without expecting any solace or comfort of this world but walking towards Cross decidedly and voluntarily.

For Mark, discipleship is not something that implies to fulfill only certain laws and ethical principles, but an intimate adherence and allegiance to the person of Jesus. From the literary point of view, the rich man is presented as an incomplete character to follow Jesus. The two facets of this man, positive and negative are presented for our understanding. The positive face is that he is the one who better follows the law and commandments that represent the Jewish legacy. For Markan Jesus, it concerns to him enough, but 'lacks' something more. The negative face is that he willfully turns down the invitation to the disciples, that is to follow the person of Jesus, which is the remedy to his lacking. From this, Mark goes on to suggest what the norm of discipleship does mean in the ambience of richness and wealth. Discipleship means a conversion from the legacy of law to the experience of the person of Christ and his message. It is a self-denial. This is a requirement for Jesus-movement; a transformation from the bindings of law to the person, the person of Christ. Christ is the fulfillment of law and he resolves all lacking pertain to the legalistic culture.

Conclusion

We have been so far attempting to understand the norms and attitudes of the discipleship that Mark presents, but this attempt is not exhaustive but just a vague outline. In the first section, the idea of discipleship as disposition is encased into an all permeating reality of Cross and resurrection. From this point of view, we understand that the Markan idea of following Jesus is not an easy task, for the discourse itself is clear that, it demands self-denial and Cross-bearing. This demand includes the rupture of the culturally inspired institutions like family relations and inheritance. As he moves on instructing, we see that this rupture is not a real rupture in the destructive sense but is constructive in view

[71] For example Qumran, Diogenes and his disciples.

of a 'new alternative family', where not human authority reigns but only God. The radicalism that presupposes the loosing is not a real loosing but an extensive gaining of what is foregone mundanely. The discipleship is in making of this fictive family, wherein all who adhere to Christ and to his name are received and receptive to each other, irrespective of the outcaste or the little ones. It is the responsibility of the followers to keep the sanctity and integrity of the 'new family' in solidarity through acceptance and service that is even extended to the children, the weak and the little ones. In this sense, Markan discipleship is open and inclusive to 'whoever wishes' to follow Jesus Christ. This dimension of following is a living reality 'on the way' of the journey of disciples, whose ultimate hope is in the eschatological in-break of God's dominion at the coming of the Son of Man. All these are possible only through the inseparable allegiance to Jesus Christ; his name, message, memory, and faith in his power.

In the second section of discipleship as vocation, Mark gives no discourse of discipleship, but shows what does the following Jesus mean by and its purpose, through various call episodes. When taken into account the entire episodes, we see a progressive maturation of Markan idea of discipleship. He treats mainly three aspects of discipleship in this section: call and following, call to be with him, and sending out for mission with authority. These aspects are not separable to each other but all-encompassing even when the focus of Mark varies from one to other in consecutive episodes of the calling. In 1:16-20 and 2:14, the Markan focus is on 'calling and following' though its purpose of 'fishers of men' is inherent; in 3:13-19 his focus falls on 'call of disciples to be with him' though 'sending out' is mentioned but not yet realized; in 6:6b-13 the already mentioned purpose of the call culminates in mission. This maturation is symbolically an idea of Mark that one in the community as a follower is initially being present closer to Christ and to the 'fellow Christians' in communion, in order to take up in the long run the mission of Jesus by witness.

If, in the discursive part as we have seen above, disciples are subject to the norms and attitudes of discipleship, in these call narratives, Jesus is the subject, author and origin of disciples' new way of life. Their status and mission as 'Christians' proceed from the status and mission of Jesus. His initiative and choice shape the community of disciples. He gathers the *new Israel* and guides them, so they are to be after him. Here, the disposition of self-denial becomes praxis of the followers who left their kinship ties and occupations of the past life for the formation of a *new household*. This formation that pertains to the discipleship is really a social transformation. Hereafter, nothing of their culture and instinct should bind them, not even law, for their adherence to the superseding authentic law and the new culture of the Kingdom dispense them from any of their cultural, traditional and legal barriers.

This mission account has the historical frame of Jesus' mission and adumbrates the Markan community's future mission. The disciples' mission is an extension and perpetuation of the same mission of Jesus. Their sending out with the same mission of Jesus is for the apocalyptic battle against demonic power and through which the God's dominion will become a subject for hope and trust. In this battle, rejection and opposition are indispensable components. They are not in itself the goal but inescapable consequences on the way of the establishment of God's dominion. Jesus' earthly ministry as well as that of the disciples are the proleptic prelude to the final victory of God's reign, and the Markan community to whom this Markan story is told has been given that hope of imminent new age of God's dominion, the eschatological end.

Are these norms of discipleship, pragmatic in the concrete life of the disciples? Mark will show that, it is not impossible with the power of God and not possible with one's own effort, through his dramatization of characters in various plots and settings of his story. In this chapter, we have inferred the norms of discipleship from the words of Markan Jesus and settings of the disciples. In the next chapter, we would decode the characterization of the characters in the Markan story in order to understand how they form to be either prototypes or antitypes of discipleship.

Chapter 4

CHARACTERIZATION AND IDENTITY DESCRIPTORS

The biographer's task was to capture the gesture which laid bare the soul.

(Patricia Cox, *Biography in Late Antiquity*, xi)

The task of this chapter[1] is to unpack the characterization of the Markan characters in order to describe the values, traits and point of views they represent as a result of reading the text as a coherent unit.[2] Method used for this is the Narrative Criticism. Markan story is a drama with scenes, settings, plots, characters and conflicts with a unifying thread of ideological viewpoint. The Markan story-world is a very dynamic interactive one that consists of major and minor groups and individuals of characters, powerful and weak groups interacting and co-existing each other. Now we look at the characters and see how Mark does the characterization.

The story of Mark is about characters; characters in plots carry out actions in the story. They are brought on stage to the implied reader by the implied author. Author communicates them to the reader through their actions and words or through that of other characters. The character traits communicated are finally meant to elicit in the reader sympathy, empathy or antipathy towards the respective character. The character building could be done through direct and indirect ways and various rhetoric patterns like comparing and contrasting,

[1] For a more expansive version of this chapter - the characterization of the Markan characters, see CYPRIAN E. FERNANDEZ, *Identity in Conflict: A Socio-rhetorical Reading of the Markan Story of Jesus*, Asian Trading Corporation, Bangalore, 2016, pp. 267-343.

[2] cf., S. BAR-EFRAT, *Narrative Art in the Bible*, (JSOTsup. 70), The Almond Press, GA (USA), 1989, p. 48.

epithets and descriptions of the narrator. Since we presume that Mark redefines the identity of his community through the retelling of the story of Jesus with the disciples in his creative background and narrative settings, our task is to bring into light, how Mark constructs his characters as being configured or indifferent to the norms, values, and point of view of discipleship, because characters are 'windows and mirrors' of the community to which the story is told. It is hardly to be mentioned again that this study restricted to expose the ideological plane of characters' viewpoints.[3]

We will see here the Markan characterization of two groups: the in-group of disciples and a few minor characters; the out-group of opponents. The mode of literary analysis[4] of the characters that we follow here is to understand, what the characters say and do that illuminates them, what others say about them that illuminates their character, what the narrator says about the character that illuminates them. Reviewing these by comparing and contrasting, we will be able to get some insights on traits, beliefs, values and points of view they represent. Moreover, we analyse their motivation, desire, relation to other characters and insights, the narrator gives into the thoughts and feelings of them. It is important to see how the narrator persuades the reader to identify with some characters and to alienate himself/herself with the others.

In-group Characters

The in-group, according to the general understanding of the social identity theory, constitutes positive members that share the identity of the group and stand in favour of it. In the Markan story, the disciples and the minor characters are virtually the constituent figures of the Jesus-movement, the in-group of the story, favoring for Jesus' values and for his group. Being sympathizers of the Jesus-group, they are expected to be the prototypes of the story.

The Twelve and the Disciples

As we go through the Markan narrative, the reader could generally experience that the imagery of the twelve is placed *en masse* with that of the disciples. But, there are important moments where the twelve retains its identity as a special group of disciples, who are called, appointed, and given the authority of Jesus (3:14; 4:10; 6:7; 9:35; 10:32; 11:11; 14:10, 17, 20, 43). The term *mathētēs* is used forty six times in the Gospel of Mark. It is generally used to signify the disciples of Jesus except in a couple of instances to refer the disciples of John and

[3] According to Boris Upensky's opinion, characterization could occur on four planes: the spatial temporal plane refers to action; the phraseological plane refers to speech; the psychological plane refers to thoughts; the ideological plane refers to beliefs and values. cf., M. A. POWELL, *What is Narrative Criticism?*, Fortress Press, Minneapolis, 1990, p. 52.

[4] cf., *Ibid.*, pp. 103-105; D. RHOADS - J. DEWEY - D. MICHIE, *Mark as Story: An Introduction to the Narrative of a Gospel* (2nd ed.), Fortress Press, Minneapolis, 1999, pp. 165-175.

of Pharisees (2:18; 6:29). It is a wider group consists of those following Jesus throughout the story. The narrator use *mathētēs* in a wider sense to include all those who follow Jesus. He tapestries a complex picture of disciples having a net relation of their presence and interactions within a wider space.[5] In other words, the implied author creates an imaginary world of a community of the followers of Jesus with a suggested traits and characters, which would in turn capacitate the readers from various streams of life to mirror themselves and decide on their following Jesus. In this respect, the reader will be convinced that in the narrative world of Mark, the twelve is a symbolic component of a wider group of disciples. Twelve represents the starting point of the discipleship in the Markan setup that grows in its horizon further more. This view is justifiable, for we have seen that discipleship for Mark is inclusive and open without limits and frontiers not for a few but for "all" who "wishes" to abide by proper demands (10:44,45;10:44). Therefore, as the traits of the twelve are symbolic and representative, we approach the characterization of disciples as general category than making any distinction between the disciples and the twelve.[6]

Disciples as Followers

Mark shows disciples as those who configure with certain norms of discipleship which we have already elucidated in the last chapter. The disciples become real disciples because of those qualities they bear and the foremost among them is that they earn their identity because of Jesus' choice for them. Mark shows that the disciples follow Jesus because their 'vocation' originates from the authorship of Jesus. Jesus forms the twelve according to his wish (*hous ēthelen autos* 3:13). Jesus calls them from a larger crowd (3:13-19), appointed them and renamed

---

[5] The group called disciples is also found along with the anonymous crowd that comes along Jesus (10:46; 12:43; 8:34), and Jesus is found to summon the crowd and the disciples together before he expounds some of his teachings (8:34). Disciples are also found in the company of Jesus with sinners and tax collectors (2:15).

[6] According to the proposal of Meyer, Markan usage of the title 'the twelve' and 'the disciples' is an indicative of two sources used - 'the twelve source' and 'a disciple source'. cf., S. FREYNE, *The Twelve: Disciples and Apostles; A Study in the Theology of the First Three Gospels*, Sheed and Ward, London – Sydney, 1968, p. 109. According to Ernest Best, 'the twelve' and 'the disciples' are distinguished. 'The twelve' is traditional and 'the disciples' is redactional. The disciples constitute a wider group but Mark does not make any distinction in the sense that there is not any identification of the twelve with the disciples, but on the other way round, twelve is to be understood as signifying the wider group, the disciples. cf., E. BEST, pp. 183, 188(n.4), 204. Malbon suggests that "at the level of story, 'the twelve' and 'the disciples' refers to the same group of characters. At the levels of the relation of story and narration, and story and narrating, however, there is an expansive movement from this group (twelve and disciples) to additional characters (4:10; 10:32), to the implied reader and at the levels "disciples" is a more flexible term than "the twelve."" Other scholars also consider and support her view that twelve and the disciples are identical. cf., E. S. MALBON, *In the Company of Jesus: Characters in Mark's Gospel*, Westminster John Knox Press, Louisville – Kentucky, 2000, p. 74.

some by surnames (3:13). Some of them have already been called individually who were formerly fishermen and tax collectors (1.16-20; 2:13-14). They are individuals handpicked by Jesus, a new collective entity and not simply a sum of its parts. Apart from the call and appointment of the twelve, narrator shows Jesus calling the disciples along with the crowd to himself (8:34). When he calls his disciples and the twelve, it is to teach about the demands of discipleship or to show the examples of virtues of discipleship (8:34; 9:35; 10:42; 12:43). For Mark no disciple is spared to the choice of Jesus' call since the very being in the *new family* of the disciples is efficacious to share in the power of Jesus' authentic choice.

Disciples are obedient to the choice and mandate of Jesus. Their report of first missionary journey is positive and proves their aptitude to be followers. After the missionary journey, Jesus invites them for a rest (6:30-33). "It is worth stressing, especially in view of the frequent negative comments about the disciples that increasingly crop up after this point of [missionary journey] 6:6-13 makes clear that the disciples did do some positive things in obedience to Jesus' commissioning. They seem to be better at doing the ministry than understanding what it is all about."[7] Jesus is assisted by the disciples obediently in preaching, teaching, feeding and healing (3:14-15; 6:12, 30, 41; 8:6; 6:7, 13; 8:6).

Mark portrays disciples always going with Jesus (1:29; 13:3; 5:37; 9:2; 14:33-36; 6:31,32; 7:17; 8:10-27; 9:28; 10:32) in contrast to the crowd that always seen coming to Jesus (1:32; 2:2; 3:8; 4:1; 10:1; 2:2; 6:31-42; 8:1; 5:21; 9:15-25; 6:33; 9:14; 14:43).[8] It creates an allusion to an important sense of discipleship that they were called to be "with him" (3:14). The omniscient narrator use *mathētēs* for the first time in the plot of Levi's call. From there until the plot of Gethsemane, the reader feels an indubitable and dynamic presence of the disciples along with Jesus in the story discourse. Disciples are spatially found with Jesus (2.15; 3:7); moving up and down from place to place with Jesus; coming to Jesus' hometown; coming to the region of Delmanutha in the boat (8:109); moving to Caesarea Philippe (8.27); conversing with Jesus privately (9:28); led by Jesus to Jerusalem going up (10:32); going to Jericho along with some crowd (10:46); coming to Jerusalem to enter the Temple (11:11; 11:27); moving up and down in the city of Jerusalem and finally accompanying Jesus to Gethsemane (14:32). The disciples follow Jesus until the courtyard of the chief priests and not more (14:66). Their presence with Jesus is not mere physical one but dynamic. They are not simply moving with him like crowd, which is mere beneficiary rather witnessing all his experiences even at the moment of his pain (14:33-42). They are eager to learn the reason for their failure (9:28). They are the conveyers of his popular feedback (8.27). Jesus asks

---

[7] B. WITHERINGTON, *The Gospel of Mark: A Socio-rhetoric Commentary*, Eerdmans, Grand Rapids, 2001, p. 152.

[8] The major distinguishing factor between 'the disciples' and 'the crowd' is that Jesus withdraw with the disciples for private teaching (3:9; 4:36; 6:31-33, 45; 7:17,33).

help from the disciples to keep boat ready (3:9), bring colt (11:7), prepare place for Passover (14:16), explaining the parables to his own disciples (4.34) privately (*kat' idian*). They are entrusted responsibility to serve the crowd with the blessed broken bread (6:41).

If disciples are with Jesus then they are at the defense and providence of God. The norm of discipleship that Mark frequently underscores is the possibility of God's power at the moments of impossibilities and trials of the disciples. Markan disciples are subject to such experience of God's defense. There are moments of accusations and polemic dialogues between Jesus and the 'guardians' of traditions due to the provocative breach of tradition by Jesus' disciples (2:18; 7:1-23). Jesus defends them distinguishing from other patterns of discipleship, those of Pharisees and John the Baptist. Disciples are exemplified as the dispensed from the clutches of law and tradition to a level of life taken up by the Spirit of Jesus and his personal presence.

Mark projects disciples literally leaving their occupation and kinship ties in order to follow Jesus that is conformed to the important norms of discipleship and to its nature of exigency and radicalism. The narrator places Peter, the fishermen, along with his brother Andrew as the first among the disciples who are called by Jesus alongside the Sea of Galilee (1:16). The Levi, the son of Alphaeus (2:14) is called from his place of occupation to the state of discipleship.

Disciples of Jesus are not like disciples of Rabbis who focus on learning law or not like Hellenistic disciples who interests in learning philosophies. The disciples of Jesus instead have a personal allegiance and an emotional adherence to their master. Disciples are called and renamed personally by Jesus (3.16). Peter's responses shows that he has a tendency to be prominent as somebody in the company of the disciples. It may express his desire to be first in closeness to Jesus. It is expressed through his hasty responses and emphatic over-confidence even to die for Jesus (14:29-31). This personal mutual relation of Jesus and disciples results in disclosing his identity as messianic secret to his intimate disciples. By the virtue of Jesus' allowance, some disciples are permitted (*aphēken*) to witness the power of Jesus in raising the Jairus' daughter when others from the crowd are not allowed for the same. In the transfiguration and Gethsemane episodes, (14:32-34) they are taken alone privately (9:2, 9:8) to experience his life.[9]

Mark shows that disciples are participating in the same mission of Jesus and it is reported that they were success. The agenda of their calling is shown materialized

---

[9] Being privately and alone signifies disciples as 'inside group': private teaching of parables (4:34, 6:31-34); disciples in private with Jesus (7:33) Jesus takes deaf and mute man in private for curing (9:28); private interrogation of the disciples (13:3-4). In this 'privateness', Jesus discloses to the three, his loneliness and isolation at the face of his death. Ironically narrator says that they see 'Jesus alone with them' (*Iēsoun monon meth' heautōn*Å 9:8; 14:33-34). This aloneness of Jesus is a contrasting prelude to the concrete loneliness that he is going to suffer, abandoned on the real way of the Cross (15:33).

as a test dose, when the twelve is sent out for mission (6:7-13).[10] Jesus sends the twelve with his authority (6:7) and they preach (6:12), cast out demons and anoint sick (6:13). The subject of their preaching is repentance (6:12) which takes back the reader to the inaugural moment of Jesus' call for repentance. The thrust of their mission is evident by now that the disciples form a distinguished group by their role as participators of the very prophetic mission of Jesus (1.32-34; 3:7-12). They are his authorized agents and their ministry is the extension of Jesus' own. Meyer finds a very suiting allusion of the discipleship with the rejection of Jesus in his own home town and family (3:21, 31; 6.1-6). "Like Jesus who just been renounced in his own 'home', are to take on the status of a sojourner in the land. We might note that the 'donning of sandals' is a Markan metaphor for discipleship (1:7)."[11] Their outfit is austere. Their opposition is forewarned (6:11). "The way" would remind the reader proleptically, the way of Jesus to Jerusalem (10:32) and likewise the same experience of rejection and unwelcoming (*mē dexētai* 6:11). In essence, their acceptance of the call with readiness, their following together with Jesus and the nature of their mission (6:7-13) seem to tell the reader that they responded to the radical demands of discipleship, leaving family relations, traditional occupations and households (2:1:16-20).

Mark builds up some disciple characters as models of service. There are occasions when Jesus sends two of his disciples with specific missions; they are reported from the climatic settings around Jerusalem (sending for a colt, 11:1-7; sending to prepare a room, 14:13-16). These anonymous disciples take up the instructions of Jesus and fulfill them silently. These pair disciples are similar to the woman anointing at Bethany. Both are anonymous in the narrative; both are at the service of Jesus. They prepare that are needed for Jesus to make the Jerusalem events significant (11:4-7; 14: 16). The woman at Bethany does a service that is significant for his burial ceremony. They are the models of disciples who are at the disposal of the Master and their memory of service is much persisting.

Disciples as Fallible Followers

We have seen so far how Mark presents disciples as positive followers of Jesus. The first part of the Markan story is considerably positive to present them as model characters. As the story escalates through its first half of boat-scenes, parable settings and loaves scenes, disciples fall under the dark spot of non-understanding. They fail at most important messianic manifestations. In the second half of the story, we meet them who are at the verge of understanding Jesus' identity but unfortunately it becomes "inappropriate understanding."[12] Finally, when they

[10] 'to be with him' (*hina ōsin met' autou*)/ and 'to be sent out' to proclaim the message (*apostellē autous kēryssein*) and 'to have authority' (*echein exousian*) to cast out demons (3:14-15).

[11] C. Myers, *Binding the Strong Man: A Political Reading of Mark's Story of Jesus*, Orbis – Mary knoll, New York, 1988, p. 213. in B. WITHERINGTON, p. 209.

[12] cf., E. S. MALBON, p. 90.

are at the brink of understanding Jesus at the close of the story, they abandon him. Mark presents them not as negative but fallible followers with their own weaknesses. Let us see how Mark shows the other face of the disciples.

Towards the middle of the story, to a greater surprise of the reader, Mark brings in an anonymous father of a possessed boy who blatantly announces the failure of the disciples (9:17, 18). We hear his voice from the crowd informing Jesus; "I asked your disciples to cast it [dump spirit] out, but they could [*ouk ischysan* 9:18] not do so." *ouk ischysan* is literally translated as; "they were not strong enough."[13] For Jesus, they belong to a "faithless generation" (*Ō genea apistos* 9:18). They are incapable to cast out demons when exorcism is considered as one of the most important missions for which they are appointed for (9:18). Jesus interprets their impairment saying, "this kind can come out only through prayer" (*en proseuchē* 9:29). They can be strong against the demonic power only if they remain "awake and pray" in faith (*grēgoreite kai proseuchesthe* 14:38).

The lack of faith and prayer lead the disciples to a state of fear. It is a surprise that Mark portrays disciples as terribly fearful at sea even in the presence of their master (4.41; 6:50). Jesus' words are enlightening for the reader to understand the reason of their fear that they did not have faith (4:40). The narrator views their inside and reason out for their lack of faith as hardness of their heart and non-understanding of the miracle of loaves (6:52). Mark does not say that their problem is incomprehension at sea-miracles (6:45-6:52) but rather misunderstanding about the loaves, which somewhat links the disciples' perceptual failure in the boat scene with their obtuseness in the previous miracle (6:35-37). They are unable to recall the happenings and find meaning related to God's providence of the past. When they ask for meaning of the parable, Jesus scolds them saying, "are you without understanding?" (7:17-18). The failure to understanding becomes their second nature so that they fear and frighten; for instance, Jesus was leading them to Jerusalem telling that "I am going to Jerusalem" (10:32). This causes in them fear and astonishment (*kai* ***ethambounto*** *hoi oí de akolouthountes* ***ephobounto*** 10:32). It is a tactic of narrative anachronism in the story to preview the tragic event that is going to happen ahead in Jerusalem and to foreshadow the future reaction of disciples' abandoning of Jesus at the shadow of the Cross because of their fear (10:33).[14]

---

[13] cf., NGEINT, p. 155.

[14] Disciples are wonderstruck, amazing and astonished at the powerful presence of Jesus and his radical teaching of discipleship (10:24). It is doubtful if Mark intends this behaviour of disciples as negative. Some scholars consider it as part of the messianic motif. Timothy Dwyer has made an enquiry on it. According to him, the wonder expressed in the first half of the Markan narrative (till 9:6), "co-exist with obedience rather than rejection". In the second half, the wonder operates in response to the variant manifestation of the same power of Jesus oriented in his death and resurrection. cf. T. DWYER, *The Motif of Wonder in the Gospel of Mark*, JSNTSup.128, Sheffield Academic Press, England, 1996.

Disciples are portrayed as characters with a restrained temporal outlook. Their viewpoint is limited to the spacio-temporal and material dimensions. When they were asked to feed the crowd, they find excuses and limited possibilities saying 'it is a desert place...time is late... (6:35). They find material solutions like 'buying bread for two denarius and giving them to eat' (6:37) in contrast to Jesus who is empowered to feed people abundantly without any money (6:38, 10:26). They look for material means in front of their impossibilities and limited source ("How to feed in the wilderness..." 8:4). Mark presents them crazy for worldly greatness, craving for pride and vying for position (9:38-40). Their narrow mindedness is exposed when John, one of the twelve, comes forward with an allegation against an outsider who cast out demons in Jesus' name (9:38-40). When Jesus is compassionate and sympathetic to the children, contrastingly his disciples rebuke the children permitting not to come near to him (10:13-16). They are blind to see service and humility as the means for achieving greatness in the Kingdom. On the way of Journey, disciples show passion for power, position and honor in the kingdom (10:35-45). All their culturally formed negative attitudes, desires and worldly requests become stumbling blocks to their discipleship because of their misunderstanding of Jesus and his Kingdom.

Disciples, even at the close of Jerusalem, remain 'blind' to the reality of the Cross, though they were taught the value of self-sacrifice by pointing out concrete example of a poor widow's offering (12:41-43). In this respect, no reader can ride over the passion narrative without observing two contrasting disciples, Judas Iscariot and Peter. In them, Mark shows disciples as gravely fallible even to an extent of abandoning and betraying their Master in Jerusalem. Judas 'forms another group' to which he is the leader and he leads them to arrest Jesus (14:43) by his 'sign of betrayal'. Peter becomes an embodiment of all the disciples' failure. This abandoning is a culmination of his thinking 'in human terms rather than in God's terms' and thus he is lost to the viewpoint of Satan (8:33; 9:6; 14:37). Nevertheless, his emotion of remorse gets a special attention to the reader so his name is not vanished but remembered to the end of the story.

The narrative contrasts the trial of Jesus in parallel to the trial of the disciples. The interpolation of Jesus' trial before the Council of Chief priests between the scenes of Peter's following of Jesus till the courtyard and his denial, is a narrative device to contrast between the trial of Jesus and the trial of Peter (14:53,54 - [14:55-65] - 14:66-72). The episode of two trials echoes two prophesies of Jesus: Jesus endures at the trial, a mode of which his followers also will have to face trials in future outside the story world (13:9-13); Peter's denial is exactly the kind of behavior pronounced by Jesus in 8:34-38. While Jesus perseveres his trial without failing before the opponents, Peter on the contrary looses his perseverance to end himself in a complete denial of Jesus. Auerbach says that Peter's story "speaks to everybody; everybody is urged to take side for or against it...the incident [denial of Peter is]... entirely realistic ... [it] is replete with problem and tragedy. Peter is no more an accessory figure serving as illustration...He is the image of man in the highest and deepest and most tragic sense."[15]

Minor Characters

Mark makes some minor figures that are apparently seen insignificant to the readers, into major figures. This makeup of the little ones into some one great is founded on the undefeatable attitudes and norms of discipleship. Though "follow me" has pride of place in descriptions of disciples, the minor characters never are invited to this relationship, yet they exemplify many characteristics of the discipleship that are essential to make following Jesus meaningful. Those characters are put in contrast to the fallible disciples and shown to the reader what is meant to be really a disciple. They are prototypes of believers who become part of the Gospel of Christ, the Son of God (1:1), experience the in-breaking of the reign of God and respond to his call "repent and believe the Good news of eternal life" (1:14 -15). Now let us turn to see a few of those characters and how Mark characterizes them to configure so aptly with the values of discipleship.

The lineage of the minor characters is open with the healing stories of the unclean (1:23-28) and the leper (1:40-45) placed in the background of Jesus' ministry in the vicinity of or in the Synagogue in Galilee. **The leper**, the man of confident reverence gets our attention by his kernel of prayer made to Jesus to "choose" him (*eanthelēs*) in mercy to be clean and correspondently he is chosen by Jesus like any of his disciples chosen personally. After being healed, the narrator comments that he "preached" (*kēryssein*), the same term used to indicate preaching of John the Baptist and Jesus. Narrator specifies what he preached, that is "word" (*logon* 2:2).[16] In short, the 'word' refers to different dimensions of Jesus' life, his mission and teaching and it is proleptically suggested that the leper as a preacher of the many things of Jesus' life participates in the project of Jesus' mission. It is a surprise in the story world that Mark presents the leper as preacher of the word, even before the disciples are sent as preachers of the same word.

The **man possessed** of an unclean spirit in the gentile region of **Gerasene** is another minor character of a major event of conflict (5:1-20). He serves to be an agent for the author to present a great conflict and confrontation between Jesus and the unclean spirit. The possessed is like a spokesperson of the indwelt spirit (5:7-9). The narrator's verbose and repetitious description about the possessed

[15] AUERBACH, *Mimesis; The Representation of Reality in Western Literature*, (trans. W. R.Trask), Princeton University Press - Princeton, NJ, 1953. in D. RHOADS - K. SYREENI (eds.), *Characterization in the Gospel : Reconceiving Narrative Criticism*, (JSNTsup.) Sheffield, England, 1999, pp. 56-59.

[16] It is the word Jesus refers to in his parable of seed (4:14); Jesus was speaking in word (4:33; 7:13,29); the word of God and the will of God (8:32); passion prediction (8:38); words of Jesus (9:10); the words of warning of Jesus (10:22); invitation to follow Jesus (10:24); the teaching of disciples of Jesus (16:20); question of Jesus (11:29); Jesus' prayer of Gethsemane (14:32); the word as Jesus' preaching (12:13).

underlines the severity of his situation (5:3-5). The contrasting elements[17] between this healing and earlier healing in 1:23-26 give an understanding that Jesus' permanent nature of his misión of exercising the authority of power to cast-out evil spirit will generate hope in the reader that this mission is to be continued. We may now pass on to see how Mark presents this man as a model of discipleship in the mission of Jesus.

The liberated man expresses his desire to follow Jesus but Jesus commands; "Go home to your friends, and tell them how much the Lord has done for you, and what mercy he has shown you" (5:19).[18] Unlike leper's case, Jesus does not insist here complete silence but limits the range of his proclamation to his own family and what is to be proclaimed. This man also disobeys the command of Jesus not negatively rejecting it but positively making an unlimited proclamation concerning Jesus (*ērxato kēryssein,* 1:45 = 5:20). It is ironic that now this man is a preacher of Jesus and his mission field is not a limited family but an extended family of all who wishes to hear and follow Jesus. The onlookers of this miracle, similar to the disciples in the boat scene, are frightened (5:15; 4:41 *ephobēthēsan*) and further more ask Jesus to leave their place. In contrast to them, the converted man is fearless "to leave to be with him" (5:18 *hina met' autou ē).* Mark shows this man as without *Christophobia* instead with personal allegiance to Jesus.

From the gentile area Jesus is now welcomed by some "standard characters"[19] – Jewish crowd and a **Jewish leader Jairus**. The healing of the **woman with hemorrhage** and the story of the raising of Jairus' daughter are sandwich episodes (5:22-24 [25-34] 35-43).[20] It serves to clarify the meaning and significance of both the episodes and enhance each other the characterization of the individual

---

17

5:7 *kraxas phone megalē*	**1:26** *phōnēsan phōnē megalē*
5:7 *Ti emoi kai soi*	**1:24** *Ti hēmin kai soi*
5:7 *Iēsou huie tou theou tou hypsistou*	**1:24** *Iēsou Nazarēne … oida se tis ei ho hagios tou theou*
5:7 *mē me basanisēs*	**1:24** *ēlthes apolesai hēmas*
5:8 *exelthe*	**1:25** *phimōthēti kai exelthe ex autou*
5:13 *kai exelthonta ta pneumata ta akatharta*	**1:26** *to pneuma to akatharton kai phōnēsan phone megalē exēlthen ex autou*

18 "To be" (*met'autou* 5:18) is not meaning merely 'to be with him', originates with the initiative of Jesus. It is a privileged position granted only to the Twelve whom Jesus called (3:14). Though admirable, the man's request is beyond his own prerogative." cf., K. R. IVERSON, *Gentiles in the Gospel of Mark,* (LNTS) T & T Clark International, London, 2007, p. 32.

19 J. MARCUS, p. 365.

20 There are more examples for the interpolated scenes in Mark: (3:20-21[22-30]31-35); (5:21-24[25-34]35-43); (6:7-13[14-29]30-32); (11:12-14[15-19]20-26); (14:1-2[3-9]10-11); (14:12-16[17-21]22-25); (14:54[55-65]66-72).

characters, for they have internal as well as external similarities and allusions.[21] When the reader meets Jairus and the anonymous woman in the same narrative, he/she can still hear the echo of a clear rebuke to the chosen disciples, "why are you so afraid? Do you still have no faith?" (4:40). Further, the characters in this twin episode pay heed to Jesus' advice, "do not fear, only believe" (5:36). The narrative enables the reader to see that the faithful response of Jairus and the woman really impugn the mere worldly logic of the disciples[22] and the faithlessness of the crowd that gathers at the house of Jairus' house.[23] Jairus is a highly esteemed person in the Jewish community (5:21-23) as one of the leaders of the synagogue.[24] Despite his lofty position, he is humble (5:22, 23) to fall at the feet of Jesus and beg, in front of the crowd and disciples. Jairus humbles himself before the authority of Jesus and his request reveals his confidence in Jesus.[25]

Among many physically challenged suppliants in Mark, the hemorrhage woman is the only said to be worn out both physically and economically by the protracted therapy. This conveys the seriousness of her condition and the intensity of her need to rely ultimately to Jesus' power. Though healing will certainly trespasses the incurability and hopelessness plotted in the narrative, the narrator favors much to her inner emotions like fear and tremble and describes her soliloquy; "If I but touch his clothes, I will be made well." (5.28). She is shown from an inside view, underscores that she is strongly convinced of Jesus' power in her faith which brings her out of fear of public embarrassment and exposure. The narrator qualifies her as truthful woman attaining her share of peace (5.34) for she is rewarded with wholeness of the person which reminds the reader, the Markan wish of peace to those who follow Jesus (9:50).

Her touch at the fringe of Jesus' garment is notable as various other characters in the scene (v.27-narrator, v28-woman, v30- Jesus, v.31-disciples) frequently refer to her touch. It is a Markan symbolic description that she is personally adhered to Jesus and this quality of discipleship could be acquired by anyone irrespective of outcaste, impurity and gender differences, for discipleship to Jesus Christ is open and inclusive for whoever wishes. Moreover, the narrator suggests that she has a

---

[21] Some significant similarities are: The woman and the girl both have something to do with the number twelve (12). The 12 years of the growth and suffering is equal for the both clients of the miracles. The woman's affliction continued for 12 years, the age of the young girl. "The beginning of misery and the beginning of life happened at the same time." B. M. F. VAN IERSEL, *Mark: A Reader Response Commentary*, T & T Clark International, London- NY, 2004, p. 363.

[22] Mk 5:31, And his disciples said to him, "You see the crowd pressing in on you; how can you say, 'Who touched me?"

[23] Mk 5:40, And they laughed at him.

[24] He is responsible to the supervision of the synagogue building and the arrangements of the synagogue service. cf., J. MARCUS, p. 365.

[25] *One of the Scribes* in 12:28-34; Judas as *one of the twelve* in 14:10, 43. Markan narrator shows some exceptionals in each character groups, who behave contrary to their stereotyped traits. Mark's phrase (5:22) may intend to emphasize that not all of the Jewish authorities are opposed to Jesus.

magic-tainted belief on Jesus, thinking that even a touching of his garment would transfer enough holiness of healing power into her.[26] By her faith, she is welcomed as daughter (*thygatēr* 5.34) to belong to Jesus' new community of family who has faith in him and would do the will of God. She exemplifies in a radical way the depths of trust/faith for all disciples. Jairus on the other hand evokes proud and challenge in the readers' side to risk any high position of life without fear even to be humble and trustful to Jesus.

Narrator exemplifies another **woman from a Greek Syrophoenician race** who is rather fearless to war in faith. [27] He narrates the supplication of the woman on behalf of her daughter (7:25-30) and obtains the favor by a debating dialogue with Jesus. There are many features to compare and contrast her with the previous characters but here it is fitting to see her how she is made up more a disciple at the back scene of the disciples' failure. The disciples, although they are insiders of Jesus' company to whom given the mystery of the kingdom of God (4:11), comprehend neither the loaves-sign (6:52) nor the parables (7:17, 18). In contrast to these disciples, this woman, though she was initially treated like an outsider by Jesus, becomes an insider to Jesus' company through her insight into his annoying parabolic question concerning bread (2:27).[28] She stands as a great blow to the Jewish authorities who honor [God] with their lips but their hearts are far from [Him] (7:6-7). Because she seems dissenting to Jesus by her lips saying, "even the dogs under the table eat the children's crumbs", but her heart is close to Jesus in faith.[29]

---

[26] cf., B. WITHERINGTON, p. 187.

[27] There are a number of unique features of this character in Mark. She is the only example in the Markan narrative and whole of the Gospels, who wins an argument with Jesus. Her 'womanness' is emphasized (*akousasa gynē, thygatrion autēs, elthousa prosepesen, gynē ēn Hellēnis, Syrophoinikissa, aphelthousa*) than her 'gentileness'. She is the only Markan woman who speaks in the narrative. Gerald Downing shows a number of examples to tell that in the antiquity, Christian tradition and OT, women do not speak first or not at all. In Mark, it is uncommon and unexpected. cf., F. G. DOWNING, *Making Sense in (and of) the First Christian Century*, (JSNTsup.197,) Sheffield Academic Press, Sheffield, 2000, p. 107.

[28] Joel Marcus refers in his commentary to both the negative and positive connotations of the 'dog-expression' in the OT and the early Judaic culture. The OT tradition to call some one dog is an insult because this negative imagery is related to "the fact that the dogs pictured in the Bible and in the Jewish tradition are generally the wild, scavenger sort rather than the domestic variety" (1Sam 17:43, Isa 56:10-11). The NT follows this belief, picturing it as a symbol for "opponents and heretics" (2Pet 2:22; Phil 3:2; Rev 22:15). On the other, it would be also exaggerating that the image of dog is always negative. There are also appealing images of dogs like domestic ones, which compares righteous gentiles to dogs at the eschatological banquet. The scholars also find it a connotation of *God-fearer*. "The Syrophoenician woman's self-description as a dog that is with in the house, but that is in a position inferior to that of the children corresponds to the way in which Gentile sympathizers with in Judaism (God-fearers) were regarded by some Jews." cf., J. MARCUS, p. 470; K. R. IVERSON, pp. 55-57.

[29] Her address to Jesus as *Kyrie* (7:28) affirms her faith, though the very term 'faith' is not denoted by the implied author for it. It is a divine title than being it a deferential address of mere

The reply of the woman to Jesus creates an image of the character that she is convinced of her hope and trust, irrespective of whatever feeling her reply might generate in Jesus. She does not have inferior feeling being a gentile to make a request to Jesus, a Jew male, and neither has any superior feeling which might object in any manner for putting her request falling at the feet of Jesus, acknowledging him powerful (7:25/). She acknowledges Israel's privilege and simply appeals unconditionally to Jesus' kindness. Her humility overcomes Jesus' reluctance.

The character of **Blind man at Bethsaida** (8:22-26) is catchy when Mark projects him as a prototype of discipleship because he is set at the background of passion prediction, 'blindness' of disciples and teachings of discipleship. The reader can understand the purpose of Mark in setting all the blind suppliants 'on the way' section (8.22-26; 10:46-52). The disciples need clear sight to see Jesus on the way while following him for whom this blind man is a model. This healing story has many similarities with the just previous healing of the deaf and dumb man.[30] But, the distinguishing factor of his healing is that he attains a gradual transition of sight from partial to complete. It will have an externally proleptic allusion to the gradual transition of the disciples from their blindness to a complete insight into Jesus in future, but now it is faulty, as the reader understand that Peter makes a confession out of his partial understanding of Messianic identity (8:31-38). His example of discipleship becomes ripen in the character of blind Bartimaeus who earns complete sight and even totally follows Jesus.

By the very first reading of the story of **Bartimaeus**, (10:46-52) the simplicity of his own person covets our hearts leaving an emotional imprint on us. He seems to be like a child, who is very plane in his request; 'I want sight'. This impression would impel the reader to recall Jesus' invitation to become like a child to inherit the Kingdom of God (9:36-37; 10:15). Bartimaeus appears 'hounding' after Jesus with his earnest faith, an exceptional trait that distinguishes him from other suppliants.

Bartimaeus on the wayside reminds the reader the call of Levi who was called from the place of occupation. Bartimaeus[31] sit on the way side for begging, his

---

reverence. Mark is familiar with the use of *Kyrie*, as divine connotation (1:3,12:29-30,36; 13:20; 2:28; 5:19;11:3; 9:12, 36-37; 13:35). cf., J. MARCUS, p. 470.

[30] Most of the similarities are conjunct, with the verbal forms like *pherō / parakaleō / haptomai / epitithēmi / apokatastēmi* (1:32; 2:3; 8:22 / 1:40; 5:18, 23; 8:22 / 1:41; 5:27-31; 8:22 / 5:23; 8:23-25 / 3:5; 8:25). Like the deaf and dumb man of 7:31-37, he is also brought by others and they beg for his healing. Jesus takes him outside the village, similar to the private healing. It is ironically contrasting to the private (*apolabomenos* 7:33; *epilabomenos* 8:23; *proslabomenos* 8:32) rebuke of Peter in the succeeding episode in Caesarea Philippi.

[31] The name 'Bartimaeus' and 'son of Timaeus' is effectively the same. It is a conflation of Greek with Aramaic. Mark's unusual giving of his name signifies his mind to give an authenticity to his person and the story. cf., C. S. MANN, *Mark: A New Translation with Introduction and Commentary*, (AB) Doubleday and Company Inc., Garden city – New York, 1986, p. 421.

occupation, and metaphorically his story turns to be a vocation-story when he encounters Jesus. The movement of Bartimaeus in the scene draws reader's attention to the essential qualities of discipleship. From the sitting posture, he moves to Jesus jumping by leaving aside his garments and finally he follows Jesus (10:46, 50, 52).[32] More over Mark is particular to show Bartimaeus as following Jesus on his way (*ēkolouthei auto en tē hodō*). The *way* has a symbolic significance in the Markan narrative, since Jesus' way to Jerusalem is also a way of discipleship, the way of Jesus is the way which is according to the divine will (1:2, 3; 6:8; 8:27; 9:33, 34; 10:17; 10:32; 12:14). There is also a sign of discipleship of leaving material possessions behind (1:18, 20; 10:21, 28). He fulfills what the rich man could not, by leaving behind what he has, to be with Jesus. He succeeds the movement even there are hurdles of people's silencing (10:48). Bartimaeus cry, as reported twice ("Jesus, Son of David, have mercy on me" 10:47; "Son of David, have mercy on me" 10:48) reveals his staunch and unbeatable faith in Jesus. His faith is finally attested by Jesus; "Go, your faith has made you well" (10:52).

Bartimaeus is a man of courage. Though the crowd insist him to take up courage, (10:49b) he is already courageous in fact. This advice is coming from the crowd and not from Jesus who had already advised disciples to take courage at the boat scene (4:40-41). Bartimaeus is called by Jesus (*phōnēsate... phōnousin... phōnei* 10:49), therefore, as Jesus called his disciples, figuratively Bartimaeus is also called to that status of discipleship.[33] The disciples are 'blind' to request for power and authority whereas Bartimaeus is also blind but his request is to have sight and for the removal of blindness (*Rabbouni hina anablepsō* 10:51). Mark invites his readers to get easily identify with this character in view of his faith, courage, enthusiasm and following Jesus. He inspires the reader to become aware of the real sense of following, viz. following not by mere faith alone, but also by praxis to be 'on his way' with clear in-sight.

Mark portrays another possible self for his readers in the character of a **poor widow** (12:42, 43). She is a poor widow so she is needy. Yet she behaves in a heroic way by self-denying sacrifice. "...she out of her poverty has put in everything she had, all she had to live on" (12:44). She is not showy but genuine, and silent in

[32] It is not merely a following in the physical sense. The narrative explicitly shows the characteristics and signs of discipleship and the word used for the following also signify that he follows Jesus in its true meaning, taking up a commitment. In Mark, the verb *akoloutheō* is used to signify both the physical and psychological following to Jesus; the crowd follows Jesus (3:7; 5:24; 11:9) and the disciples follow him. In both sense, it is 'following'. The object of it is always a group or a person in following. In the NT, this word is used for 90 times and out of which 73 times it refers to the following Jesus especially in the Gospels. cf., DENT, Vol.1, col. 146; J. F. WILLIAMS, *Other Followers of Jesus: Minor Characters as Major Figures,* (JSNTsup.) JSOT Press, Sheffield, 1994, pp. 156-159.

[33] A narrative allusion between the Jesus' interaction with the Bartimaeus and the disciples, affirm it. Jesus asks Bartimaeus *Ti soi theleis poiēsō* (10.51) like Jesus asking John and James *Ti thelete [me] poiēsō hymin* (10:36).

piety. Perhaps her offering may be insignificant in the eyes of the world but it is great and visible to God. Jesus summons his disciples to see her outstanding and amazing act of sharing and total self-giving (12:43). Mark exemplifies the poor widows as silent devotee and prototype of sacrifice, which is radical to discipleship. she is placed in contrast to the rich man who left Jesus because of his love for richness[34] and Scribes who devours widows (12:40); instead this widow stands out in giving sacrificially "all" (12:44) that she has.[35] As scribes are showy in their pretentious piety (12:38-40), this widow silently does her true piety.

Mark presents another silent woman (14:3-9) but very assertive in action to represent another dimension of discipleship where the chosen disciples fail. She is the one **who anoints Jesus in the 'holy week'** and in turn, Jesus appraises her as 'Gospel-memory' to be pronounced (14:9) in the evangelical history for her undivided loyalty and courage. Mark positions her exemplary mode of following within the frame of passion narrative. Her action is symbolized as a last rite done for Jesus (like disciples of John the Baptist who lay his body in the tomb 6:29), in contrast to, the disciples who would flee away undoing this (14:7, 8). Her action is put in the middle of the conspiracy of Jesus' opponents and contract of Judas for betrayal. When on one side a conspiracy of hatred takes place, on the other side, takes place the anointing of love and devotion.

The narrative gives an indirect hint of woman's economic position. In 14:3, 4 she is anointing Jesus with a precious and costly nard and this preciousness makes the onlookers indignant to observe it as a waste.[36] "If so, this woman is acting very much like the widow with the two lepta, using all her social security for an

---

[34] This narrative contrast serves as an instructive means for the narrator to expose his readers the values of the Kingdom:

10: 17-31 Rich Man	12:41-44 Poor Widow
Rich and poor: 10:25 *plousion*, 10:21 *ptōchois*	Rich and Poor: 12:41 *plousioi* 12:42 *ptōchē*
Truly I say to you :10:29 *Amēn legō hymin*	Truly I say to you: 12:43 *Amēn legō hymin*
He refuses to give he has: 10:21 *hosa echeis*	She gives all she has: 12:44 *hosa eichen*
He lacks one thing : 10:21 *hen se hysterei*	She gives out of her lack: 12:44 *hysterēseōs*

[35] A. G. Wright does not admit the interpretation of this widow as an example of sacrifice (12:38-40). He reads Jesus' attitude as a lament over the sympathetic gift of her. As a widow who is devoured by the scribes, her gift is not a subject matter for Jesus to praise but to lament over it with compassion for her and the social situation that exploits them. cf., A. G. WRIGHT, "The Widow's Mites: Praise or Lament?- A Matter of Context", *CBQ* 44(1982), pp. 256-265; C. S. MANN, pp. 493-496. Malbon admits this contextual reading as such, but she objects Wrights' view of a single contextual reading by calling for a "multiple contextual reading and …[a] multiple contextual readers" to read the widow's mite-passage. cf., E. S. MALBON, pp. 166-188; J. F. WILLIAMS, p. 177.

[36] What the woman pours on Jesus' head is a nard, "which is an eastern perfume with a very potent fragrance which came from a root found in India." cf., B. WITHERINGTON, p. 367.

act of devotion."[37] The narrator speaks little about the profile of this woman but what author wants to convey is put at the authentic mouth of Jesus. Jesus' praise designates her as subject of Gospel proclamation, so the reader will not be skeptic to take her as a prototype of discipleship.

Mark brings in a vivacious model of discipleship in the portrayal of **Simon of Cyrene** (15:21). He bears the Cross of Jesus. There is no much social identification of him in the narrative than the narrator's introduction that he is the father of Alexander and Rufus. The author takes for granted that the real reader of the story must know ahead the children of Simon - Alexander and Rufus - and through them their father. But in the narrative world his real identity consists in the literal Cross-bearing. He is a figure that brings shame and satire to disciples, who have escaped out of fear in the moments of their master's pain. When the chosen disciples get rid of the shadow of the Cross and flee away from the Master, this minor figure of the story walk along with Jesus carrying the cross. Simon is bearing the Cross (*hina arē ton stauron autoul*), is a paradigm of fulfilling the important demand of discipleship; "If any want to become my followers, let them deny themselves and take up their Cross and follow me" (8:34). The reader will have in him a visual representation of Jesus' injunction (8:34) regarding the self-denial, taking up of the Cross and following him.[38]

The mystery of Jesus' death and resurrection throws up other exemplary disciples. The first is **the centurion** (15:39-45) who is gifted with great insight and reminds all disciples over the ages that Jesus Christ, the Son of God (1:1) can only be understood fully, adequately and appropriately at the foot of the Cross. According to the lexical understanding, he is the head of a band of hundred roman soldiers.[39] Until this point of the narrative, soldiers are negative figures. They mock Jesus, assault him and crucify him (15:16-20, 31, 32, 36). In contrary to the image of those cruel soldiers, this centurion is an exception as he is open to the truth, and by his confessional statement he recognizes Jesus' identity as the Son of God (15:39). He has the insight to perceive Jesus in divine point of view. His confession becomes true and genuine with his profound Christological insight in contrast to the confession of Peter (8:29) which is objectively true in itself but subjectively lacking a true personal perception of Jesus' identity.

Mark shows him as a man of faith and courage to confess Jesus in public without any fear, when disciples are escaped out of fear. He is courageous to declare what he is convinced of - Jesus is the Son of God -and to attest Jesus' death to Pilate (15:44, 45). He is ironically portrayed as the authoritative to declare both the human death as well as the divine sonship of Jesus. Markan narrative reaches almost to a saturate point in centurion in its molding of the prototypes of discipleship.

---

[37] *Ibid.*

[38] cf., B. M. F. VAN IERSEL, p. 468.

[39] cf., DENT, Vol.1, cols, 2298-2299.

We have another prominent model in **Joseph of Arimathea**, a Council Member (15:42-47). Joel Williams assumes the Council as Sanhedrin. The Sanhedrin members are negative and utterly opposing "united front" against Jesus (14:55-59, 65; 15:1).[40] The narrator informs us that the whole Sanhedrin seeks to find testimony against Jesus. Among this malicious unified move of the opponents, Joseph remains as a convinced faithful of the Kingdom of God (15.43) who dares to pay the last rite and a decent burial to Jesus. His conviction is courageous to believe persistently that the Kingdom has come in the life of Jesus, even when Jesus lies dead at his hands. This character contrasts with the centurion who declares ironically both divine and human reality of Jesus. Like centurion, his conviction makes him to approach Pilate to request for the body of the one who was crucified among the robbers even risking his honour and safety. His act of paying a decent burial is supposedly a responsibility of the disciples (6:29).[41] In their striking absence, he takes up that responsibility as a worthy disciple (15:46) and becomes a model for them.

Mark exemplifies the emotional aspect of discipleship through **the models of women** who follows Jesus until the tomb. So far, Mark was concentrating the characters who respond by actions and attitudes and now we are told how women had been accompanying Jesus in a very committed way for a long period (15:41). This group has been silent and anonymous and Mark expresses the intimacy of discipleship by this group.

In the scene of crucifixion, a group of women is reported and among them three women are named individually: Mary Magdalene, Mary the mother of James the younger and of Joses, and Salome (15:40). They never speak in the story but just witness the crucifixion at a distance. These women are literally following Jesus on his way not only up to the cross but even beyond his tomb, in contrast to the disciples who failed to move beyond the courtyard of the High Priest in following Jesus.[42] At the tomb, we can say that by their silence and profound puzzling emotional responses to the core of faith, these women are exemplified with an attitude required for discipleship – standing in an attitude of

---

[40] cf., J. F. WILLIAMS, pp. 188-191. Since the Jewish authorities, as unified bonded front against Jesus, Malbon argue in her thesis that Joseph of Arimathea could not be a member of the Sanhedrin. Mark cannot break that front with an exception. cf., E. Struthers Malbon, p. 149. It is convincing to consider that since Markan narrative is always optimistic to find a space for exceptional persons like exceptional scribe, exceptional centurion, and exceptional synagogue leader in Jairus, it is possible for Mark to 'exceptionalize' Joseph of Arimathea out of the Sanhedrin members, to exemplify him as a believer in God's rule.

[41] See, what John's disciples do after his death (6:29).

[42] It is not potent for these women to fail in there following because, they are following at a "distance" like Peter, who was also following but at a distance (*makrothen* 14:54 = 15:40)? I mean, in the Markan perspective, following at a distance is dangerous. There is no middle term position in following Jesus, but only a radical one, leaving 'all' behind, focusing Jesus alone and his values.

profound amazement and incomprehension before the key and kernel message of resurrection (16:6).

We have seen so far sufficient models of discipleship. They are many simple needy and faithful minor characters who are emotionally and personally opted so courageously for Jesus, hail not from the group of disciples but from the unorganized crowd. Mark uses the source of crowd, an anonymous undesignated group to draw his prototypes for the disciples of all ages. Now we turn to see the source ground of all categories of characters – the crowd.

Characterization of the Crowd

We now place crowd in between the in-group and out-group for they are a wide indefinite group inclined either to discipleship or to any impulse of opposition. The crowd lacks a definite identity, for any favoring as well as opposing attitude could be expected from it. In our story, the crowd serves as a 'background curtain' in the drama that makes the reader to take for granted its permanent presence in the plots. Mark foresees potential disciples in crowd. His "whoever"[43] expression implies a sound of invitation for the crowd to the discipleship as he does not leave them unchallenged. It is noteworthy that Mark sets the 'whoever' sayings of Jesus preferably at the settings of Jesus' discipleship discourse to the crowd and disciples. Therefore, the disciples, the crowd and 'whoever' of the Markan narrative serve to open the story of Jesus outward to a larger group.

We can see that Mark attributes some of the characteristics of discipleship to crowd. Jesus calls the crowd to himself before he instructs about the discipleship and the Kingdom of God in parables (7:14, 8:34), the crowd accompanies Jesus in multitude (2:15; 3:7; 5:24; 10:23-24, 48, 52, 46; 11:8,9-10). This striking similarity between the crowd and the disciples illumines the reader to consider the discipleship in a broader sense, which is open neither to some individuals alone but to 'whoever' wishes (8:34) as far as one is able to deny oneself and take up the Cross.

The crowd is the chief beneficiary of Jesus similar to minor characters, which approach Jesus with their need for assistance. So it becomes the subject of Jesus' compassion for they are like "sheep without a shepherd" (6:34).[44] In spite of its presence with Jesus and benefiting of his power, it tends to deny, distrust and

---

[43] cf., Whoever blasphemes against the Holy Spirit .... (Mk 3:29); Whoever does the will of God is... (3:35 – 4:1); Whoever would save his life will ... (8:35); Whoever is ashamed of me ...(8: 38 - 9:1); Whoever receives one such child ...(9:37); Whoever gives you a cup of....(9:41); Whoever causes one of these little ones ...(9:42); Whoever divorces his wife and ...(10:11); Whoever does not receive the kingdom of ... (10:15); Whoever would be great among you ...and Whoever would be first ...(10:43-44); Whoever says to this mountain ...(11:23).

[44] The crowd comes to Jesus seeking healing (1:32; 2:2,13; 3:8,20, 32; 4:1 10:1; 6:31). Jesus offers them food (6:39,41,42; 8:1). They are also beneficent in hearing the teachings of Jesus and his parables along with his disciples (7:14). The parable of the sower is presented with an end of Jesus' exhortation to the crowd (4:1, 9, 23-24).

abandon Jesus. The crowd occasionally seems believing not in Jesus "and he could do no mighty work there, except that he laid his hands upon a few sick people and healed them. And he marveled because of their unbelief" (6:5-6). Finally, the reader will experience the disgraceful attitude of the crowd that join with the opponents of Jesus in the arrest (14:43), bear false witness against him (14:53, 56), opt for Barabbas to Jesus and cry for the crucifixion of Jesus (15:8-14) and mock Jesus (the passersby with opponents mock at Jesus on the Cross 15.31-35, 36).

At the start of Jesus' Galilean ministry, Mark assumes the crowd as a band of 'ad agent' that conveys fame of Jesus.[45] Many come to Jesus hearing the hearsay of the crowd. Yet it retains its mob nature being unidentified and incompetent to take up any commissioning from Jesus. Best identifies them as "the unevangelised mass" or "the uncommitted."[46] We can consider them as fallible anonymous Christians. It is a round character group with variants of positive and negative traits. The compassion of Jesus for the crowd evokes in the reader sympathy to the desperate situation of their lack of proper leadership. Jesus is the real leader when the human authorities become unjust, corrupt and antitypes with egoism. We now meet some of the antagonistic characters exposed in the story.

Out-group Characters

Here, we look at how Mark constructs the world of out-group in contrast to the world of in-group. This section will undertake the prominent groups that appear to be opponents in character and viewpoint in the whole Markan story. They are classified into three groups:[47] 1. Pharisees and Scribes, 2. Sadducees

---

[45] Not only they hear Jesus but also they hear about Jesus from their surroundings. In Capernaum many gathered hearing Jesus (2:2). People from Palestine and beyond gathered to Jesus hearing about him (3:8). There are many occasions the narrator reports that the crowd rushed to Jesus just hearing about him; hearing about his fame and name (6:55, even individuals from the crowd came to earn benefits by hearing about him - 5:27; 7:24-25; 10:47). These multi-activities of hearsays, hearing and gathering to Jesus, take place with in the crowd.

[46] cf., E. BEST, *Following Jesus*, pp. 29,101,136,154; Idem., "The Role of the Disciples in Mark", *NTS* 23(1977), pp. 392-393.

[47] It is fitting to discuss some of the scholarly opinion on the historical relevance of Markan portrayal of Jewish leaders and the antagonism that is experienced by the reader. NT scholars do not, of course, accept the antagonism between the Markan Jesus and the Jewish leaders as "descriptive of the historical Jesus but rather as reflective of the subsequent struggles of the early Christian church and the Judaism." They are the images of collective Christian memory. The very important principle, as Malbon says, is that 'Gospel of Mark is not an allegory in which characters or a group of characters in the story may be equated with person or a group of persons beyond the narrative'. cf., E. S. MALBON, pp. 123, 136. Markan portrayal of Pharisees seems *accurate, though biased,* on the aspect of their location, it is puzzling. Josephus locates them mainly in Jerusalem, but Mark locates them in Galilee. cf., J. MARCUS, p. 523; *JW* 2:569; A. J. SALDARINI, Pharisees, *Scribes and Sadducees in Palestine Society : A Sociological Approach*, Eerdmans, Grand Rapids – Cambridge, Michigan – U.K., 2001, 146-149; L. LEGRAND, *The Bible on Culture*, TPI, Bangalore, 2001, pp. 90-94. As it is impossible to speak of an organized Judaism in the first century context of various

and priests, 3. Family of Jesus.[48] By the narrativization of out-group characters, Mark brings to the light positive identity factors of his design through his in-group characters and models, which we have already seen above. The in-group positive image is made as worth as role model under the dark spot of out-group characters. Any search for their historical reliability is shunned by the narrator since his principle motif behind the construct of out-group is to set a contrasting opposition to the in-group characters as his task of illustrating identity markers for his readers.

Pharisees and Scribes

Pharisees are absent from the arrest, trail and death scenes of Jesus in Jerusalem. But, they are present to confront Jesus in several occasions: once they go with the disciples of John 2:18; other time they are united with some of the scribes from Jerusalem (7:5); at another moment, they are delegates of Scribes and Chief Priests to trap Jesus (12:13). At another occasion, they themselves confront Jesus to ask sign for his authority (8:11). The reader will have an impression of this group as less dangerous in comparing to the Scribes who are unreservedly join with all the groups to move the plot against Jesus until he is crucified.

Pharisees have affinity to law, tradition and external customs than to have a personal relation to Jesus. Jesus is deeply sorry for their distrustful ignorance on the real authority of Jesus when asking signs from heaven (8:11). They are deeply interested in the culturally bound traditions and authority than paying obedience to God's dominance.[49] The Pharisees often poses puzzling and polemic questions with an intention to try (8.11 *peirazontes*) and test Jesus (12:13 *auton agreusōsin*). Jesus responds to them in parables when they raise question about the disciples regarding the fasting. This reminds the reader that they are 'outsiders' to whom Jesus always speaks on similes and parables (4:10, 11). They are outsiders who do not understand things from the view point of Jesus but purely from their cultural viewpoint. Mark is prudent to judge their inner world through the prophetic mouth of Jesus. Citing Isaiah, their hypocrisy is deplored (7:6-13); they honour God with their lips but their heart is away from Him, leaving His commandments into thin air so that strive to sustain their convenient man-made

---

sects, it is questionable the coalition move of Pharisees, Scribes, Sadducees and Priests together in Mark. Therefore, it is importantly a literary and theological motif of Mark to picture them as opponents to Jesus and disciples. To our concern, Mark is pro-oriented to the in-group identity than that of the opponents. These opponent groups are only a literary instrument of Mark for his identity formation of his community.

[48] The antagonist out-group category can be expanded with political characters in the story namely Herod and Pilate. cf., CYPRIAN E. FERNANDEZ, *Identity in Conflict*, pp. 278-279.

[49] They interrogate Jesus for disciples' breach of tradition and customs. 'Why do John's disciples and the disciples of the Pharisees fast but your disciples do not fast? (2:18); Look, why are they doing what is not permitted? (2:25); why do your disciples not live according to the tradition of the elders?' (7:5).

traditions. "They condemn Jesus for healing on the Sabbath, yet on the very same day they plot with the herodians to destroy him."[50] They become vicious and wicked to test Jesus blending the religious and political motives on paying tax to Caesar. When they are too bothered of the externals to forget the inner heart of faith and devotion, they really tend to nullify the word of God (7:6-13). By nullifying the Word (7:13.) they in fact nullify Jesus and his teachings (1:45; 2:2; 4:14-16-20, 33).

In the Markan story, Scribes are ushers of conflicts with Jesus leading to controversial dialogues.[51] Scribes as teachers are in conflict with the authority of Jesus as a teacher. Mark presents Scribes, in contrast to Jesus, as incompetent teachers with false authority. Jesus' authority comes from the Holy Spirit to forgive sins, the *ultimatum* of all authorities (1:22). Above all, they are not people-oriented but self-oriented teachers with vested interest for their own honour and sheen appearance in the public (12:38-40). Will they not become envious against Jesus when Jesus' authentic authority among the crowd challenges their public fame? (11:18). As defense mechanism, they question the authority of Jesus and further more misinterpret the same to bring defamation to him. They said, "he has Beelzebul, and by the ruler of the demons he casts out demons" (3:22). They are green with envy at Jesus that subsequently operates as the basic evil to defame him and deform the mighty works of the Kingdom among the 'little believers' (9:42). Here, are they not scandalous to the little ones? (9:42-48). Markan Jesus is harsh in his tone to criticise any scandals to the little ones. With the same tone of hardness, Scribes' malicious act is warned as blasphemy against the Holy Spirit. Anything other than this eternal sin will be forgiven (3:28, 29). Can't we say that scribes are liable to this eternal sin and thus doomed to an eternal punishment?

Priests-Group

The first reference to priests in the story comes from the command of Jesus to the leper healed, to give testimony to the priest, which occurs prior to the in-break of the Jewish opposition in the story (1.44). Jesus' command is to testify his power of authority as well as adherence to the Mosaic Law. This mandate of Jesus is understood as his exhortation to witness the eschatological action of God open in him. It renders the reader to presume that the opposition and subsequent conflict between the priests and Jesus is not initiated by Jesus but proceeds from the priests. Before the passion scenes, Jesus has only once an encounter with the priestly clan; the controversy with Sadducees on resurrection (12:18-27).

The narrator shows them as grave enemies of Jesus who wants to kill him. They love the death of Jesus. There are many instances of their seeking for Jesus,

---

[50] D. RHOADS - J. DEWEY- D. MICHIE, p. 118.

[51] cf., Healing and forgiving the paralytic (2:6); eating with tax collectors and sinners (2:16); the question of possession by Beelzebub (3:22); eating with hands defiled (7:1, 5); Scribes are also in conflict with disciples of Jesus (9:14) and argue with them.

not to follow him but to destroy him. They seek him after hearing about the cleansing of the temple (11:18); seek him how to seize him by deceit and to kill (*apokteinōsin* 14:1); seek a witness against him in order to convict and they were not finding any (14:55); seek him as a robber who later appears with a crowd of clubs and swords to seize him. They are deadly antagonists to Jesus and his Kingdom (14:43). Their character does not leave any trace of repentance and possibility of discipleship in them.

The conflict over the Jesus' authority initiated by Scribes gets into a vertex point when priest questions the same in the passion scene. "What kind of authority to have to do all these things? Who gave you this authority?" (11:28-29). The authority factor is that which links both Jesus and priests with the crowd. The chief priests are shown as very sensitive to the feelings and movements of the crowd as they are afraid (*ephobounto*) of Jesus because the crowd were amazed of his teaching (11:8). They feared the violent power of the crowd (14:2). Jesus as the true servant from God is a genuine benefactor of the crowd, but the crowd in turn becomes a benefactor of the opponent priests-group whom served by the public recognition and subjection. They not only fear the crowd but also use and abuse the power of the crowd to incite the mob sentiments against Jesus (15:11). All the reasons for their antagonism against Jesus root in their envy of him. Pilate judges correctly their inside thoughts; "for he [Pilate] realized that it was out of jealousy that the chief priests had handed him over" (15:10). In the words of Hagedon and Neyrey, the word envy is the skeleton of a long cultural process, and the "anatomy of envy" could be viewed throughout the conflict between Jesus and priests.[52]

Family of Jesus

In the literary reading of Mark, we do not find any intentional description of the profile of Jesus' family as in the infancy narratives of Mathew and Luke. His family is presumed to be in Nazareth from where Jesus leaves for his baptism (1:9). When he returns to his hometown (6:1), he is not welcomed. Mark pictures his home of origin in hostile colours. Nazareth is often substituted by Capernaum as his place of house (1:21; 2:1; 9:33). Iersel says that Nazareth becomes a Galilean Jerusalem, a place fraught with opposition.[53] Therefore, the disciples replace his kith and kin; Capernaum replaces his native place.[54]

[52] "Chief priests are distressed at Jesus' success and seek to destroy his prestige...[for] Jesus not only invaded the physical space of the elite priests by entering the temple, he challenged their priestly role in his critique of the way the temple was run (11:15-19; 12:9,12,40-44)." in A. C. HAGEDOM - J. H. NEYREY, "It was out of Envy that they handed over : the Anatomy of Envy and the Gospel of Mark", *JSNT* 69 (1998), pp. 15-56.

[53] cf., B. M. F. VAN IERSEL, p. 93.

[54] cf., S. C. BARTON, pp. 67-96.

The 3:20-21 is a redactional seam raises much confusions and doubts on its meaning.[55] Most important among them is to answer the question, to whom *hoi par'autou* refers to in 3:21? It literally means 'his friends' or 'his relatives.'[56] Because of the difficulty of interpreting *auton* (3:21) and *elegon* (3:21) in the literary context wherein has a reference to four set of characters - Jesus, crowd, the disciples, and scribes - it is dubious to say who went out to restrain whom. The major opinions reach a consensus that Jesus' family try to restrain him for 'he is beside himself.'[57] From the narrative reading, we understand that 3:20-21 seems to be the first part of a sandwich episode (3:20-21 [322-30] 3:31-35). The Markan order in his mind about the happenings of this episode would be that Jesus' family members set out (may be from Nazareth) to restrain him in belief that he was demented. To add weight on their misunderstanding, Mark brings in meanwhile, a further accusation of the Scribes of Jerusalem (3:22) and Jesus responds so harshly to them. Meantime his family arrives and sends for him. Here, Jesus gives the reply for them that a *new family* of his is already constituted.[58]

It is usual that when Mark inserts materials in the intercalating episodes, the parts absorb certain meaning of the whole framework of the episode. In this sense, the odium of blasphemy that Mark attributes to the scribes, to some degree could be extended to the story of Jesus' family and the harsh judgment on scribes against their blasphemy is servable to the family members too. Ultimately, the severity of the family's charge is expressed in his definition of the *new family.*[59] Jesus' family is outside to the circle of the followers who are ought to do the will of God (3:35). We see here Jesus replying to the Scribes in parables (3.23) as it is natural that Markan Jesus speaks in parable to the outsiders (4:11). Consequently, both Scribes and family members become outsiders in the Markan story who do not do the will of God. Nothing more is needed to confirm the hostile nature of Jesus' own family to the works of the incoming Kingdom of God.

In this episode, while Mark has his focus on natural family of Jesus, his Jesus is shown oriented much towards the *new family* of disciples. We cannot speak Jesus' family without speaking about this *new family*. In relation to Jesus, the evangelist

---

[55] *Ibid.*

[56] cf., B. M. METZGER, p. 70.

[57] This subject has been widely dealt by a few authors. cf., H. WANSBROUGH, "Mark III.21-Was Jesus out of His Mind?", *NTS* 18 (1972), pp. 233-235; D. WENHAM, "The Meaning of Mark III.21", *NTS* 21(1975), pp. 295-300 ; J. PAINTER, "When is a house not home? Disciples and family in Mark 3: 13 – 35", *NTS* 45 (1999), pp. 498-513.

[58] *kai erchetai hē meter autou kai hoi adelphoi autou* (3:31) reminds the similar Markan catchphrase in 3:21, *exēlthon* which enables us to identity mother and brothers of Jesus of v.31 with *hoi par' autou* of v.21.

[59] But we cannot completely equate Jesus' relatives with the scribes as hostiles since scribes has a sustaining role through out the narrative while family members are restricted to this part. They fade out of the story after 6:1-6a. They do not deny Jesus, nor do they betray. The unbelief is caused by the rumor of the public and it is relative. cf., S.C. BARTON, pp. 67-96.

is implying that Jesus' relations with his own family are being superseded by his relations with his disciples; that those chosen by him have precedence over those to whom he belonged naturally; that his mission has priority over family ties. This rupture of Jesus' family becomes an experience to disciples in their relationship with their families. To the view of Mark, Jesus enters a house and the house to which he enters now becomes no longer a dwelling place of family but a gathering place of the new community.[60] A new self-understanding of the new group is given that its identity is not forged around the natural ties of family and religion but it is voluntary to who does the will of God. This *new family* is fictive; it does not deny the existence and legitimacy of the natural family. We may commit errors in understanding the Markan vision of this *new family* in a plain sense. "Jesus brought into being a new community based not on ties of blood and heredity, but a voluntary association opens in a quite novel way to anyone who repents, believes in the Gospel and does the will of God."[61] Jesus' own family was blind on what Spirit was doing in Him and so they restrain him. They are culturally inspired than spiritually. Their familial image founded on the pivotal values of honour and shame so they go out to protect the honour of the family damaged by their madden member of their family, Jesus. Jesus neither does value the honour nor does shame his family, rather, claims for a higher legitimating norm for his true family. He claims for a priority of the acquired honor of kinship by doing the will of God over the ascribed honour of the natural family.[62] He is, in fact, not discrediting his own family members but extending them an invitation to join his new family circle.

Distinctive Traits of In-group and Out-group

Mark characterizes two sets of characters in contrasting manner guided by the principles according to the prescribed charter of discipleship. The narrative is well coherent with its own rhetorical application of suspense and gaps for readers concern, to draw out the desired interconnections and inspiration of discipleship from the character project of the author.

The out-group is generally antagonistic in behaviour to the views and norms represented by the in-group. Pharisees and scribes are opponents but priests group is exceptionally dangerous and criminal, craving for the murder of the Son of God. Mark tries to expose the out-group as indifferent to the viewpoint of God made manifest in Christ – the Son of God. They find themselves unfavorable to the gestures of the Kingdom of God because of their culturally inspired human

---

[60] cf., E. S. MALBON, *Narrative Space and Mythic Meaning in Mark*, Harper and Row, San Francisco, 1986, p. 140.

[61] S.C. BARTON, p. 85.

[62] cf., B. J. MALINA – R. L. ROHRBAUGH, *Social Science Commentary on the Synoptic Gospels* (2nd ed.), Fortress Press, Minneapolis, 2003, pp. 158-159; B. J. MALINA, *The New Testament World: Insights from Cultural Anthropology*, pp. 27-57.

viewpoint which does not transcend itself to get tuned with the viewpoint of God. This ignites the whole conflict between out-group and Jesus' group in the story. The whole conflict is fundamentally one that of between the human authority and divine authority out of which Mark instructs his community that the in-group enjoys the real authority uncorrupted and non-abusive and rather liberative. Mark shows that this true leadership is realized in Jesus to whom the people under the human load of authority are sheep without real shepherd and he is the true shepherd who serves them with his own life.

The warning Mark reminds the reader by showing the fallible disciples that even disciples can become prey to these attitudes manifested by those out-group characters if they are not vigilant in faith and sustained in the memory of Christ. In contrast to the exclusivist attitudes of out-group, Markan *new family* of insiders is open and inclusive without any enslavement to the fencing of laws and traditions. The fictive boundaries that the insiders enjoy are defined, not in the cultic and legalistic canon or in any cultural and institutional terms but in the inward spirit of allegiance to Jesus Christ, his memory and through living a life of loving and vibrant relationship in the community. Their true devotion comes from their hearts, than merely becoming a lip service (7:6). The out-group features serve as a prelude to the Markan orientation to characterize the in-group identity.

In the section of disciples, we have seen the characterization as rather complex on the whole wherein they start their tour with an impression of reliability, being called by Jesus, being with Jesus leaving all, following him, and assisting him by sharing even in his own mission. They are obedient to the definite choice of Jesus and seem privileged to be defended under the providence of God. To certain extend they are shown as models for the allegiance to Jesus Christ. However, as the story is wound up, they terminate being non-examples and fallible, ironically leaving every hope in Jesus Christ for their restoration in Galilee. A considerable part of the Markan characterization of disciples occupies to display their fear and lack of faith and understanding. These basic drawbacks lead them to be unsympathetic to the little ones, weak in Spirit, exclusive and temporal in outlook, and further to abandon and betray their master. It is dialectically interconnected, that the lack of understanding generates in them the lack of faith and the lack of faith in turn generates fear and lack of understanding. It is clearly shown by Mark that the Cross aspect is scandalous to them; crucifixion is a saturate point of the story, at the juncture which all these drawbacks of them are at disclosure. They are on the way, on move with Jesus yet unwelcoming to the same reality of this way; manifest the existential fact of discipleship that there would be a conflict to live according to the terms of God than in terms of humans. They saw the "honour as their identity, power as their privilege, richness as their blessing and the security as their salvation" [63] for it was the cultural understanding of the time. They fail to understand appropriately the call of discipleship that it is meant for a cultural

[63] cf., D. RHOADS – J . DEWEY – D. MICHIE, pp. 122-129.

breakdown to the cause of a new culture and dominion of God inaugurated by Christ.

The characterisation of the disciples elicits in reader the sentiments ambivalent towards them. Through the Markan paraenetic device[64] of presenting disciples, the reader is opportune to put on the shoes of the disciples and feel the privilege of being with Jesus. At the same time, the author wants the reader to evaluate and judge the weakness, capacity and failures and to make themselves strong to genuinely follow Jesus. Markan author creates sympathy in the reader for the failures and weakness of the disciples (16:7). The repeated failures of the disciples support his emphasis on Jesus as the only true, positive and incomparable archetype of discipleship for readers and the fallible disciples are contrasting examples intended to warn readers to take the demands of following Jesus seriously.[65] Describing the incomprehension motif of Mark, D. J. Hawkin explains what Mark wants from the reader. "It is evident that Mark is not inviting his readership to repudiate the suffering of the Messiah as Peter does in 8:31-33. Just the opposite; precisely what Peter repudiates, the Church is called on to embrace. The mystery that the disciples fail to understand is precisely the mystery into which the Church is called to enter. The incomprehension motif is to be classified as *typology per contrariam.* It sets in sharper focus what has to be grasped about the mystery of Christ....The destiny of Jesus is the paradigm of Christian existence. To "comprehend" is to discover and affirm the law of the Cross as the supreme eschatological reversal. The dimensions of Mark's pedagogical task, then, are considerable. His strategy is to thematize incomprehension not only as superficiality and as ignorance but above all as blindness, that comes from the contradiction of human appetites and ambitions. The disciples are limited by the instinctive willingness to identify the good as the good for me."[66]

Mark rules out absolutism of having a perfect disciple or does not rule out none to the possibility to become a disciple since any one can be a disciple of Jesus Christ. No one can be perfect in following since anyone who follows can be fallible. Mark has shown the disciples as those who positively configure more with the discipleship pattern in the vocation stories. They are the symbolic meaning to whoever wishes to follow Jesus in order to understand that discipleship is a gift and status which proceeds from the very life and authority of Jesus. Regarding the willingness to follow, the disciples are exemplars but to follow Jesus and to be his

[64] It is pedagogy through negative examples after the model of Greco-Roman teaching and exhortation. cf., M. A. BEAVIS, *Mark's Audience: The Literary and Social Setting of Mark 4:11-12*, (JSNTsup.) JSOT Press, Sheffield, 1989, pp. 181-182; B. FIONE. S. J., "Covert Allusion in 1 Cor 1-4", *CBQ* 47(1985), pp. 85-102.

[65] cf., L .W. HUTARDO, *Lord Jesus Christ: Devotion to Jesus in Earliest Christianity*, Eerdmans, Michigan-Cambridge, 2005, pp. 306-316.

[66] D. J. HAWKIN, "The Incomprehension of Disciples in the Markan Redaction", *JBL* 91 (1972, 4), p. 500.

disciples understandably and distinctively in the pluralistic culture may become a matter of fallibility for them. It is the point of departure from which Mark now turns to show us more and better exemplary models of discipleship or prototypes that configure very profoundly with the values of discipleship.

A group will always accredit certain individuals as prototypes than others on a strong motivational basis. It is a social phenomenon where certain individuals typify the identity of the in-group aiming at consistent and positive group behaviour. The minor characters are more prototypes to tell to his community, what positive attitude they should have regarding their in-group status as disciples of Jesus. As Mark use the metaphor of family to define the community of the disciples headed by God, the minor figures are configured as real 'sons' and 'daughters' (5:34; 2:5) in this family, as Markan Jesus address with these familial epithets, not his adherents but minor characters. They are living symbols of faith and insights in the Kingdom of God. All their imitable gestures of words and actions are shown to have come out of their deep-seated faith and trust in Jesus in whom God's Spirit abode. Their expression of faith-driven emotions and loyalty to Jesus Christ are vivid and outstanding. Some of them are converted to be active preachers of the Word without fear. Some fulfils the radical demands of discipleship by Cross-bearing and self-denial. Mark goes in extend to show the dignity of living in this newly inaugurated family of disciples through the metaphor of Joseph of Arimathea who leaves not the body of Jesus shameful but in decent to the satisfaction of human dignity. Mark tells to his readers through these minor characters that the discipleship is possible despite any embarrassing social factors, only through an invincible faith in Christ and convincing hope in the reign of God.

These minor characters represent the symbol of desired social transformation, which has been stipulated in the inaugural project of the Kingdom – repent and believe in the Good News. Encountering Jesus personally and to be converted to the *new family* is a great social process which is exemplified in the instances of each minor characters. Mark follows a stereotypic pattern in this. When they meet Jesus, they are generally categorized as needy, physically challenged, socially alienated, possessed, ritually unclean and outcaste, parentally responsible and burdened. Some among them are socially respectful, authoritative, wealthy and influential. This situation is ontological to them. At the point of their encounter with Jesus, they are of faith and insight, fearless, reverential, truthful, humble, bold, persevering, repentant, courageous, enthusiastic, service minded and perceptive. After they meet Jesus, they become people who are wholly sane, converted, receptors of Jesus' compassion, calm, peaceful and servants of the Word. Their conversion is an adequate response to the in-break of the Kingdom initiated by Jesus' mission and at the same time a beginning of their participation in the same mission perpetuated for the eschatological end.

Before we conclude this chapter, it is appropriate to answer a quite expectable question regarding in-group out-group differences drawn out from the Markan story. We have shown some characters that conform to the principles of following Jesus and some are conflictive to them so as to call them respectively in-group and out-group. Is this in-group versus out-group a reader's construct or an author's concept? Is there internal and direct reference in Mark to show this mentality of in-group and out-group inherent in the text?

In 4:10-12 after Jesus' teaching of the parables, those around him with the twelve (4:10) ask him about the meaning of the parables. In this setting, the author shows the presence of two groups of people; 1. those around Jesus with the twelve, 2. the twelve. It is narrated that these people - two groups - jointly ask Jesus the meaning of the parables. It is presumable for the reader that the twelve is a group chosen and commissioned by Jesus (3:31-35) and those around the twelve with Jesus (4:10) is a crowd. This crowd has already appeared prior to this setting as who sit around him in 3.32. In 3:31-35 Jesus looks at those in circle around him and map them as his new relatives or family members. From the above premises, it could be inferred that in 4:10-12, "those around him with the twelve" is an audience of Jesus' teaching including both the disciples (twelve) and others, those who listen to him and seek further instructions in order that they might do the will of God. Their presence declares their option for the side of Jesus and his values.

If the aforementioned are the in-group members who are listening to Jesus, there are normally out-group members who are emotionally and subjectively distanced from him and his company. In 4:11, Jesus explicitly refers to a group designated as outsiders; "And he said to them, to you has been given the secret of the Kingdom of God, but for those outside, everything comes in parables". The outsiders are those who are being out of the circle which is formed by the insiders who are in the presence of Jesus. In contrast to the outer group, this circle of in-group people are, who remain with Jesus owing to the dispersion of a group (huge crowd) that hear the parable alone but waiting not to hear the mystery of it (4:1-9). Those 'dispersed' have listened the parable but have shown no further interest in what he has to say about it. Therefore, those of the 'outside' form the unreceptive members of the crowd.

In 3:31-45, the family relatives of Jesus are mentioned twice as those who are outside in contrast to those who are seated around him. The narrative says as follows: "Then his mother and his brothers came; and standing outside, they sent to him and called him. A crowd was sitting around him; and they said to him, your mother and your brothers and sisters are outside, asking for you." (3:31-32). Therefore, the outsiders comprise also his family relatives. The family members are those who are non-understanding and unreceptive to Jesus and his values. In 3:20-21, family members are made belief by others' accusations on Jesus as the one who has demented and they try to seize him (3:20-21).

Again we see the scribes saying that Jesus is working miracles through the power of Beelzebub (3:22) and Jesus respond to them in parables (3:23-28). It could possibly be inferred that speaking of parables by Jesus is a sign of treating certain as outsider/s (4:11); for them "everything comes in parables". The scribes, the opponents of Jesus are unperceptive of his values, are thus outsiders. It means that he gives two forms of the same instructions. On the one hand, he lays the original form of parables un-interpreted in a larger audience. On the other hand, he lays the parables interpreted for those who are with him in circles. It does not mean that the interpretation of Jesus' parables would bring the insiders exceptionally to a complete comprehension of his identity and his values. In contrast to the outsiders, insiders, though they show the characteristics of the outsiders like incomprehension, are restrained from rejecting Jesus intentionally and destroying him, due to their emotional favoring for Jesus. This distinguishing mark separates them identically as two entities within the story world of Mark.

The best definition for the outsider and insiders could be seen from Jesus' response to the disciples in 9:38-41. John mentions about an unknown exorcist as who does not belong to "us", that is, to the company of Jesus and his disciples. "Whoever is not against us is for us." (9:40). It is the reply of Jesus to John's arrogance. It is clear from Jesus' reply, however, that an outsider, who calls upon the name of Jesus can also share in that power, provided his appeal imply a positive attitude towards Jesus. The horizon of the in-group is not limited to a single geographical space or a small group, rather it is extensive to the extent of admitting positively the viewpoint of the Kingdom and open to overwhelm more faithful.

In the scene of explaining the tradition of Jews, the narrator makes an intrusion with an assumption that the hearers/readers need explanation of "things pharisaical" or even "things Jewish" (7:3-4) like *Corban* (v.11). These intrusions therefore manifest the distance assumed by the narrator to be existed between the hearer/reader and the Pharisees/Jews. To view from the other side, the intrusion itself serves to distance the hearer/reader from the Pharisee/Jews. In his explanation, "all the Jews" are "them" (third person plural form); therefore, the narrator and the hearer/reader are "us". The crowd and the disciples are thereby not unlike the hearer/reader but are "us" as opposed to "them."[67]

Conclusion

The chapters three and four are not an end in itself but they would carry us forward to have a synthesis on this study, answering to, how Mark suggests a new social identity to his community? We have been informed well by the social identity model about those required properties to be explored from the text of Mark for explaining the social identity of the Markan group. As a result,

---

[67] E. S. MALBON, p. 152.

we have seen in the above chapters the elaboration of the identity descriptors[68] of discipleship, which is the salient category of the Markan group. The disciples who follow Jesus must hear his voice obediently and follow him fulfilling the required demands of self-denial and Cross-bearing. The radical exigency of following Jesus includes the norms of service with humility even to the little ones. Mark has adapted a very creative way of proposing those categories of discipleship, not by mere saying of dialogues and narrative discourses but through showing of resolute and strong characters. Those categories that are constituent in shaping of group identity are personified through the Markan characterization of in-group in contrast to the out-group. The positive dimensions of the Markan community are exemplified in the disciples and more in prototypic characters through whom Mark goes to tell his group *how they ought to behave* and *what attitude they ought to have* as a group of disciples. On to the contrary, he has a set of characters to tell that *what their identity is not.* In the text, Mark is on shaping of a new identity for his group.

Now we have at our hand almost the basic ideological elements and properties to reconstruct the desired social identity of the Markan community. In the concluding chapter, we are going to see on whole a new counterculture that Mark proposes to his in-group at the backdrop of a dominant culture of out-group. In other words, what should be his community in comparison to other social groups and their behaviours?

---

[68] See, a table of the identity descriptors attached to the end of this chapter.

Identity Descriptors of the Markan Community

	NORMS (*Discipleship as the Category of the Community*)	IN-GROUP		OUT-GROUP	
		VALUES	PROTOTYPES	VALUES	ANTITYPES
COGNITIVE	<u>**EXCLUSIVENESS**</u> **Christocentrisim:** Adherence and allegiance to Christ – Knowledge on the revelation of Christ - Following Christ has precedence to Parousia – Sharing the Mission of Christ, his authority to exorcise, preaching as ambulants – conversion from law and tradition to Christ. (1:16-20; 3:13-19; 6:6-13;10:17-31).	**Faith - trust – confidence- prayer – needy of Christ's help**	The Leper (1:40-45) Jairus (5:22-43) Hemorrhaged woman (5:22) Bartimaeus (10:52) Centurion (15:39-45) Syrophoenician (7:25-30) Woman at Bethany (14:3) Majority of the minor characters are models of faith	**Faithlessness-testing-questioning-rebuking-incompetent authority and self-reliant**	Disciples, Peter (9:18;14:38) Crowd (5:35-43) Pharisees, Scribes (3:22; 9:42-48).
		Insight-understanding the identity of Christ	Centurion Bartimaeus Syrophoenician woman (7:25-30)	**Incomprehension-Miscomprehension-Blindness to the view point of Christ**	Disciples (6:52) Pharisees, Scribes (7:6:13) Priest-group Family members of Christ (3.21f, 31ff)
	<u>**INCLUSIVENESS**</u> Open to all and accept whoever wish to follow the will of Christ, children, women, little believers, outcaste, gentiles, sinners.(8:34-9:1; 2:13-17)	**Preaching-Witnessing-Mission-following as full-time itinerants**	Disciples – The leper (1:40) – Gerasene Demoniac (5:1) Bartimaeus – Centurion – Women at the cross and tomb (15:40,41; 16:1)	**Defamation False witness Betrayal – denial Abandoning**	Scribes –Family members (3:22; 9:42-48) – Sanhedrin members – Disciples-Peter, Judas Iscariot. – Richman (10:17ff)

contd...

VALORATIVE	**SELF-DETACHMENT** **Radicalism & Exigency** Cross-bearing- self-denial- detachment of kinship ties and worldly possessions – avoiding scandals, service and humility – recognize children, woman and little believers. (8:34-9:1; 9:33-50)	**Self-sacrifice-cross bearing and leaving kinship ties - shame**	Poor widow (12:4-43) Simon of Cyrene (15:21) Disciples	**Temporal out-look- Power, honour, wealth, authority, rejection of cross**	Disciples, Peter, James and John (9:38-40;10:26-9:38-40; 6:35,37)- Richman (10:17-31) – Pharisees, Scribes, Priests.
		Courage – loyalty	Jairus (5:22-43) Bartimaeus (10:52) Centurion (15:39-45) Syrophoenician woman (7:25-30) Women at Bethany and at cross Joseph of Arimathea (15:42-47) Gerasene Demoniac (5:1)	**Fear - cowardice**	Disciples (4:41; 6:50) Priests group fearing crowd
		Service **Charity**	Pair Disciples (11:1-17;14:13-16) Woman at Bethany Joseph of Arimathea	**Murder –** **Crucifixion** **Hatred- enmity- be served-honour**	Priests – Soldiers Pharisees, Scribes, Sadducees
		Humility	Jairus Syrophoenician woman Woman at Bethany Joseph of Arimathea	**Mockery** **Hypocrisy** **Assault – Envy-** **Jealousy- Authority**	Pharisees – scribes – Sadducees- soldiers – priests group.
EMOTIVE	**COMMUNION** Members of a new family- House of God – a New Israel- who does the will of God- sons and daughters of God – relationship as brothers and sisters in Christ-Spirit of the community.	**Love** **Solidarity** **Fraternity** **Compassion** **Sharing** **Sympathy** **'We' feeling** **Unity** **Empathy**	Holy Spirit All the insiders of the Markan community is united in this emotional impulse and have living, loving and vibrant relationship	**Antipathy** **Hatred** **Enmity** **Division**	Evil Spirit All the outsiders who are not in conformity with the emotions and viewpoints of the Markan community

Chapter 5

IMAGING CHRISTIAN IDENTITY AND MARKAN COMMUNITY

A narration is brief if it is told in such a way that, at times, that which has not been mentioned may be understood from that which has been said.

(Cicero, *De Inventione,* I: 20.28)

We have outlined in the second chapter of models and methods, how a group does constitute its identity. The Social Identity theory addresses mainly this question by the way of explaining inter-group process. The identity of a group is determined through the means of social comparison and differentiation with their corresponding out-group.

From the integrated view of the social memory theory and the social identity theory, we are subsequently able to consider that the Markan text is the evidence of the identity of the group to which it was addressed. The ideological agon between the in-group and out-group in the text explains very well, for what the in-group stands for. We have seen this in the preceding chapters, that Mark has been presenting his in-group with a uniform conduct of living the values and norms of discipleship. The uniform behaviour, especially of the minor characters as Mark concerned, is conducive for the identity description because the stronger the social identification of a group, the more pronounced would be the tendencies towards the perception of similarity and difference between the in-group and out-group members.

Hence, it is understood that we find it necessary to make this study from the author's viewpoint. We need to keep in mind that Mark is addressing an already formed group of the followers of Jesus that was living in the shadow of then persecution and the Jewish war of 70-72 C.E. In the scholarly survey, we have been informed that the majority of the scholars doubtlessly agree that Mark was writing his Gospel for his community. To the core of the purpose, Mark intends to give a new life and identity to his group that already cherished the memory and tradition of Jesus. He uses the same Jesus memory and tradition, told and retold, to reinterpret the social self-definition of his group. As Mack makes out, "Mark appropriated the Christ myth and linked it with the Jesus tradition...to give to Christian imagination its sense of a radical and dramatic origin in time."[1] The point becomes clear now that Mack is using the term imagination, which is alias to our term identity. It means that the identity still remains as a project to be materialized in the cultural context. The ideal identity that Mark suggests will be realized only through its interaction with the cultural context of the community. The social identity of the community is obtained by the cultural interaction of their memory and tradition and Mark is trying to show, how that memory and tradition of Jesus ought to be inculturated in his social world. In other words, he prompts them, how the values of the Jesus-memory are to be lived out in the cultural situation of the group. Perhaps this 'cultural incarnation' of the identity would call for a revolutionary rupture and breakdown of the cultural structures in view of a new self-definition.[2] So now, we will have a picture of what the Markan community should be. To say inversely, we do not know exactly what had been the shape of his community before he wrote the Gospel for them.

In this concluding synthesis, with an application of social comparison strategy of SIT, we will have a certain overview on the Markan reconstruction of the social image of his group. By comparing the out-group and in-group values, we observe what the identity of the Markan community must be - the valorative, cognitive and emotive factors that constitute it. The cognitive factors are the logos of the Markan group; the valorative factors are ethos and the emotive factors are pathos of the Markan community. These three factors are fundamental to any sound and full-fledged living social entity of this world. Subsequently, it will prompt us what the social situation of the community that had occasioned Mark, for such a reinterpretation of his group image. It would further more lead us to confirm the location of the community, but by limiting itself to a convincing scholarly position.

The Logos of the Community: Cognitive Aspect

The conceptual foundation is indispensable for any motivated group or community by which the members are mutually identified as members of the same group, as well as enhance their sense of belongingness. The essential cognitive aspects or the mental principles which would operate as the basis for

---

[1] B. L. MACK, *A Myth of Innocence*, Fortress Press, Philadelphia, 1991, p. 355.

[2] cf., B. HOLMBERG, "Jewish Versus Christian Identity in the Early Church", *RevBib* 105 (1998), pp. 423.

the category of the Markan community of Jesus are mainly its Christo-centrisim and inclusivism.

Christo-centrism

The ideal community designed by Mark is fundamentally Christo-centric. This should be the cognitive base of the social identity - the logos - of his community, that they are of Jesus Christ, to be lived in Jesus Christ and guided by Jesus Christ. This awareness should be the distinguishing factor that primarily should differentiate them from the out-groups of the time.

The antagonists in the Markan text are primarily having an anti-Jesus attitude, expressing themselves their non-belief and distrust in the person of Jesus. They are portrayed as those who do not agree with his viewpoint and reluctant to acknowledge his authority, especially in forgiving sins. Their affinity to the law, tradition and external cultic purity observances, power and honour conscious keep them aloof from having any positive relation with Jesus personally. In the story world, their hypocrisy is subjected to the criticism of Jesus, their self-oriented leadership is being overturned by the authentic leadership of Jesus Christ, their attempt to defame Christ's name is neutralized by a band of people who are bold enough to give fame and name to Jesus' authority by following him totally.

This inner antagonism in the text may be a *model of* the experience of the Markan community in its multi-sectarian ambience.[3] The author does not leave this antagonism unvalued but considers it as a counterpoint of his identity thesis, to suggest a *model for* his community. Markan community is called to build up a sound attitude and awareness on the person and mission of Jesus, contrary to that of the out-group and in contrast to the fallible disciples. Here, it is necessary for us to look at the Christology of Mark in gist, before we understand his 'painting' of his group as Christo-centric.

Jesus is the anointed Son of Man crucified. He is mightier with the power of spirit and authority but become weak and powerless on the Cross (1:1-15). It is the parody and paradox of the Markan story as well the novelty in the vision of the Markan Christology. Mark attempts to reconcile these bipolar Christological

---

[3] It is truly understood that the Markan group in a social world was among the multi Jewish sects. According to Josephus, "the Jews had for a great while had three sects of philosophy peculiar to themselves; the sect of the Essenes, and the sect of the Sadducees, and the third sort of opinions was that of those called Pharisees; of which sects, although I have already spoken in the second book of the Jewish War, yet will I a little touch upon them now." (*Ant* 18:1.2). M. Hengel argues that Christianity as a messianic movement in the early period was not born out of any syncretism of pagan religions and beliefs rather it was a 'child of Judaism', though the pagan influence was directed to the Jesus movement thought the Jewish mediation. "...it was not until the first decades of the second century that the separation between mother and daughter [Judaism and Christianity] was finally completed and the former Jewish eschatological movement had been transformed into a new more universal religion." cf., M. HENGEL – C. K. BARRETT (ed., D. A. Hagner), *Conflicts and Challenges in Early Christianity*, Trinity Press International, Harrisburg - Pennsylvania, 1999, p. 6.

images symbolized in Galilee and Jerusalem. He tries to put them face to face in order to reconcile the Cristic images of 'the Son of God' and 'the Son of man'. The Son of God of the opponent priests (14:61-62) is the same 'the Son of man' marching on to the Cross. Markan reconciliation of these two poles is gestured typically by making the divine voice of Baptism reechoed at the foot of the Cross through the Roman centurion. His confession along with the subsequent empty tomb restores the generated hope of the Galilean phase. After all, hope is reborn in Christ, which marks a new beginning. The author does not miss to tell the reader that this Jesus would be the same who is to come at the eschatological end in power. Mark put the designation 'the Son of man' always in the mouth of Jesus who while speaks of himself in reference to his passion. The title 'the Son of God' is often put in the mouth of other characters in the story world when speak of in reference to Jesus. This attempt is to show that both notions of Christ are same and Mark needs to reconcile them avoiding one-sidedness of emphasis.[4] The centurion, who is a complete contrast to the mocking Jewish leaders, is the Markan arbitrate to link both the reality of Jesus at a single point, the Cross.

The proportionate partition of the story between the Galilean ministry and Jerusalem orientation indicates that the author likes to take a balancing view on Christology. The Galilean-Jesus, whose power is manifested through the casting out of demonic dominions through his indwelling Spirit, was to be reconciled with the Jerusalem-Jesus who is despised and rejected helplessly. The theme of Jewish apocalyptic eschatology has begun in the Galilean ministry of Jesus. In him shown, the Kingdom has its in-break through his healings and table fellowship. This Kingdom that arrived in Jesus has double facets; on the one hand, the present reality of the overpowering of the evil power and his call to share in that warfare by being adherent to him which is symbolized in banqueting; on the other hand, at the same time, this eschatological event is awaited to fulfill in the future. Within the narrative, the eschatological event that inaugurated in Galilee will have to be fulfilled in Jerusalem, but analeptically the fulfillment of the same eschatological event is awaited for a future time, which is even unknown to the Son of Man.

It is a strenuous effort to give a cognizable account of Mark's story in communicating his new vision of a world, its identity and human destiny from the sociological point of view of the first century Mediterranean world, since the Cross was a symbol of scandal, and the crucified, an utter failure. But, with this paradoxical reality, Mark summons his community to follow and to be faithful to

---

[4] The Son of Man is not a title, but a self-designation. The NT expression *ho huios tou anthrōpou*, is a fixed formulaic construction with specific, exclusive reference. It is an *idiolect*, functions like a name to identify or distinguish a person. It was used to show Jesus at the same time a human descendant and a distinctive figure with reverence. cf., L. W. HUTARDO, *Lord Jesus Christ: Devotion to Jesus in Early Christianity*, Eerdmans, Grand Rapids - Cambridge, Michigan - UK, 2005, pp. 290-306.

Jesus who has been devoted as the Son of God, the crucified. This call is hard and socially provocateur.

The pronounced conviction of the Markan group must be that Jesus is the sole 'architect' of their existence. The total intention and design of the Markan community proceed from the mind of Jesus, who has 'legislated' the vision and perception of the community, where their voluntary obedience takes precedence to any human psychological decision. They need to pay heed to Jesus' call for a reorientation of their social life, for which have been gathered and created as his own. This primary aspect of identity is exposed in the vocation scenes. The Markan community is given an image of 'fishermen', a conventional image to elicit in them a higher meaning of their existence. In the cultural background, this metaphor had various significances; in the Greco-Roman set up, it connotes teacher; in Jewish culture, it means different kinds of pupils; in Qumran set up, it means elected members who are warned of three nets of *ḇəlîya'al*[5]; for OT prophets, it connotes eschatological warfare and restoration of hope by the re-gathering of the people of God (Jer 16:16; Ezek 29:2-5; Am 4:2; Hab1:14-17). In Mark, it is a paradigm reintegrated to indicate their mission with all those implications of the OT Community. The community gathered by Jesus Christ comprises not merely of disciples of law or philosophy, but obedient followers of Christ who are called to partake in the eschatological warfare. The election of a new community on the mountain top is a reliving memory for the community that recalls the Mosaic tradition of God's choice for a new Israel (Ex 19:24, 34; Num 27; Deut 9:10, 32). Like Moses who stood between God and the Old tribes of Israel, Jesus is presented as intermediary between God and the new tribe of Israel, the Jesus movement. This inculcates a consciousness in the community that they are the *new Israel* and Jesus is the *new Moses* equipped with the authority to guide them.

The Christic-consciousness of the Markan community is not an ephemeral thought but a deep-seated conviction. They should cherish the relation of Jesus Christ who is shown as the person of authority with Spirit and his authority is not only to forgive sins but also to form a community, open to the sinners, outcaste and despised. The vocation instance like calling of Levi is formulated to illumine his group that their interest should lie in their peccable nature and the authority of the caller. Thus, they must have the distinctive awareness that they have relation with the one who has the authority over sins and sinners, made worthy to share his table fellowship in the breaking of the bread.[6]

The Markan community becomes more Christo-centric not only by the Christic-conviction but also by a Christ-oriented mission. The intrinsic relation

---

[5] *ḇəlîya'al :* 264Q258 (The Community Rule, *Serekh ha-Yahad*); also see, Judg 20:13; 1 Sam 10:27; 30:22 cf., HELOT, p. 116.

[6] cf., J. MARCUS, *Mark 1-8*, (AB) Doubleday, NY, London, Toronto, Sydney, Auckland, 2000, pp. 230-232.

to Jesus Christ is more concretized in a visible manner by the very participation in the historic mission of their Master and by perpetuating his activities as a sign and reality of the coming of the Kingdom. Mark suggests the followers of his community that they are not disjunct as mere ecstatic enchanters or hearers about the glorified Christ, but are enlisted as agents in the showdown of the Kingdom, meriting also the persecution. Jesus Christ is the archetype of this uprooted persecuted (10:30) members, as Mack points out, Jesus, the obedient martyr, becomes the community's myth for their experiences of trials and tribulations.[7]

The Christological convictions and mission of the community are intimately correlated to the virtue of faith and understanding in Jesus. The vitality of the group is anchored on their faith and insight in Christ, the crucified and the glorified. This should become, as Mark expect of his group, its most basic identity marker in their social milieu. The disciples, as seen in the previous chapters, are shown as models for the allegiance to Jesus Christ. However, as the story gets into its apex, they terminate themselves being non-examples and fallible, leaving every hope in Christ for their restoration in Galilee.[8] A considerable part of the Markan characterization of disciples, occupy to display their fear, lack of faith and understanding. These drawbacks lead them further to be unsympathetic to the children, weak in Spirit, exclusive and temporal in outlook, and further to abandon and betray their master. These are interrelated, that the lack of understanding generates in them the lack of faith and the lack of faith in turn generates fear and lack of understanding. Their non-understanding of Jesus Christ will result in the non-understanding of their own position in the community. Thinking not of the human things but of God (8:33) is the "code for the values of the Gospel."[9] But, they are 'on the way' on move with Jesus, yet unwelcoming of the same reality of this way, manifests the existential reality of the community that there would be a conflict to live according to the terms of God than in terms of humans.

The behaviour of the disciples would elicit in the Markan group certain sentiments ambivalent to them. Through the Markan paraenetic presentation of the disciples, the community is opportune to put on the shoes of the disciples and feel the privilege of being with Jesus. At the same time, the author wants his group to evaluate and judge its weakness, and failures and to brace themselves strong to follow Jesus. The repeated failures of the disciples support his emphasis on Jesus as the only true, positive and incomparable archetype of discipleship for his community, and the fallible disciples are contrasting examples intended to warn readers to take the demands of following Jesus seriously.

---

[7] cf., B. L. MACK, pp. 353-371.

[8] T. Weeden observes three stages of disciples' fallibility exposed by Mark: "Imperceptiveness", "Misconception" (of Jesus' messiahship), 'Betrayal/Denial/Abandonment'. He proposed that the disciples represent the false theology of glory in Mark's Community. cf., J. R. DONAHUE, "Windows and Mirrors: The Setting of Mark's Gospel", *CBQ* 57 (1995), p. 15.

[9] *Ibid.*, pp. 26.

The disciples' failure is the point of departure from which Mark shows his group more and better exemplaries that configure profoundly with the values of discipleship. A group will always accredit certain individuals among them as prototypes on a strong motivational basis. Similarly, these minor characters are so, to tell to his community, what positive attitude they should have regarding their in-group status. Most of the minor characters are shown as living symbols of an invincible faith against the cowardice and fear of disciples. Their expression of faith-driven emotions and loyalty to Jesus Christ is vivid and outstanding. By their portrayal, Mark is really defining the *modus vivendi* of faith and insight. The faith does not stand alone, but goes along with the understanding the person of Jesus. The indispensability of human response to Jesus in faith and understanding is an emphatic idea of Mark. This human response in faith is essential than any psychological human decisions for the enactment of God's reign. When the flow of faith is blocked, as Mark shows, the flow of Jesus' ministry is also being interrupted, but divine course of action will take its shift to other locations (gentiles) where faith and understanding is fertile. Hence, Mark exhorts his community through these minor characters that the discipleship is possible despite any embarrassing social factors but only through an invincible faith in Jesus Christ and convincing hope in the reign of God.

From a bird's eye view on the whole story, we understand that for Mark, 'faith', 'believing', 'prayer', 'name of Jesus', 'preaching of the Word', 'repentance' are coherent symbolic languages and concepts that signify the human existential response to the contingent eschatological in-break begun in Jesus.[10] While we realise what does these positive response of faith really mean through the minor characters, it is also necessary to know what does the non-understanding of the fallible disciples mean. In the miracles of feeding and walking on the sea, the misunderstanding of disciples are not of the very miracles as such but consists in the failure to recognize the action of God in them; in other words, the central operative formula of those miracles is unrecognized by the disciples. Even parables as such (7:14, 17) were understood intellectually but not ontologically, that is to say, the essence of the miracles was not captured by them. The misunderstanding is nothing but the failure to recognise God's action existentially revealed in Jesus Christ and that in turn incurs difficulty in them to come into agreement with Jesus' real identity as God's agent. The best metaphor to tell this secret of failure is that, they did not understand because of their 'hardness of heart' (6:52; 8:17). The community of Mark is encouraged, therefore, to prepare for the struggle of understanding ontologically the meaning of the action of Jesus that would in no time make them to come into agreement with the agenda of God.[11]

---

[10] cf., J. C. BEKER , "Recasting Pauline Theology", in J. M. BASSLER (ed.), *Pauline Theology*, Vol. 1, Fortress Press, Minneapolis, 1994, pp. 15-24.

[11] cf., J. M. ROBINSON, *The Problem of History in Mark*, SCM Press, London, 1971, pp. 73-78.

So far, we were observing the basic cognitive factor of the identity of Markan group. However, there also involves some emotive concerns inherent in the relationship of the Jesus-movement. An inseparable union between the community and Jesus is identified in the Markan concept of bearing and acting upon his 'name'. The use of Jesus' *word* is as powerful as his *name* in Mark. As Kee says, "neither conceptually nor in literary ways it is possible ...to draw an absolute distinction in Mark between Jesus and his followers, or in theological terms, between Christology and Ecclesiology."[12] This powerful attachment to the Master is the key and clue of their success. Any mission without Jesus Christ is doomed to failures and meaningless. In this sense, the Markan presentation of the fallible followers is intended, not to accuse any historical images of disciples but to tell the present time of Mark that the value of his community could be understood fully and retrospectively by re-living the past memory of Jesus's messianic action. If any misunderstanding of the messianic identity happens, it could be resolved only through a turning back to the past memories of messianic events. Moreover, this emotional allegiance to Jesus Christ is not an abstract conception but contingent, by being faithful and loyal to his name in public and stand for the sake of his Good news. The personal adherence to Jesus as well as his message dynamically preached makes realize the presence of Christ experiential.

Another aspect of the Christo-centric life includes that the community that moves after Jesus Christ always has the priority and precedence to Jesus Christ over law and tradition. The identity of the Markan community becomes competent and higher in a multi-religious context not because of their allegiance to the letters of law and their observance, rather their commitment to the person of Jesus Christ - who renders life to all law and prophets. As the community proceeds from the choice of Jesus Christ and is gathered in response to his prophetic call for a reorientation, this response to the conversion will include a conversion from the legacy of law to the experience of the person of Jesus Christ. The rich man who is challenged by this demand of conversion to the person of Jesus Christ could be often misinterpreted as a call to do charity. Nevertheless, the Markan community knew already that the charity was accepted as lofty in the legalistic culture of Jews. Even renunciation factor was not alien to the Hellenistic and Jewish culture. But, for the community, one thing that was new and an unknown would have been the radical transformation of life from law to the person of Jesus Christ. This deepest level of response is possible only through the adherence to Jesus who is full in the Spirit of God. The self-denial and Cross-bearing becomes possible only through Christ's spirit because they are not an imitation of what Jesus did but they are the result of one's following of the same Spirit in which he faced the humiliation of the Cross.

---

[12] H. C. KEE, *The Community of the New Age: Studies in Mark's Gospel*, The Westminster Press, Philadelphia - Pennsylvania, 1977, pp. 143-144.

The awareness that Mark tries to affirm is that his community is an apocalyptic and eschatological one. It is an attribute wedded intimately with the Christological awareness. Mark is not only conscious to reconstruct their cognitive identity in the temporal dimension of the past as well as the present but also to map out a future of their social consciousness as Christo-centric community. He clarifies that his is a community that should move further in the history not in a vain hope but with an undefeatable hope, oriented to the coming of Christ in Power. While setting the eschatological hope for the community, Mark advances from presenting the memories of the 'past Jesus' for the present living of the community, to a 'future Jesus Christ' in whom culminates all the time of their belief and action. The shaping of a communal identity is not a task with fractional time conscious but is concerned of micro as well as macro time. This concept of time-conscious as an entity continuing and developing to the future, will solve the tension that is found in the Markan narrative about the eschatological Kingdom inaugurated on earth (1:15) and the kingdom that is to be established in the parousia (8:38-9:1; 13: 24-27). The foretaste of the future apocalyptic *escaton* is shown pre-figured in some of the experiences in the events like transfiguration and Jesus' Passion and apocalyptic predictions.[13]

Hence, the way of Jesus Christ is tested and proved credible by himself; the 'middle time'[14] that falls between the death and the return of Jesus Christ is the time of and in which the Markan community is engaged in the same pattern of his mission preaching and living with an imminent hope of Parousia, for 'there will be some who will not die without witnessing it' (9:1). In the earliest time, especially for agrarian society, the concern of time was present-oriented and imminent future, not in an uncertain future. But, with a slight twist, Mark ascertains to his community the coming of the Kingdom by reinterpreting the Parousia and establishment of the kingdom as one and the same entity that would be fulfilled in Christ.[15] The establishment of the Kingdom will happen imminently but it does not mean that no one will die before that, rather some

---

[13] According to Mack, this apocalyptic vision is the remarkable feature of Markan vision of identity. "... Jesus' appearance in Galilee was a dazzling entrance of God's Son into the world with the power and authority to set things right. The world was wrong, set against the rule of God and in league with powers under the control of Satan. Ultimately, these forces could be no match for the rightful rule of God. Unfortunately, however the evil forces were still firmly enough in control to plot against the Son of God and kill him. That sealed the fate of the temple of the Jews and all it stood for, and inaugurated the time of the end. Judgments were called for and woes unleashed. The citadel of opposition would be destroyed and another brilliant appearance of Jesus as the Son of Man with power and glory would be necessary to bring the hostilities to an end and vindicate with finality the cause of God's kingdom. Those who understood that secret and endure until the end belonged and would belong to the new and perfect order of things." B. L. MACK, p. 355.

[14] cf., W. H. KELBER, *The Kingdom in Mark: A New Place and a New Time*, Fortress Press, Philadelphia, 1974, p. 140.

[15] cf., E. BEST, *Following Jesus: Discipleship in the Gospel of Mark*, (JSNTsup.) Sheffield, England, 1981, p. 45.

will certainly witness it.[16] As Norman Perrin interprets, it is a promise to a limited and specific group of people, those members of the Church who will remain steadfast under the threat of persecution (9:1).[17] Mark does not intend to make an ideological transition on the matter of the delay of Parousia, rather to reassure it. His reinterpretation of Parousia is progressive and clearer in chapter 13:30-32, when he speaks about the certainty of Parousia but uncertainty of its time, igniting his community to continue his mission on this world with vigilance on the establishment of the Kingdom. Markan hope is that the community, in spite of any trial and persecutions, is set ultimately to witness and participate in the establishment of the Kingdom. Mark rejuvenates the eschatological hope as time-bound; meanwhile the community of disciples is one that constantly engages for the cause of the Gospel, being oriented permanently to the coming of Christ.

As a whole, Markan effort is to provide his community an auto suggestive formula that, they ought to be a group gathered by the power of the death of Jesus as life-ransom; they ought to be a group guided in action by the awakened memorial presence of Jesus, a permanent Christ consciousness; they ought to be a group in march in the hope of Parousia. When designate the Markan community as Christo-centric, it does not mean that the community was in absence of a Christo-centric life ever since its origin, rather it would mean a balancing of Christology that was necessary for the community. To conjoin the life of the community with the life of Christ, it was indispensable to bring Christ on to the ground as crucified. As the community was under the shadow of temor and persecution, the Cross-bearing Christ was seemed more encouraging and meaningful to survive the trials of the time.

Inclusivism and Exclusivism in Social Nature

Mark is constructing an awareness of his community that they should be simultaneously inclusive and exclusive. As an exclusive group, they are privileged to have the revelation of the Kingdom, which is expressed through the private instruction of Jesus to his disciples. Their inclusive nature is represented through the openness of Jesus' ministry in public sphere that brings good news to the wider world of gentiles.

By starting from the text, there is a privileged group as depicted as insiders (Mk. 3:31-35; 4:10) whose presence declares their option for Jesus and his values. It is, to whom, said to be given the esoteric meaning of the parables. Markan parables are enigmas, which are directed to the out-siders, but its meaning is exclusively revealed to the insiders. This view point of Mark runs throughout his narrative and could be detected from the usage of *kat' idian* by which Mark stresses the nature of private disclosure (7:33; 9:18; 10:10, 23; 8:30; 9:2; 13:3).

---

[16] B. J. MALINA – R. L. ROHRBAUGH, *Social-Science Commentary on the Synoptic Gospels* (2nd ed.), Fortress Press, Minneapolis, 2003, pp. 182-183.

[17] cf., N. PERRIN, "The Composition of Mark ix 1", *NovT* 11 (1969), p. 69.

The exclusive presence and interaction of Jesus with his inner circle of disciples in the last supper, paschal arrangements of his disciples, are all colored with this desired aspect of closeness of the community to Jesus. Importantly than all these instances, Mark reflects the clandestine nature of the community through the private disclosure of the messianic secrecy to his disciples. According to Wrede, the messianic secret is not the silencing of his healing and performance of exorcism rather it involves mainly the disclosing of his imminent death and resurrection.[18] These textual lessons direct us to think of the community as a social group distinguished by its unique knowledge of the identity and mission of Jesus. As Kee opines, "the secret is not apologetic or a literary device invented by Mark and employed by him somewhat clumsily to explain why a non-messianic Jesus came to be acclaimed as Messiah after his death, but is a central, pervasive element in the community's understanding of itself and of Jesus as those to whom it has been revealed that the Kingdom of God is given – not to those who seize power – but to those who in faithful, suffering obedience, receive it as gift."[19]

For Mark the horizon of the community is not limited to a single material space or to a specific sects by faith or birth, rather it is extensive and open to those who admit positively the viewpoint of the Kingdom. By placing the crowd in contraposition to the in-group, its boundaries are made fictive even to an extent, to include anyone who 'wishes' to follow Jesus from the crowd. The "whoever" expression implies a tone of invitation directed to the crowd as he does not leave them unchallenged of the discipleship. Therefore, the disciples, the crowd and 'whoever' of the Markan narrative serve to open the story of Jesus outward to a larger group. In similar way, the call of Levi would mean to the community broader in its vision and wider in its 'membership' to include anyone of the society irrespective of their sinful, despised or any moral, gender or social status.

From the above notions, we understand that the community should have the cognitive awareness that it is simultaneously open to Jesus Christ and to the fellow believers. All the members of the community must be made closer to feel one in Jesus Christ. For such a fraternal end, the community members will have to undergo a process of depersonalization converting their personal self to a communal self, to turn to be Jesus's followers and to have a 'we' feeling in Jesus Christ among them. The consciousness of one being in the group because of the conception that they are adhered to Jesus Christ is fundamental which in turn brings cohesiveness, solidarity, uniformity, broadmindedness, mutual acceptance and sharing in the group that initiates interpersonal relations. This process of 'depersonalization' is plausible only if the community pays heed to the evangelical call to a radical way of life, as we would see below.

[18] cf., H. C. KEE, p. 96. Kee has expressed the idea of Wrede to argue for his idea.

[19] *Ibid.*

The Ethos of the Community: Evaluative Aspect

The *normativeness* and *prototypicality* of a group or any motivated community are essential in qualifying the behavior of the group members for which it is necessary to create and maintain social norms, values, attitudes and beliefs as characteristics of the group. They are even abstracted as distinguishing features of their social categorization in the wider world they live. The Markan story highlights certain evaluative norms, attitudes and their prototypical images as the defining and distinguishing features for the Markan community, among them, radical values and countercultural motives are outstanding.

Radicalism in Life and Mission

We observed that the out-group in Mark is characterized as a dominant culture having a stereotyped pattern of actions, beliefs and reactions in contrast to the countercultural movement of the Markan community. In the historical context, these constituent groups had their own identity, but in the story, they are shown as a unified front as if the Jewishness is the sole opposition to the Markan concerns. The out-group focuses on permanency and stability of their beliefs and traditions, being adamant to any type of social and cultural changes. The questioning of Pharisees, Scribes and Sadducees of Mark on the breach of tradition and purity observances is a single example that shows their stereotype mentality and stubbornness to any change. In this situation, they are arrogant to any type of countermovement and they would come out with strategies of punishment, casting out counterparts as traitors and blasphemous. Those unchanging institutions of the religion in Judaism were sponsored by the primary social factors like family and state.[20] "Sadducees rooted in aristocratic families, Pharisees rooted in Abrahamic pedigree and herodians rooted in a monarchic family clearly aim at well-guarded permanence."[21] Correspondingly, "the Sadducees insist on Torah and only applicable Torah. The Pharisees allow for a growing tradition that must necessarily fit some presumed practice of the ancients. The herodians focus on a single set of properly rooted heirs. In all cases…[they have] established doctrine, ceremonies that ask participants to revere an unchanging set of beliefs…"[22] They become representatives of honour, power, authority and unjust social structures. As Malina continues to observe that even with the destruction of Jerusalem in 70A.D, Israelite counter-movements to the Jesus movement saw no real need for change – just adaptation to a new situation.[23]

---

[20] cf., D. M. BOSSMAN, "Authority and Tradition in first Century Judaism and Tradition", *BTB* 17 (1997, 1), pp. 3-9.

[21] B. J. MALINA, *The New Testament World: Insights from Cultural Anthropology* (3rd ed.), Westminster John Knox Press, Louisville – Kentucky, 2001, p. 213.

[22] *Ibid.*

[23] cf., *Ibid.*, p. 214.

Not only the antagonist group, but the fallible disciples are far from the view point of Christ and thus they seem to be blind to Jesus as well as to their position in the community; as Tyson discusses, it is due to their fundamental misunderstanding of Jesus' messiahship.[24] They crave instinctively for power and position, they are unsympathetic to the children, and they are narrow-minded to exclude the believers who act in the name of Jesus.

In contrast to these fundamental out-group establishments and fallible disciples of the story, the Markan group is socially designed to respond in a different and indefinite manner in its given social situation. It is called to be radical in the social and cultural aspects. Here, we treat the basic valorative factors of the social identity of the Markan community. By the values and radical norms suggested by Mark, we do not mean them as clearly formulated code of laws but a set of personal values to be interiorized by the community. These attitudes and norms will cue them in what disposition is appropriate to be in the community.

Value of Detachment

The value of detachment is stipulated as the primmest radical response of the Markan community in their social situation. The demands of leaving behind the kinship ties, ownership status and material possession, confirming oneself practically to the virtue of self-denial and Cross-bearing are important norms that distinguish the community. How does it become a distinguishing norm against those movements of itinerant stoic philosophers and other sects of the time? The radical missionary instruction of Jesus is set before the community to make aware that the abstinence from the material and cultural ties is aimed solely at the mission of the community. The ordinary human ties and obligations are to set aside, not to make a retreat from the world to be ascetic but for the worldwide mission. The Markan demand is unique in style and form, being lenient than that of its Q version and rigorous than that of the cynic stoic charismatic preachers. The 'foregoing everything' in view of the full-time mission is meant to have a deep trust in the providence of God; nor does it mean any animosity to family relations or material possessions. God is the owner and they belong to Him; the *modus operandi* of their mission resembles that of Jesus, going around the villages, preaching, healing and casting out demons.

The detachment includes not only one's possessions but also one's self. Malina interprets the self-denial as kin-denial since the Markan pattern of the discourse (8:34) is as such; *self-denial - Cross bearing - following*, which is similar to the pattern of Q where it is; *family denial – Cross bearing – following*.[25] In Mark, 'family denial' of Q is replaced with the 'self-denial' because Mark has a communitarian interest to relate this radical value with the family metaphor. The

---

[24] cf., J. B. TYSON, "The Blindness of the Disciples in Mark", *JBL* 80 (1961, 3), pp. 261-268.

[25] cf., B. J. MALINA, ""Let Him Deny Himself" (Mark 8:34): A Social-Psychological Model of Self-Denial", *BTB* 24(1994, 3), pp. 106-119.

kin denial is a collectivistic self-denial that incurs the negation of the family and all that this primary in-group provides to its member. For the Mediterranean society, the detachment of a male from the family is suicidal and of a female by marriage is integration to another family. In the similar way, this collectivistic denial is metaphorically meant by Mark to give preference to one's integration to a *new family* through a detachment from the patriarchal dominion and ties. The self-denial is, not something is denied to self (like asceticism), but for Mark, it is the denial of very him/herself, because the direct object of the verb *aparnēsasthō* (8:34) is himself *heauton* which is opposite to any self-affirmation, putting value on oneself or one's life position before man or God. Therefore, now it is clear to his community that self-denial destined to, not a self-affirmation but an affirmation of God's head by integration into His *new family*. From the sociological point of view, this formation of the newly elected people aims at a social transformation in a culture that considers "honour as their identity, power as their privilege, richness as their blessing and the security as their salvation."[26] The inversion of social values into values of God's dominion should become visible now through the revolutionary life of the Markan community.

Mark shows the community some examples to practice these radical values. The self-denial includes the community's groundbreaking attitudes to the children and the weak ones. In a culture where a child is insignificant, weak and non-ideal; in a culture where lacks emotional sympathy for them, Markan community must be different to have a rupture with that cultural value which is detrimental to the human dignity. They are ought to be ready to accept, welcome and recognize such unimportant ones, like Jesus receives them (10:13-16); they are ought to give attention to the children the insignificant and the least, in the name of Jesus, the Son of God who becomes the least, the last and insignificant on the Cross. To restrict the community by exclusive hard and fast lines and to ignore the little ones (anonymous and simple believers) will be a great offence deserving *geenna*. Therefore, the greatness of a disciple in the community lies in accepting also, who are physically weak, spiritually ingenious and psychologically simple. The ruling over the other under the pretext of authority is totally ruled out by the norms of service. This is vital to their identity image.

The self-denial will be doubly harder when it becomes Cross-bearing, in the sense that they are to be ready to be ashamed of and face the consequences of being allegiant to the crucified Christ and his Gospel in public. Due to this radical conduct of the community that its very nature is self-denial, the stable cultural system will reward them 'Cross' of persecutions and rejections. Cross is a metaphor of uneasiness, challenge and risk even to death over the radicalism of discipleship modeled after Christ.

---

[26] cf., D. RHOADS – J. DEWEY – D. MICHIE, *Mark as Story: An introduction to the Narrative of a Gospel* (2nd ed.), Fortress Press, Minneapolis, 1999, pp. 122-129.

Notwithstanding its pain, moreover the community must strive to maintain the sanctity and integrity of the communion. They must be adventurous even to fight against anything of scandalous to the community by renunciation. Contrary to the stagnant attitude, any radical change must be welcomed in view of configuring with the viewpoint of the Kingdom. Markan metaphor of "amputation" of the bodily organ underscores the intensity of radicalism in the communitarian life. All those scandalous elements are considered threat to the unity and cohesiveness of disciples. The choice of the members in the community either for the eternal life or for losing one's life is not a personal affair rather a demand for the integrity of the community of believers.

The one conforming to these values and attitudes is actually deigned for a social transformation through personal conversion to the cause of the Kingdom. The norms, beliefs and attitudes of the communitarian life that confers social identification to the Markan community profoundly demand personal as well as a social conversion. This call for transformation is stipulated in the inaugural project of the Kingdom – repent and believe in the Good News. The minor characters are modelled as symbols of this desired social transformation. Encountering Christ personally and be transformed to the *new family* is viewed as part of the social process as such. Mark follows a stereotypic pattern in showing this process in secondary characters. When they meet Jesus, they are generally categorized as needy, physically challenged, socially alienated, possessed, ritually unclean and outcaste, parentally responsible and burdened. Some among them are socially respectful, authoritative, wealthy and influential. At the point of their encounter with Jesus, they are of faith and insight, fearless, reverential, truthful, humble, bold, persevering, repentant, courageous, enthusiastic, service minded and perceptive. After they meet Jesus, they become people who are wholly sane, converted, receptors of Jesus' compassion, calm, peaceful and servants of the word. Their conversion is the adequate response to the in-break of the Kingdom initiated in Jesus' mission and their beginning of the participation in the same mission of Jesus to be in perpetuated until the eschatological end.

We have seen above the important valorative factors that constitute the social identity of the Markan community. Those values and attitudes of the community are radical in nature and exigent in time. By these norms, we cannot make them equal in social status with their prominent contemporary sects like Pharisees, Scribes, Sadducees and Essenes.[27] Though the Markan image of the community shows some sectarian features, there are enough impulses to be distinct to the sects of the times, as a marginal grouping within the Judaism of the second half of the first century.[28] The point of view of the community should consistent with

---

[27] cf., H. KEE, pp. 97-100.

[28] John Riches enumerates basic features of sects from the work of Bryan Wilson. According to them, sects are exclusive with monopoly of religious truth and tendency to be lay. They reject the division of labours and remain voluntarists, that is, membership requires some merits. They

the point of view and way of life that Jesus had exposed. Mark keeps pace with the spirit of Jesus to stipulate these norms and attitude to his community, which enable it to stand itself distinct against all other sects and antagonist groups. The norm of cross-bearing and self-denial is in conformity with the life of Christ, the spirit of humility in service is in agreement with the total, and unique humble self-sacrifice of Christ; the ambulant missionary style is in agreement with the itinerant Jesus in villages of Palestine with the message of God's dominion and power. Total renunciation of even kinship is in view of forming an eschatological family of disciples wherein they are to live in solidarity and fraternity. Mark wants his community to get identified with those norms in a cohesive manner and all the members of the community while behaving according to these norms and basic attitudes would engage in the formation of their social selves in the world.

The Pathos of the Community: Emotive Aspect

The affective dimension of the group identity presupposes an intra-group emotional bias. It means members of the same group will have a strong emotional affinity and intimate favoritism towards their group. There will be an emotional contagion that creates a solid bonding among the members. Markan story provides with certain metaphors and emotive concepts to elicit a strong bond and mutual affiliation in the Markan community, among which a new fictive house image and its associated feelings are very telling.

A New House of Kinship

We have seen the principles of behaviours and attitudes of the Markan community, which made us to look at it 'from within'. Now we are going to see how the Markan community should be experienced 'from outwith'. In other words, what should be the relational concept of the Markan group in its social world of the first century Mediterranean world? Mark is using the primordial, powerful social reality of his own time - family and kinship relation - to reconstruct the social image of his community.

Unlike Luke and Mathew, Mark does not give any profile of Jesus' family, neither infancy narratives nor accounts of his adolescence at home. Besides, we know that Markan Jesus is presented apparently as an advocate for the renunciation of the kinship ties for the sake of discipleship (1:20, 29, 36; 10:17, 21, 23-26, 28, 29; 12:25; 13:12). His family is depicted in hostile, paralleling them with the scribes who defame him, though they are relatively mentioned by pass in a couple of scenes. His response to his family members who set out to get him back

---

are protest group against dominant ethos and maintain some standards. Markan group does not fit strictly into all these features of a sect for example; it is inclusive as well as exclusive. Markan group intends to be a 'supra sect' transcending even the normal criterion that constitute a sect. cf., B. WILSON, *Religion in Sociological Perspective*, Oxford University Press, Oxford, 1982 in K. RICHES, *Conflicting Mythologies*, T & T Clark, Edinburgh, 2000, p. 91.

mistaking that he has gone off mentally, is not a rebuke but a declaration, that his *new family* of disciples is inaugurated. His natural family presumes to be in Nazareth, which is a place he leaves for his baptism. When he returns later to his hometown, he is not welcomed. There are more instances as such where, instead of Nazareth, Capernaum is substituted to show his place of house (1:21; 2:1; 9:33). In Capernaum, the disciples replace his family.

But above these dissenting descriptions, our attention needs to be diverted from the antagonistic features of Jesus' family and demands of kinship denials, to Markan Jesus who is in search of a 'family', asking 'who is my mother and brothers?' (3:33). Pointing out the group of his disciples, he identifies his *new family*. Jesus' family is the family that does the will of God. Therefore, the disciples replace his blood-kins; his native place is replaced by Capernaum. This replacement is put in contrast to his natural family with a literary motif, to depict them as antagonists in order to publicize the institution of *the new family*. Why Mark use family metaphor to identify his community and what is the meaning of this new identity?

There is a redundancy of the catchphrases of 'mother' and 'brothers' in Markan pericopes, which affirms the evidence of Markan mind favored for the family metaphor. It shows that he is not denegating the validity and essentiality of the natural family ties.[29] His strong defense for the integrity of marriage is all outstanding among the synoptic concept on the same (10:2-12). Furthermore, it is not polemic against Jesus' natural family or his family leadership in Jerusalem Church (Acts 15; Gal 2:9) as Tyson, Trocme and Crossan hold.[30] From the anthropological view, culturally inspired family of Jesus could be observed as who go out to protect their honour, deformed by their 'mad-gone' member, Jesus. In a counter way, Jesus neither values up the honour nor does he shame his family, rather claims for a higher legitimate norm for his true family. It underscores the priority of the acquired honour of a kinship by doing the will of God, over the ascribed honour achieved by the birth. It is not a discredit to his natural family members but an invitation extended to them too, to become part of the new family circle of disciples.

It is more convincing that, the natural family ties, as Barton suggests, takes the second place to the priority of doing the will of God, which is very much represented by the *new family* (3:35). This contrasting of the natural family ties with the *new family* of the followers of Jesus is a 'relativization' than any literal rejection of family, as Kee understands.[31] By this a new self-understanding of his community is formed and by this way of identification for which the family

---

[29] See in Mark where home and natural family has importance: 7:10-13; 10.2-12; 5:21ff.; 7:24ff.; 9:14ff.; 5:36; 7:28; 9 :24;5:40; 2:11; 5:19; 8:26; 1:16,19; 3:17; 5:17; 15:21,40.

[30] cf., K. RICHES, p. 77; J. B. TYSON, pp. 261-268.

[31] Kee loses sight of its metaphorical sense while he says that Mark denies, "all generic, familial, and sex distinctions are eradicated in this new concept of the true family "which seems incongruent

metaphor was sounded effective and strong in the Mediterranean ambience where family is an emotive and primary factor of the social structure. As Riches views, "this fictive tie replaces natural ties as definitive of group membership through which "one of the key makers of Jewish identity is undermined."[32] This explanation may rule out the possibility of committing an error in understanding the Markan view of the new family as literal and simple. The community of Jesus' followers is a fictive family. "Jesus brought into being a new community based not on ties of blood and heredity, but a voluntary association, opens in a quite novel way to anyone who repents, believes in the Gospel and does the will of God."[33]

In the historical context, Markan community as an eschatological fictive family has an alternative role to be played by its very being in a world of warfare for a social-political and religious freedom as well as against the dominance of a patriarchal system. Primarily, the call for any detachment to kinship as a prerequisite preferring to the new form of a family, had probably elicited in the real audience of Mark a sense of revolutionary situation of their time, a time of nationalistic movements in pursuit of freedom; a time of wars and upsurges in pursuit of freedom from the political dominion.[34] Mark reconstructs an image of Jesus' world as radical and rebel in an alternative new way, where the hope is to have a dominion of God than of the worldly powers and shelter under possessions. The call to discipleship is preparatory for a new battalion of this new mode of war for a new world. The war is fared against the demonic power than human

---

to the of 5th commandment of 7:10-13 and 10:19 and teaching of divorce 10:1-12. cf., H.C. KEE, pp. 109.

[32] cf., J. RICHES, p. 77.

[33] S. C. BARTON, *Disciples and Family ties in Mark and Mathew*, Cambridge University Press, Cambridge, 1994, p. 85.

[34] It was a general history of Jews that there had been a constant resistance against the religious syncretism and political domination. There were attempts at the same time for the national unification and to have *status quo* resisting the unification efforts. This led to the formation of various sects and fights, which was instigated by internal and external conflicts. To brief out the sects and conflict; According to Josephus (*Ant.* 18:1.2), Pharisees Sadducees and Essenes were three main sects of Palestine in Jesus' time. Whereas the Pharisees and the Sadducees together constituted official Judaism, in which their rivalry was the dominant factor, the Essenes were located on the fringes from the very first. To speak from the angle of the Essenes, 'like the Pharisees, they had begun as a voluntarily segregated group separated from the masses, whom they considered to be impure and impious. They were separated from the Sadducees who in their eyes represented an illegitimate priesthood. They were separated from the Pharisees, despite certain affinities of spirit, practices and doctrine, because in general they exceeded the Pharisees in the strictness and the completeness of their observances of law. They were separated from the zealots despite craving belated convergences, because Essenism by nature was not at all a manifestation of militant nationalism.' cf., A. R. CARMONA, *La Religión Judía: Historia y Teología*, BAC 611, Madrid, 2001, pp. 145-151; M. SIMON (tran. J. H. Farley), *Jewish Sects at the Time of Jesus*, Fortress Press, Philadelphia, 1967, pp. 47-84 ; L. M. WHITE, (trans. J. P. Escobar), *De Jesús al Cristianismo*, Verbo Divino, Navarra, 2007, pp. 106-110 ; M. D. COOGAN, *The Oxford History of the Biblical World*, Oxford University Press, Oxford, 1998, pp. 455-459, 486-489.

powers, for the former influences the latter. The means of violence is substituted by the culture of service even unto the persecution. This way of being is the way of discovering the authentic human identity amidst the corrupted cultural institutions and values. Its norms restore this authentic identity in two ways; by being with Jesus as disciple and by exercising the mission that pertains to the call. As Barton's study reveals; "there is no sign, however, of antipathy toward familial and occupational ties *per se*. The motivation for leaving is presented, not in negative terms, but in terms of the prophetic call to a mission to the people of all kinds (2.15-17)...The leaving of familial and occupational ties for the sake of Jesus and the Gospel (8:35b) dramatizes powerfully the movement's sense of new priorities, while intimating, at the same time, what those new priorities might cost in personal and social terms."[35]

Secondly, Mark is silent of leaving wife when the list of forgoing is given even twice (10:28-31). In addition to that, Mark is in favour of securing the integrity and dignity of marriage by prohibiting divorce categorically (10:1-12). Here, the subject of giving up is the family of ones origin. In the patriarchal system, father is the owner of the family, family members are his wealth and possessions, and even female members and wives were considered equivalent to slaves.[36] Mark expects from his community to bring in a rupture in that cultural system of household domination substituting with a fictive kinship or *new family* where God is the Father and owner; the disciples, the new Israel are the possession of God. Jesus is their 'big-brother' who has the delegated ownership of this family. Therefore, this new family is an eschatological family that is desired to bring about a radical social transformation.[37]

Emotions are assumed to play a significant role in the intra-group attitudes and relations. One major function of emotional contagion is affiliation or bonding: the joint experience and expression of emotions is assumed to strengthen the social bonds between individuals. The Markan community with 'we feeling' of a family of God will have its members with a deep sense of belonging to their group as sons and daughters of God. The dominations and ruling over on to each other has no room because the reign of God is upon this new household. This sense of belonging and emotive adhesion should fuel for a fraternal communion among the members as brothers and sisters. This group cohesion should presuppose an intra-group emotional bias, that members have a strong emotional affinity and intimate favouritism for the group, or to say in clear terms, they have love and affection for their group. It is to presume that Mark inculcate this familial feeling

---

[35] S. C. BARTON, pp. 66-67.

[36] In the list of family members of Jesus both of natural and fictive, 'father' is omitted. Mark has the concept of God as the father of Jesus (1:1 the Son of God) and Jesus also calls God as the father of disciples (11:25). God becomes the father of Jesus' new family. cf., J. M. ROBINSON, p. 81.

[37] Robinson calls these Markan phenomena as creation of a new history of society and culture through constitution of a new family and house of table fellowship. *Ibid.*, pp. 80-85.

to have an effect of emotional contagion when there arise the situations of group crisis or of persecutions so that group members may have the same emotional reactions towards those moments of crisis in order to console each other and maintain solidarity.

A Possible Situation of the Markan Community

Now we turn up to answer the next question raised at the very beginning of this study: What should have prompted Mark to suggest these images of identity to his group? It is not such an easy task to articulate the situation and circumstances of the Markan community with crystal clarity, but we intend to extrapolate the situation from the above result of the study. This becomes a difficult task as said, because unlike Pauline letters, it lacks direct mentioning of any crisis or predicaments of the community. Therefore, the picture that we draw upon the situation of the Markan community will be a patch up image because of its speculative nature.

From the principles of the Social Identity and Social Memory theory, we understood that the text is one of the responses to the emerging crisis and changing realities of the group. The past bedrock events used in the text will assume the pedagogical character in suggesting to the community, distinctive norms that form and transform their identities. We presume that Mark is a fictive leader who stands as an in-group prototype to persuade the members as a whole, to positively differentiate between in-group and out-group, and to make their group 'special'. Mark by suggesting a 'possible selves', is doing the same, facing the challenges of his community with a 'new genre of Gospel' and strategies. Hence, the text is an encoded memory of the community and any study of it in understanding the reinterpreted aspects of tradition could be considered as the very act of knowing somehow what the community was.

What are the challenges and predicaments of the community that paved the way for Mark to address his Gospel? We have seen that Mark is curious to articulate the social identity of his community by stressing on community's position in their social world as Christo-centric, articulating their way of behaviours and dispositions in the values and norms which are radical and exigent, and their position in the social world as concurrently exclusive and inclusive, moreover underscoring its mode of being in the pluralistic sectarian culture as an eschatological family than any power vying voluntary union. From the above analysis, we may infer that the community indeed had internal crisis mainly in two areas; 1. the misunderstanding of the identity of Christ or, to say, the Christological crisis, 2. the misunderstanding of their own position in the community. These two crises that might have been faced by the community are interconnected. The Christological challenge as well as the predicaments that had to be faced regarding the discipleship could be read within a single frame; the identity of being a disciple in the community is to live according to the Christological essence. There had been certainly external challenges like persecutions, Jewish war and destruction of the temple, which acted as catalysis for the inner crisis of the community, yet the Markan orientation, is pro-in-group and apologetic than anti-out-group and polemic.

Christological Crisis

It is evident from the Markan emphasis given to the authority of Jesus and the centrality of Cross in the life of disciples, that something had gone wrong with regard to their Christ-awareness. It is an indisputable argument that Mark brings the Christology on to the ground. Before we come to our own position on this crisis, first we may reproduce some scholars' opinion in this regard. As some opines,[38] there should have been a situation when Mark wanted to concretize the Christology - a divine man Christology - that was being propounded by the Pauline rivals. Weeden supports this view explicitly by linking to those Pauline antagonists at Corinth. According to this view, Mark was in a situation to butt the incipient Docetism and the prevalent tendencies of false claims of Messiah. Simon Magus was a type of confusing figure of that time with his conjuring acts, having references in the Book of Acts (8:9) and in the early Christian writings.[39] In this background, Markan text could be seen as polemical.[40]

Another probable scholarly suggestion is that there was an opposition of law observant Jewish Christians like whom Paul confronted in Antioch, Galatia, Jerusalem and Rome (Rom 15:31; 14:1 – 15:13 ; Acts 15). Some scholars are precise to tell that this opposition was from the law observant Jerusalem Christian community.[41] Kelber is one among these scholars. To him, Mark affirms the Galilean position over Jerusalem mother Church that had an upper hand in traditions and remained in root traditions of Jewish life (Sabbath, purity, fasting and traditions). Among them developed the faith in eschatological Parousia in a vulnerable manner even to an extent of ignoring the importance of Cross in the life of Jesus. They became exclusivists leaving no room for gentiles in their ministry. For Kelber, the fallible disciples in the story are the representatives of what appeared to be the Jerusalem Church.

[38] Marcus refers this view to Schweitzer and H. Martin. cf., J. MARCUS, p. 75.

[39] Justin Martyr, *I Apology* 26. Justin Martyr's account drags us to the location of Rome where Simon was erected with an inscription, "Simoni Deo Sancto,"

[40] This corrective Christology of *divine man* is refuted by Kingsbury. cf., J: MARCUS, p. 77. His arguments based on the following points: 1. divine man is not an affixed term in the Hellenistic ambience of first century as to use it referring to Jesus' miracles or the Son of Man title, 2. Since divine man epithet is more related with the miracle works, Mark is not negative about his miracles but evaluated positively by Markan onlookers; Jesus' opponents evaluate them negatively, 3. disciples are not traitors who negate Christ but fallible followers, 4. In 14:61-62, Jesus' response of the Son of God is not with a sense of suffering figure but of a glorious figure of him.

[41] cf., J. B. TYSON, pp. 261-268.

Another suggestion holds that Mark was responding to the Jewish opposition to the Christ devotion of the early Christian community, before 70 C.E. As L. Hutardo presupposes, the Markan first readers would have been the direct witnesses to the Jesus' trial on the blasphemy and condemnation to death because of the eschatological claim. The blasphemy charge therefore portrays the religious and theological-Christian heritage, and the intended readership was likely to have been heavily gentile in make-up; the experiences of being arraigned before synagogue authorities on charges of blasphemy must extend back sometime before the date of Mark.[42] All the NT authors witness to this situation of the readers, on what happened to Jesus. Mk 13 indicates that the author was writing for readers who knew such experiences, either directly or indirectly and who were in danger of facing similar sufferings in their immediate future wherein Jesus' trial was a prototype for them. "It is all the more likely that Jews would have responded with cries of blasphemy to the kind of Christological claims we have in Mk 14:61-62, for these Christological claims were accompanied by a devotional practice in which the exalted Jesus was invoked, hymned and acclaimed in gathered cultic settings within the first couple of decades of the Christian movement..."[43]

For B. Mack, Mark wrote his story of Jesus as obedient martyr, had little to do with the historical Jesus rather with the recent history of the Jesus-movement to which he belonged. "A failure to reform the Diaspora synagogues, from which this group or groups had finally found it necessary to withdraw, resulted in confusion about the group's purposes, hostility against Judaism, and withdrawal into a sectarian mentality and enclave. Mark associated the death of Jesus with the group's rejection by the synagogue and then linked both to the destruction of the temple. The end of the temple was, according to Mark, a righteous judgment, a vindication of the rightness of the cause and kingdom for which the group stood. Before Mark made that connection, neither the Jesus movements nor the congregations of the Christ had imagined Second Temple institutions as their nemesis. When Mark did make that connection, the Christian myth of succession or substitution was born. Jesus had been the rightful heir to a Kingdom in conflict with Second Temple Judaism. Its leaders had sought to destroy him, but had succeeded only in destroying themselves. Jesus, the once and future king, now was to reign in the place of the vanquished high priests. It was a myth written during a brief period of threat to a particular Jesus-movement in danger of losing its bearings, its confidence, and it's cool."[44]

Ecclesial Crisis

The demands for a radical following of Jesus and his teachings are to be considered to learn the inner crisis of the community. Our analysis on discipleship

[42] cf., L. HURTADO, "Pre-70 CE Jewish Opposition to Christ-devotion", *JTS* 50 (1999, 1), p. 48.

[43] *Ibid.*, p. 49.

[44] B. L. MACK., p. 356.

leaves no doubt in us that Markan community had a grave failure in understanding and living their role as followers of Jesus Christ.

In accordance with 1 Cor 12:3, all Christians were capable to have various charismatic gifts and power of exorcism. At that stage of Jesus-movement, leaders would have been jealous of the ordinary members and had perhaps fallen to exclude them. The crisis was not only of the generational transition of the community that was struggling to get attuned with the original spirit of the Jesus-movement but also involved a tension within the group which was heading to get organized and be hierarchical. In 9:14-29 evince out this inner tension, which the attention of the community is being deviated to and their interest (of leaders?) concentrates on power, status, and institution of order as such, so that they were incapacitated to do their original mission. An instance in the story of the disciples who couldn't exorcise the evil spirit reflects this historical reality of the Christian, oriented towards getting disconnected from the original charisma of the mission. The division between the important and the unimportant, 'first and the least' must have crept into the community life. The newly converts as strangers who remain loyal to the original charisma of the movement were excluded because of jealousy and inferiority feelings of the community leaders.[45] The question of the rich man reflects the tone of confusion existing at the time of Mark regarding salvation and Mark is trying to give an answer to his community regarding the overwhelming question. By this reading of the text from within, we can probably contend that Markan effort here is to elicit the Jesus-memory of the community and get the community be reconnected to the original bedrock charisma at the face of its internal crisis and predicaments.

According to Iersel, the persecution of Nero in 70 CE caused crisis in the community; they had remorse and shame in the world because Christians betrayed their fellow Christians in front of their authorities. Those among them who survived persecution felt guilty and agony of frustrations. "They needed figures with whom they could identify themselves and who could help them come to terms with their failure."[46] It was in this context Mark wrote his Gospel, which deals with betrayal by relatives, persecutions, theme of failure, and examples of following as well as the followers who failed.

For Mack, Mark was aware of a numerous problems of pluralities in bearing a view on Jesus but in spite of all those, much mind-boggling problem was the internal confusions, regarding the apocalyptic time, messianic understanding and excitements, betrayals, denials and apostasies - in a single term, crisis of

---

[45] According to J. Weirs, the strange anonymous exorcist in Mk 9:38 is supposed as Paul. Mark refers to Paul anonymously to support his ideological view of defending against "the official Jewish Christian leadership of Church." cf., Foot note No. 67 in E. BEST, *Following Jesus: Discipleship in the Gospel of Mark*, p. 96.

[46] B. M. F. VAN IERSEL, *Mark*, p. 52.

discipleship. In this situation, Mark was concerned of proposing a conceptual foundation for the continuing existence of his community.

External threats of Persecution and War

It is doubtless among the scholars that persecution and war was an influencing factor for the origin of the Gospel of Mark, because the text itself is preoccupied with the description of persecution and references to the destruction of Jerusalem (4:16-17; 8:34-38; 9:42-48; 10:17-31, 38-39; 13:9-13). In addition to this, the secrecy motif, the outsider and insider concept, and 'until now' expression of Mark in 13:19 regarding the persecution, hint that it was an actual situation. But there are differing opinions on it. Some argue for the Roman persecution of the Christians in Rome while others speak of the general persecution which haunted Christians for all ages.

Agreeing to the destruction of the temple and Jewish war as motivational factors of Mark, Kelber explains that the war was an apocalyptic Armageddon misguided by the oracles and apocalyptic hopes of false prophets. Christians, who shared messianic hopes and apocalyptic interests with their fellow Jews, were collaborative in that Armageddon. The crisis broke out when the Kingdom that was hoped for, did not come at its appointed time and in promised place; hence, it was necessitated to reinterpret this false notion of time and wrong choice for place of the Kingdom. Mark's task is to show the new place and a new time of the Kingdom. Galilee is the real and new place, a centre of life designated by Christ. The community is in the midst of time, 'not out of or without time'. It is a time of crisis in which persecution is 'not an end but an opening door to the world'; dislocation is not "the sign of Christian bankrupt but a chance to reach the new place of life."[47]

Kee speaks about the historical context of the Markan community during the first Jewish revolt (66-70 C.E.). There were various modes of responses from the Jewish sects to the situation; a possibility of collaborating with the roman political dominion and its allies and consequently be conformed to the Greco-roman way of life like the herodians did; yet another was an aversive mode of collaboration with the foreign rule by way of passive acquiescence, as the Pharisees did. However, the Markan community was different from these "leavens of herodians and Pharisees" (8:15); because it was in no way passive or indifferent to the oppressive situation. Markan community found itself defined to be a radically alienated social group which could be subjected to suspicion and hostility from fellow Jews and gentiles. "It was in such an era and in this sort of climate that the Gospel of Mark is most likely to have been written, to offer understanding and encouragement to this segment of primitive Christianity."[48]

---

[47] W. H. KELBER, *The Kingdom in Mark*, pp. 140-144.

[48] H. C. KEE, p. 100.

Ernest Best proposes that the purpose of Mark is internal and pastoral to his community. The Roman Church that has been suffering from the pain of persecution was guarded by the *euangelion* of encouragement in securing its faith. At the face of persecution, it might be tempted to fall easily into false understanding regarding faith and even to forego the community. Hence, persecution as such is not the direct cause of the Gospel since it was endemic to early Christianity in general. Ernest Best does not attribute any historical event as a direct cause of the Gospel as above said factors like death of eyewitnesses, fall of Jerusalem and persecutions, or threat to the divine man Christology; they are only some contributory factors.[49]

Markan Strategy in Calming the Storm

We have seen various situations of the Markan community from diverse scholarly perspectives. Now from the above analysis, we can deduce two main streams of challenges that the historical Markan community would have faced, even though such persecutions and war were a historical reality to them. As we have understood from the text, the Markan ideology is centered on understanding, believing and living the mystery of the crucified Christ by the disciples of Jesus in communion wherein the threat of persecution becomes a real reward to the witnessing community, not a cause of its destruction; war becomes not an end but a beginning of the new age of life to witness Christ. According to the Markan view, the true challenge of his community was not something that of external rather internal to his community, even when we are not able to rule out those external threats as contributive factors to the inner crisis of the community. We can generally categorize the inner challenges into two.

Primarily, as a group, there was a natural crisis of the growing Christian community. It was the temporal distancing from the heritage and patrimony - the historical Jesus-events and its memory, especially the mystery of the Cross - due to the transition of a generation. The Gospel origin becomes the part of the natural process of telling and retelling the collective memory of the group. Being different from the Pauline style of letter writing, Markan introduction of this new biographical Gospel genre to address the inner crisis of his community with a motivation to revive and reinterpret Jesus-memory, seems reasonable in this regard. It is remarkable that scholars, namely Kelber and Radcliff, have considered Markan Gospel as an emergence of a new genre in contrast to the earlier oral traditions for the reason that they were irrelevant and incapable to give sense to the challenges of the time.[50]

---

[49] cf., E. BEST, *Mark: The Gospel as Story*, pp. 21-36.

[50] cf., W. H. KELBER, *The Kingdom in Mark*, pp. 138-139 ; J. G. CROSSLEY, *The Date of Mark's Gospel: Insight from the Law in Earliest Christianity*, (JSNTsup.) T & T Clark, London – NY, 2004, p. 61.

Secondly, due to this distancing from the original memory of Cross-events of Jesus, the mythologizing of the Christ figure and consequent devotion to the glorified risen-Christ began to be emphasized. The community would have, in such a situation, faced an ideological crisis with a triumphalist messianic identity while forgetting the Cross aspect of the risen Christ. The community might have experienced a paradox in proclaiming their faith in the messianic identity of the glorified Christ and at the same time facing persecution and difficulties when witnessing Jesus. Mark had to address properly this paradox. This paradox is not of the community, but proceeds from the very being of Jesus, the Lord who obediently embraced the Cross. Joel Marcus does articulate this view with more exactitude in favour of Kingsbury's view that Mark's Christology is not corrective in the radical sense, nor does it oppose any heretical views. It addresses the tendency of the community within. They might have forgotten the vicarious impact that Jesus' death and resurrection brought about, during the concrete experience of their trials and tribulations.

Above all, we can integrate the double folded challenges *ad intra* of the Markan community into a single crucial one, to be termed as *Jesuological amnesia*.[51] Markan retelling of the story of the crucified Christ is intended to elicit the Jesus-memory in faith.[52]

As we have seen in the previous chapter of models, when a group faces crisis, inter and intra group conflicts, there are various approaches to reduce the tensions and group biases. Mark, however, does not use the method of decategorization, for he does not attempt to dissolve the group boundaries or nullify the identity of his group or the out-groups. Neither he attempts with the cross-categorization since, he does not try to replace the salient category of discipleship with another one in the face of difficulties of following Jesus. Then what he follows is the strategy of the new version of re-categorization. His strategy was a method of favoring a common in-group identity with pro-in-group orientation than anti-out-group orientation.[53] In-group members could perceive out-group members sympathetically but in-group members even more positively. Group reformation brings in-group members closer to the self without changing the distance between the self and the out-group (or non-group) members much. The out-group and the outer factors of challenges, hence become only an instrumentality to retrospect and introspect the community's past with a self-oriented motivation of

[51] cf., J. MARCUS, p. 78. I am indebted to my Professor. Dr. Jacinto Nunez Regodon for enlightening me to use in such a context the expression *Jesuological* as appropriate one, instead of *Christological*, in order to connote all that pertain to the historical Jesus, while he was responding to my paper, *The Social Identity of the Markan Community: A Study from the Discipleship Perspective*, presented in 2007 at the University of Salamanca (Pont.).

[52] *Ibid.*, 79.

[53] Gaertner and his colleagues are interpreters of this new version of the Social Identity theory. cf., J. LIPPONEN – J. LESKINEN, "Condition of Contact, Common In-group identity, and In-group Bias toward Contingent Workers", *JSP* 146 (2006, 6), pp. 671-684.

reformation. With an analogy, it could be said that the out-group is like a white screen on which the film of in-group is projected.

We do not deny that the community as a movement within the Judaism was challenged by their fellow Jews (Kee), persecutions and rejections from the Synagogues (Mack), and by the Jewish war and tribulations of the time (Joel Marcus). In spite of these external crises, Mark's concentration is in the inner fabric of the community regarding the foundational beliefs, convictions and behaviours. His effort of telling Jesus' story is mainly oriented to his community building than becoming polemic apologetics to the outer threats. By rediscovering the Christological roots of the community and affirming the overarching Christological identity to the group, which might also be included of Jews and gentile Christians, he does a process of re-categorization of his group. We cannot totally rule out the possibility of Pharisees and scribes being in-group members. They could have never been totally aliens to the community of Mark but probably associates (Acts 15:5) with divided minds on account of their Jewish legalism and orthodoxy. At the same time, there are accounts of Pharisees and Sadducees who try Paul in the Roman tribunal (Acts 23:6-8). If Markan community is a marginal group within Judaism, can't we view the Jewish antagonism as an intra-group conflict to the Markan community? If so, the Markan group can be assumed as a marginal group within the Judaism that faced intra-grupal tensions. In other words, this is what Joel Marcus says; "instead of speaking vaguely of the Gospel's context as one of "persecution", we may specify the context of intra and intercommunal tension produced by the upheaval of the Jewish War."[54]

Appendix: Location of the Markan Community

For two reasons, this final question regarding the Markan location is answered under appendix. Primarily this answer would be more hypothetical. Secondly, this short work is academically too narrow and limited to answer such serious question of Markan immediate context and geographic location. For that, we need an extensive study.

This attempt is to reconstruct the location of Markan community briefly and hypothetically. From the above analysis of this study and with the support of scholarly constructions, we can vaguely locate the Markan community in Syria/ Palestine approximately, in the shadow of Jewish revolt and Jerusalem destruction than Neronian persecution in Rome, for a few reasons that follow. The arguments of Joel Marcus along with those of Mack and Kee and of Roskam in certain points, are much convincing to us.[55] They point towards the same situation but interpret it from different viewpoint.

[54] J. MARCUS, "The Jewish War and The 'Sitz Im Leben' of Mark", *JBL* 111 (1992, 3), p. 462.

[55] For detailed view of them, see the first chapter of this study, under the title 'A Siro-Palestinian Audience to Mark'.

Most frequently, some elements like persecution and war factors of Mk 13 are considered to locate Mark. In this study, as we read the text as whole and coherent, it is found that the antagonism that is used as antitypes throughout the story is directed against Jewishness than any Roman political ruling. In contrast to that, the roman authority is comparably portrayed innocent to the cause of Christ events. It is a reflection not simply of an inner conflict between Jewish and gentile Christians, which was common to most of the Jesus-movement of that time, but rather represents a strong Jewish opposition against the Christian movement. Almost all the accounts of trial of disciples and wars in the prediction of chapter thirteen are Jewish in nature like, "nation rising against nation (13:8), destruction of Jerusalem temple (13:1-2), 'betrayals in Councils', 'beatings in synagogues', "abomination of desolation", 'appearance of false prophets' (13:6,22). Josephus describes about the appearance of false pretenders and mocking trials of revolutionaries in Jerusalem in connection with the Jewish war.[56] Jesus' purification of the temple which was a "den of brigands" (11:17 = Jer 7:11; Isa 56:7) has reference to the historic occupation of Jewish revolutionaries in the temple under the leadership of Eleazer and his habitation there until the fall of it in 70 C.E.[57] Joel Marcus points to the reason that, those Christian believers were not supporting the Second Jewish revolt of Palestinian Jews under the leadership of Bar Kocha against Romans in 132-135 C.E.[58] Likewise, he suspects, that in the first revolt of Jews, probably Christians had been persecuted, for not having had any agreement with the Jewish messianic nation for which the revolutionaries of Jews fought against Rome.[59] The Christians who were considered as gentiles became target for the persecution of Jews whose revolt was not only anti-roman but also anti-gentiles.

Roskam, with her key understanding of 13:9, is more close to place Markan community at the background of Jewish practice of handing over troublemakers in order to avoid violent Roman intervention. The community seemed to be a threat, not to the Romans but to the Jews and depiction of Jesus death as result of Jewish ill-will than of anti-roman political ambition, is a strong argument of Roskam.[60] Theissen also adhere to the interpretation of 11:15-17 linking to the

---

[56] *JW* 2:433-434, 444, 652; 6: 313; 7:29-31, 4:335-344.

[57] *JW* 4:151-157; 5:5; 4:182-183, 201, 38; 6: 95.

[58] JUSTINE MARTYR, *I Apology 31:6*.

[59] The *Enciclopedia Judaica* speaks about the spirit of nationalism of the Jewish war. Practically Zealots were a militant group of the Pharisees who represented the theoretical side of the ideology of a theocratic nation while Zealots were their pragmatic wing who fought for the realization of this theocratic nation. Their attacks were not only directed to the Romans but also to pagans, indifferent Jews, traitors and those who worked under the Roman Empire. cf., "Sicarii", *Enciclopedia Judaica*, 1971, vol.14, Par.1491-1492.

[60] cf., H. N. ROSKAM, *The Purpose of the Gospel of Mark in Its Historical and Social Context*, (NovTsup.) Brill, Leiden, 2004. cf., Review of Zeba A. Crook in RBL 08/2006, *http://www.bookreviews.org* accessed on 20-11-2006.

Jewish revolt in the background of prophetic citation of Isa 56:7 and Jer 7:11.[61] Above all Markan reference to the davidic messiahship with the both sentiments of acceptance (10:47-48; 11:9-10) and reluctance (12:35-37) reflects some claims over the davidic messiahship by Menachem and Simon bar Giora[62] experienced by the Markan community, so as to show that Jesus' Messiahship is more and different to their fake claims, that he is Son of God and he had already entered as Messiah in Jerusalem years back. Hence, we can contend that, we cannot extract the Markan community out of a Jewish ambience and its direct antagonistic influence.[63]

If persecution is considered predominant as a cause for the Gospel origin as many take it for granted attributing to Neronian age, then the persecution mentioned in Mark 13:9-13 need not necessarily be pointed toward Rome at the event of 71 C.E.[64] of Titus's triumphal procession to Rome or the earlier persecutions under Nero. The Neronian persecution was not a unique phenomenon during which Mark wrote his Gospel. Even before that, there are sources that mention the sporadic persecutions against Christians even from the mob and Jews. "Hated by all" (Mk.13:13) refers to mob violence. For example, we have records of Christian persecutions in Judea (Gal 1:13,22); particularly in Jerusalem (Acts 12:1-5; 21:27-36; 23.12-15, *Ant* 20:200): in Damascus - Syria (2 Cor 11:32-22, Acts 9:1-2,23); in Asia minor (Acts 13:50; 14:19; 19:24-34); in Greece (Acts 16:19-24; 17:5-9, 13; 18:12-13).[65] Those who speak for the Roman audience, like Brian Incigneri, paint the Markan community as pathetic and suffering like a "prisoners" of Persecution which would elicit sympathy in readers, but vice versa, for Mark, as this study observed, persecution is a reward with the new fictive community for the followers and he invites the community to withhold it like a valiant soldiers for the new eschatological warfare like Jesus. Being more Markan than Mark, the modern Markan scholars elicit this pathetic feeling towards the Markan community in readers, by embellishing the allusion of

---

[61] Theissen has the same approach like Marcus, believing Josephus' testimony that the rebellion began when the revolutionaries excluded gentiles from any participation in the cult by refusing to accept their sacrifices and gifts. Therefore, temple became no longer a house of prayer for the gentiles. Markan Jesus universalizes it as a house of all nations. (11:15-17). This house later will be replaced by the cult of Jesus when destroyed stone to stone. cf., G. THEISSEN, *Colorido Local y Contexto Historico en los Evangelios* (tran. M. O. Gaztelumendi), Sigueme, Salamanca, 1997, p. 149. Also see, J. G. CROSSLEY, pp. 71-73.

[62] cf., *JW* 2:17.8.433-434; 2:17.9.444; 2:22.2.652; 4:9.4.514; 7:2.2.29-31.

[63] cf., J. MARCUS, *The Jewish War and The 'Sitz Im Leben' of Mark,* pp. 456-460.

[64] cf., B. J. INCIGNERI, *The Gospel to the Romans: The Setting and Rhetoric of Mark's Gospel,* Brill, Leaden- Boston, 2003, p. 247; K. D. Dyer, *ABR,* Vol. 54, 2006, *http://www.fbs.org.*; D. N. Peterson, RBL, 01/2005 in *www.bookreviews.org.*, accessed on 15-03-2006; M. F. Bird, *RBL,* 11/2005, in *www.bookreviews.org,* accessed on 20-08-2006.

[65] For detailed reference, cf. J. MARCUS, *Mark 1-8,* pp. 32-33.

random elements of the text with the Roman events without considering the text as a whole and without meaning much of the mind of Mark.[66]

Joel Marcus is further inclined to argue for the Roman province of Syria, which is contiguous to Palestine. Syria was close enough with many traditions about Jesus; it was a predominantly Gentile region and an area of Pauline influence. His contention is that Mark might have written his Gospel for his community after its flight from Jerusalem and its re-formation perhaps through the incorporation into an already established, predominantly gentile Church in Syria-Palestine.[67] Perhaps it was to address the eschatological excitement of them and to make them remain intense during the temple's destruction and the end of the war. Therefore, Markan use of Latinism and Aramaism is well fit in to be appropriate.

The topographical and geographical preference of the Gospel indicates the familiarity of the places to the audience. Galilee with its surroundings is favorite to Mark; hence it could be presupposed as favorite as to his community.[68] The recent study of Roskam on the location of Markan community advocates for Galilee, in which one of her arguing points is the prominence of Galilee about which Mark is surer than the other geographical places in the Gospel. Her

---

[66] One of the criticisms of Peterson and Michael Bird against Incigneri is that he circular in his arguments and use exaggerating allusions becoming childish to observe the intelligent work of Mark simple and ridiculing. For example, Bird shows that he finds an allusion of renting of temple veil with the Vespian parading of the veil through Rome. More over the reviewers note that he is critique of all the prevalent methodology of redaction criticism, narrative criticism and reader-response criticism, delimiting him to read the text wholly and coherently. cf., K. Dyer, *ABR* 54/2006, http:// www.fbs.org. (accessed 08-06-2007); D. N. Peterson, *RBL*, 01/2005 in *www.bookreviews.org.*, accessed on 08-11-2005; M. F. Bird, *RBL*, 11/2005, in *www.bookreviews.org.*(accessed 20-02-2006).

[67] Though, there is a tradition of a warning to a Judean Christians by oracle and fled to Pella before the siege of Jerusalem, related by Eusebius and Epiphanius, Marcus favors for the Hellenistic cities according to the account of Josephus that more related to Jewish war. cf., *Eccl.Hist.* 3.5.3; *Pan.* 29.7.7-8 ; 30.2.7; J. MARCUS, *The Jewish War and The 'Sitz Im Leben' of Mark*, p. 461.

[68] Regarding inaccuracies of the geographical accounts, Dean W. Chapman has given an interesting explanation, using the colloidal space concept of the ancient agrarian world. It is unfortunate that it is seen not discussed or uncommented by any representative authors in the academic forum. For the first century agrarian community the geographical sense was more of cosmological; the topographical characteristics of colloidal geography would become 'attenuated' as distance from the subject's home increased, until references become lost in the cosmos and were no longer related in any way to experience geographical realities. Using this model of interpretation, Chapman says that Mark was a native of Palestine represents an agrarian community or peasant community who viewed geography colloidally. No peasant country in Rome or Greece or Damascus would have had this colloidal construct of the world. Mark's preoccupation with the colloidal knowledge of northern Galilee may be due to his influential members of his community but his meticulous detailing of Jerusalem elicit an assumption in Chapman that Mark had been an early Christian member of Jerusalem and later was living with an agrarian peasant community in Galilee. cf., D. W. CHAPMAN, "Locating the Gospel of Mark: A Model of Agrarian Biography", *BTB* 25 (1995, 1), pp. 24-36.

stand, though proximate of location, is indirectly supportive to our position for Palestinian location in contrast to Roman provenance.[69]

These reasons for a Palestinian provenance of the Markan Gospel are only a brief and blue print in form which could be elaborated, if the page limit and the scope of this study permits, yet the last reason but not least, could be that, the prominent advocate of the Markan community for Rome is Martin Hengel who recently amended his position thought not to place it to an alternative particular location but to speak for a universal audience to Mark. He says: "contrary to a widespread view, none of the four Gospels was written only for one particular community; far less do they simply reproduce the views of one individual community. They give primarily the views of their authors. We cannot even say with certainty whether they ever came into being only in one community, for the missionaries of the early church traveled a great deal and could be authoritative teachers at different places. So we should stop talking automatically about 'the community of Mark', 'of Luke', 'of Matthew', 'of John' as the one really responsible for the composition of a Gospel writing and its theology...Even more nonsensical is the term 'Q community', i.e., the community of the Logia source...The authors of these works do not represent the view of a collective community, but of an individual yet authoritative teacher of one or more communities (or a school), and in their quite different forms proclaim the one truth which should be binding on all believers."[70]

We may conclude that the community of Mark situated somewhere in the vicinity of Palestine under the close experience of trials, persecutions of war and the destruction of the temple. The Gospel was originated out of the immediate social situation of Jewish revolt and Jewish antagonism that experienced by the Markan community and paved the way for their internal crisis of faith and loyalty to the Jesus – memory. It is more reasonable that Mark used the proximate and immediate context and experience of the community to address and suggest it a social self-image, than to think that, he used raw materials for his Gospel, from certain remote context and events of Jewish war and destruction of the temple in Palestine for a community in Rome.

---

[69] cf., H. N. ROSKAM, in the review of Zeba A. Crook in RBL 08/2006, *http://www.bookreviews.org.*, accessed on 20-11-2006. Crook opines that Incigneri's argument for Roman provenance is more embellishing of allusions and imaginations while Roskam's argument for Galilean provenance is less problematic, less fanciful and more persuasive.

[70] cf., M. HENGEL, *The Four Gospels and the One Gospel of Jesus Christ: Investigation of the Collection and Origin of the Canonical Gospels*, Trinity Press International, Harrisburg, 2000, p. 106-107. cf., The review in *JBS* 3/2 (April 2003) pp. 63-66, in *http://journalofbiblicalstudies.org/.*

CONCLUSION

The Markan legacy is myth of innocence
that separates those who belong to
the righteous kingdom within from those without.

(Mack, *A Myth of Innocence*, 372)

In the first two chapters of the scholarly survey and the models and methods, we have been engaged in to construct the basic presumptions in order to follow the study to have a sound view of the social identity of the community to which Mark was telling the story of Jesus. The most important presumption is that Markan text is a story told and retold from the past collective memory and tradition which was available to him. His is the interpreted tradition of the story of Jesus. To tell his Jesus-story, he used the literary and rhetoric patterns with an aim to influence his audience for inculcating the identity norms and values, which he rediscovered for his group. For the decoding of the ancient text by the twentieth century modern readers like us, the help of literary criticism and its principles become necessary. The decoding of the characters, their representative values and the ideal reader of the text become important to understand the real authors and his motifs as well as the real readers who were expected to respond positively to the Markan story. The second presumption is attested from the scholarly survey that, Mark was writing a Gospel, not for fictive Christian communities but for a particular community that lived under the shadow of Jewish war and common persecutions around 69-72 C.E, to which he belonged to. He knew the impulses, problems, predicaments and crisis of his community and therefore his writing was a *response of* and a *response to* it.

These two basic presumptions really motivated to answer the basic questions of this study. What is the proposed image of social identity for the Markan community reflected in the text? What paved the way for Mark to project such identity-image? What was the immediate context of the Markan community? In order to explain the social identity in a systematic way, we rely upon the modern verified model of the Social identity theory. The social identity of the Markan group, like any group, is based mainly on a set of norms and values. They confer on them a unified auto-consciousness and self-esteem as members of their group.

In the Markan discourse of discipleship and call narrative episodes, the radical demands and norms of the community are encased within the purview of Cross and resurrection realities and *on the way* metaphor. The vocation narrative and teachings of the discipleship are ultimately directed to the vision and mission of the community. Any call of the discipleship to a rupture of the cultural systems and kinship ties are not destructive but constructive in order to facilitate the vibrancy of the communion of disciples and their coherent mission. The value of honour and authority has been substituted in order to facilitate the active recognition of the God's rule and His authority. The service and humility become an essential identity marker and practical norms for the fraternal relations within the community. All these are possible only when the community has to accept the precedence of their priorities to Jesus Christ and for their adherence to him. The maturation of a group member as disciple depends upon when he is called to the community and dynamically being adhered to the person of Christ, his name, word and way and lives with the fellow Christians in communion, in order to take up in the long run the mission of Jesus Christ, which proceeds from him.

Mark is not simply leaving the community with a block of norms and attitudes for living their life as the way of new being in their world, but he creates values that are shown lived up by a group of prototypical characters in conformity with the norms of discipleship. In short, through the presentation of prototypes and antitypes of discipleship, he addresses his community what they should believe and what they should not; how they should behave and how they should not; and how they should relate to each other and how they should not respectively. The community should believe in Christ as the Son of God as like the characters who expressed staunch faith, for instance, like the leper, Jairus, the hemorrhaged women, Bartimaeus, the centurion, the Syrophoenician woman and the woman at Bethany. In contrast to these prototypes, the community is asked not to have the values of faithlessness represented by the antitypes like Pharisees and scribes who always seek to question and test Jesus' authority over their priority to the legally inspired culture. The disciples and crowd are also fallible to become negative examples to faith. Like Bartimaeus and the Centurion, the community may have the profound insight and understanding of the identity of Christ, where as they may be cautious of and keep aloof from the blindness of disciples and hard-heartedness of Pharisees and Scribes. The community must have courage and loyalty to bear witness like the possessed of Genesaret, Bartimaeus, Woman at Bethany and so on while they must not have fear like the disciples who abandoned Christ. The behaviour of the community must be inspired by the prototypes who are shown humble like Jairus and Syrophoenician woman, while they should not behave like Pharisees and priests group who are constantly envious, jealous and hypocrite. The response of Markan community must be inspired by the self-sacrifice and the Cross-bearing of the poor widow and Simon of Cyrene respectively, while they should not behave like the rich man and the disciples who respond with a temporal and the culturally conditioned outlook of honour, power, wealth and rejection of Cross attitude. They must behave like Joseph of Arimathea who has the mind of service and charity to pay the last rite to Jesus but should not behave like soldiers and priests who enjoy murdering and mocking the 'innocent' with hatred and enmity. The community members should relate like a family members of a house, in love solidarity, and fraternity who have a common adherence to Christ and doing always the will of God.

These minor characters represent the mode of response to the call for the desired social transformation, which has been stipulated in the inaugural project of the Kingdom – repent and believe in the Good News. Encountering Christ personally and to be converted to the new family is a great social process which is exemplified in the instances of each prototypical characters. When they meet Jesus, they are generally categorized as needy, in various aspects of their life. They encounter Jesus, with faith and insight, fearless, being reverential, truthful, humble, bold, persevering, repentant, courageous, enthusiastic, service minded and perceptive. As a result, they become people who are wholly sane, converted, receptors of Jesus' compassion, calm, peaceful and servants of the Word. Their conversion is modelled as the adequate response to the in-break of the Kingdom initiated in Jesus' mission and at the same times their beginning of participation in the same mission to perpetuate for the eschatological end.

Final chapter is a synthesis on the interpretation of the social identity of the community from the ideological perspective. The Markan community should realize its identity by making itself different to the other groups of its time in the levels of its cognitive, valorative and emotional aspects. These three fundamental aspects of a group confer upon the social image in its wider ambience, as it is understood from the chapter of theory and models. By his Gospel text, Mark was attempting to give a unique social definition to his group in the ambience of the first century Mediterranean world, when it was suffering wars, persecutions, ideological confusions and faith crisis. At this point, Mark was laborious to suggest a conformable thinking pattern by affirming the fundamental and balancing ideology and a uniform mode of conduct and behaviour for his community.

The cognitive aspect of the social identity explains that what the fundamental self-awareness should be, if one is a member of the Markan community. The Markan effort is to provide his community an auto suggestive formula that, they ought to be a group gathered by the power of the death of Jesus as life-ransom; they ought to be a group guided in action by the awakened memorial presence of Christ, a permanent Christ consciousness; they ought to be a group on march in the hope of Parousia. The community becomes more Christo-centric, when it participates in the mission of Christ and his same fate. These Christological conviction and mission of the community are to be fuelled by faith and right understanding of Jesus and his identity in the middle time, a post-paschal time of the Church till the Parousia of Christ in which they have the hope for.

From the above notions, we understand that the community should have the cognitive awareness that it is simultaneously open to Christ, fellow believers and to the world. All the members of the community must be made closer to feel one in Christ. For such a fraternal end, the community members will have to undergo a process of depersonalization converting their personal self to a communal self, to turn to be Christ's followers and to have a *we-feeling* in Jesus Christ among them. The consciousness of one being in the group because of the conception that they are adhered to Christ is fundamental which in turn brings cohesiveness, solidarity, uniformity, broadmindedness, mutual acceptance and sharing in the group. This process of 'depersonalization' is plausible only if the community pays heed to the evangelical call to a radical way of life.

If the cognitive foundation of the community is relied upon the identity of Christ's authority as the Son of God, the valorative base of it proceeds predominantly from the same Christ who is crucified. The value of the Cross is the source of the fundamental values of the community. The value of detachment is the primmest among them. At the cause of the mission and the kingdom, even the material and kinship ties are to be renounced. This ascetical and radical renunciation is not because of the animosity over the natural familial relations or worldly possessions, rather is to accept the Kingdom of God. All the detachment and self-denial leads to the affirmation of the God's reign instead of human authority. This recognition of God's rule as the sole authority is a revolutionary move against the cultural setting where honour, power, authority and richness were considered the dominant values. The Markan community is therefore called upon to the revolutionary inversion of the dominant cultural values of the time. The religious culture were hypocritic where their lips accepted the God's dominion but from the heart level they were far from accepting Him and were hard heartened to His commandments.

If God is recognized, then men are also to be recognized each other irrespective of age, gender and status divisions. The recognition of the children and women as well as the weak and little believers of the community is the basic attitudinal value, where no human authority is going to dominate and rule over them. In the ambience when the rule of authority is replaced by the rule of service, the community's identity marker becomes service as Jesus its founder served the entire humanity on the Cross.

Those values and attitudes of the community are radical in nature and exigent in time. The point of view of the community should consistent with the point of view and way of life that Jesus had exposed. Mark keeps pace with the spirit of Jesus to stipulate these norms and attitude to his community, which enable to stand itself distinct against all other sects and antagonist groups. The norm of Cross-bearing and self-denial is in conformity with the life of Christ, the spirit of humility in service is in agreement with the total and unique humble self-sacrifice of Christ; the ambulant missionary style is in agreement with the circulating Jesus in villages of Palestine with the message of God's dominion and power. Total renunciation of even kinship is in view of forming an eschatological family of disciples wherein they are to live in solidarity and fraternity. Mark wants his community to get identified with those norms in a cohesive manner and all the members of the community while behave according to these norms and basic attitudes would engage in forming their social selves in the world.

The Markan community is a new family or a house of God. For this renewed self-understanding of his community, the family metaphor would have been sounded to Mark effective and strong in the Mediterranean ambience where family was an emotive and primary factor of the social structure. Mark expects from his community to bring in a rupture in that cultural system of household domination substituting with a fictive kinship or *new family* where God is the Father and owner; the disciples who 'does the will of God', are the possession of God. Jesus is their 'brother' who has the delegated ownership of this family and they are his 'brothers, sisters, and mother.' One major function of emotional contagion is affiliation or bonding: the joint experience and expression of emotions is assumed to strengthen the social bonds between individuals. The Markan community with 'we feeling' of a family of God will have its members with a deep sense of belonging to their group as sons and daughters of God. The dominations and ruling over on to each other has no room because the reign of God is upon this new household. This sense of belonging and emotive adhesion should fuel for a fraternal communion among the members as brothers and sisters, generate sympathy, compassion, respect, recognition and fearlessness, to each other. This group cohesion should presuppose an intra-group emotional bias that members have a strong emotional affinity and intimate favouritism for the group, or to say in clear terms, they have love and affection for their group. It is to be presumed that Mark inculcates a familial feeling to have an effect of emotional contagion when there arise the situations of group crisis or of persecutions so that group members may have the same emotional reactions towards those events in order to console each other and maintain solidarity.

The situation and the circumstances that prompted Mark to reconstruct the social identity of his group are drawn hypothetically due to its clandestine nature behind the text unlike Pauline letters. It is presumed that the text is a response to the emerging crisis and challenging realities of the group to which, suggests a "possible social selves" of the community.

The Markan emphasis on the Christological ideology and the normative and valorative aspects really reflects the internal and external crisis and predicaments that his community faced at a given time. Many scholars, as we have seen, had spoken for various Christological and ecclesial crisis that the community underwent like tension of the divine-man (*theos aner*) Christology, delay of the

Parousia, upper hand position of the Jerusalem authorities of the Church, general Jewish oppositions to the Christ devotion, the synagogue reforms at Diasporas and persecutions. Nevertheless, one thing is definite that the community had the difficulties in following Christ and his message of Cross; there were failures in the area of discipleship. This inner crisis is seemed to be the greatest concern of the author of Mark and the greatest curiosity as well to the Markan scholarship. These Christological and ecclesial challenges were instigated and aggravated due to the subsidiary socio-political and religious tensions of the time like Jewish war, persecutions, destructions of the temple, false prophecies and betrayals. These inner and external crises altogether could have pressed the community to search for an existential stance and a new way of looking at its existence and being in the tensed world. They were pressed to have a living of their Christian identity with a right understanding of the Christological ideology of Cross and Parousia.

At this background of the total crisis of the community, a question is relevant that why Mark wrote a Jesus-story in a biographical genre in order to address the group crisis rather than using the then well-known rhetorical medium of letter writing. As a man who had a first-hand experience of the crisis and as the one belonged to the very community, Mark writes his Gospel for reading aloud for them. Moreover, to this presumption that we have already attested in the very beginning of this study, according to Mark's observation and conception, time created a natural crisis in the being, believing and behaving of the group. That natural crisis was the generational gap, a distancing of the community from the original event of its charisma – the Christ events, his mission, passion and crucifixion. These historical events had been forgotten from the communal memory with a predominant and unbalancing emphasis on the glorified presence and coming of Christ. The 'folly of Cross' and its meaning in the Christian life had begun perhaps to be deteriorated from the cognition of the believers and it was considered by Mark to be a peril to the existence of the Markan community. It perhaps did effect adversely a shallowness and meaninglessness of the suffering and persecutions in the lives of the community. This would have necessitated him to recuperate the original charisma by recalling the past Jesus events. For Mark the *Jesuological amnesia* may be the root cause of the inner crises of his community and his approach was a pro-in-group orientation than total negation of any among them, in reducing the inner conflict of his group. It could be said so, since he is open and receptive to present even the exceptional out-group characters as prototypes like centurion or councillors like Jairus or Joseph of Arimathea.

Lastly, this mapping of the social identity for the Markan community was really driven to find out the immediate context of the text or the location of the Markan community. We have treated this question as hypothetical under appendix. We may conclude that the Community of Mark situated somewhere in the vicinity of Palestine under the close experience of trials, persecutions of war and the destruction of the temple because more than any external referents to the text, the textual referents are stronger to inform us that the Gospel was originated out of the immediate social situation of Jewish revolt and Jewish antagonism which was experienced by the Markan community and paved the way for their internal crisis of faith. Even when we conclude this study as such, in the light of differing views of scholars regarding the place and time of Markan community we cannot overrule a later possibility for an agreeable and unanimous position of scholarship to advocate for a universal readership to Mark, like that of Bauckham and Hengel. This hope may help us to overcome the pessimistic evaluation of Peterson, that "...the present state of affairs should make it impossible simply to assume that reconstructed communities behind Gospels are hermeneutically necessary to read Gospels rightly."[1]

---

[1] cf., D. N. PETERSON, *The Origin of Mark: The Markan Community in Current Debate*, Brill, Leiden, 2000, p. 202. See the review, C. A. Evans, *RLB* 12/05/2001, *www.bookreviews.org*. (accessed 08-10-200).

BIBLIOGRAPHY

Primary Biblical Source

ALAND, K. (ed.), *Synopsis Quattuor Evangeliorum*, Deutsche Biblgesellschaft, Stuttgart, 1963, 1996.

ALAND, K., - M. BLACK - B. M. METZGER - A.WIKGREN (eds.), *The Greek New Testament*, Bible Society, New York - London - Edinburgh - Amsterdam – Stuttgart, 1966.

DOUGLAS, J.D. (ed.), *The New Greek-English Interlinear New Testament* (A New interlinear translation of the Greek New Testament United bible Societies' Fourth, corrected Edition with The New Revised Standard Version, New Testament, R. K. Brown – P. W. Comfort (trans.), Tyndale House Publishers, Illinois, 1990.

ELLIGER, K., - W. RUDOLPH (eds.), *Biblia Hebraica Stuttgartensia*, Deutsche Bibelgesellschaft, Stuttgart, 1967-1977.

La Biblia: Edición popular, La casa de la Biblia (6th ed.), PPC – Sigueme-Verbo Divino, 1993.

The Holy Bible: The New Revised Standard Version, Thomas Nelson, TPI, Bangalore, 1993 & 1989.

THROCKMORTON, B. H. (ed.), *Gospel Parallels* (4th ed.), TPI, Bangalore, 1979.

Sources of Antiquity

Babylonian Talmud, in *Babylonian Talmud: Tract Sanhedrin*, M. L. Rodkinson (trans.), The Talmud Society, Boston, 1918.

CLEMENT OF ROME, in A. ROBERTS - J. DONALDSON (eds.), *Ante-Nicene Fathers*, Vol. 1, ACC, Edinburg, 1867. cf., http://www.sacredtexts.com (accessed 08-10-2006); cf., Internet Sacred Text Archive DVD-ROM 6.0.

Didache in THE APOSTOLIC FATHERS, Vol. 1, *I Clement; II. Clement; Ignatius; Polycarp; Didache; Barnabas* (trans. K. Lake, 1st ed.), Cambridge, Massachusetts: Harvard University Press, London, 1985.

EPIFANIO, *Panarion*, in *Epiphanius II. Panarion* (2nd ed.), Akademie-Verlag, Berlin, 1980.

Esdras, in R. J. COGGINS, The first and second books of Esdras, Cambridge University Press, Cambridge, 1979.

EUSEBIUS, PAMPHILUS, *The Church History*, in P. SCHAFF – H. WACE (eds.), *A Select Library of the Nicene and Post-Nicene Fathers of the Christian Church*, T & T Clark, Edinburg, 1890.

Gospel of Thomas, in A. D. De CONICK, *The Original Gospel of Thomas in Translation: With a Commentary and New English Translation of the Complete Gospel*, T & T Clark, London - New York, 2007.

IGNATIUS, *Epistle to Romans*, in A. ROBERTS - J. DONALDSON (eds.), Anti-Nicene Fathers, Vol. 1, ACC, Edinburg, 1867. cf., http://www.sacredtexts.com (accessed 08-10-2006); also cf., Internet Sacred Text Archive DVD-ROM 6.0.

IRENAEUS, *Against Heresies*, in A. ROBERTS - J. DONALDSON (eds.), Anti-Nicene Fathers, Vol. 1, ACC, Edinburg, 1867. cf., http://www.sacredtexts.com (accessed 08-10-2006) ; also cf., Internet Sacred Text Archive DVD-ROM 6.0.

JOSEPHUS, FLAVIUS, *Antiquities of the Jews,* in S. MASON (ed.), Judean antiquities 1-4 , Vol. 3, Brill, Leiden, 2000.

______, *War of the Jews*, in H. ST. J. THACKERAY, *The Jewish War* I-VII, The Loeb Classical Library- 203 & 210 (2nd imprint), London, 1961.

JUSTIN MARTYR, *Dialogue with Trypho*, in A. ROBERTS - J. DONALDSON (eds.), *Anti-Nicene Fathers*, Vol. 1, ACC, Edinburg, 1867.

Mishnah, in *Tractate Sanhedrin, Mishnah and Tosefta*, H. Danby (trans.), The Macmillan Company, NY, 1919.

PLINIO SEGUNDO, *Naturalis Historia*, in H. RACKHAM (ed.), *Natural History of Pliny*, Vol. I-XXXV, The Loeb Classical Library, London, 1938-1952.

QUINTILIANO, MARCO FABIO, *Institutio Oratoria*, in *The Institutio Oratoria of Quintilian*, H. E. Butler (trans.), The Loeb Classical library - 124, London, 1920.

SUETONIUS, TRANQUILLUS, *Claudius*, in *The Lives of the Twelve Caesars*, A. Thomson - R. Worthington (trans.), New York, 1883.

TACITUS, *Annals*, in *The Works of Tacitus* (trans. A. John Church and W.J. Brodribb), Internet Sacred Text Archive DVD-ROM 6.0.

Reference Works

ANDERSON, HUGH, *The Gospel of Mark*; New Century Bible Commentary, Eerdmans, Grand Rapids, 1981.

BALZ, H., – SCHNEIDER, G. (eds.), *Diccionario Exegético del Nuevo Testamento* (trans. C. Ruiz – Garrido), Vol. I & II, Sígueme (2nd ed.), Salamanca, 2001.

______, *Exegetical Dictionary of the New Testament*, Vol. I, II, & III, Eerdmans, Grand Rapids – Michigan, 1993.

BARNARD, A., – J. SPENCER (eds.), *Encyclopedia of Social and Cultural Anthropology*, Routledge, London – NY, 2002.

BLASS, F., - A. DERBRUNNER, *A Greek Grammar of the New Testament and other Early Christian Literature* (R. W. Funk, trans. & ed.), The University of Chicago Press (5th ed.), Chicago, 1979.

BROWN, F., – S.R. DRIVER – C.A. BRIGGS, *A Hebrew and English Lexicon of the Old Testament*, Clarendon Press, Oxford, 1951.

BROWN, R. E., *La Muerte del Mesías* (trans. S. F. Martínez), Verbo Divino, Navarra, 2005.

COOGAN, M. D., (ed.), *The Oxford History of the Biblical World*, Oxford University Press, NY – Oxford, 1998.

FEE, GORDON D., *New Testament Exegesis: A Handbook for Students and Pastors* (3rd ed.), Westminster John Knox Press, Louisville – London, 2002.

FREEDMAN, D. N., ABD, Double Day, NY – London – Toronto – Sydney – Auckland, 1992.

GNILKA, J., *El Evangelio Según San Marcos* (trans. V. A. Martinez), Vol. 1 & 2, Sígueme, Salamanca, 1996.

GOULD, E. P., *A Critical and Exegetical Commentary on the Gospel according to St. Mark*, T & T Clark, Edinburgh, 1975.

GUELICH, R. A., *Mark 1-8:26*, Vol. 34, Word Biblical Commentary, Word Books Publisher, Dallas –Texas, 1998.

GUIJARRO, S. (ed.), *El documento Q en Griego y en Español* (2nd ed.), Peeters – Sígueme, Leuven – Salamanca, 2004.

HATINA, T. R. (ed.), *Biblical Interpretation in Early Christian Gospels*, Vol. 1, T & T Clark, London-NY, 2006.

IERSEL, B. M. F. VAN, *Mark : A Reader Response Commentary*, T & T Clark, London – N.Y., 2004.

JARA, I. D., *Diccionario: Griego – Español del Nuevo Testamento*, Publicación UPSA, Salamanca, 2006.

______, *Gramática Griega del Nuevo Testamento: I. Morfología*, Publicación – UPSA, Salamanca, 2004.

JERÓNIMO, SAN., *Comentario al Evangelio de San Marcos* (trans. J. Pascual Torró), Biblioteca de Patrística-5, Ciudad Nueva (2nd ed.,), Madrid, 1995.

LAMBDIN, T. O., *Introduction to Biblical Hebrew*, Darton – Longman Todd, London, 1973.

MALINA, B. J., – R. L. ROHRBAUGH, *Social Science Commentary on the Synoptic Gospels* (2nd ed.), Fortress Press, Minneapolis, 2003.

MANN, C. S., *Mark: A New Translation with Introduction and Commentary*, The Anchor Bible, Doubleday and Company Inc., Garden City – New York, 1986.

MARCUS, J., *Mark 1-8*, The Anchor Bible – Double Day, N.Y. – London – Sydney – Auckland, 2000.

MATEOS, J., *Comentario al Evangelio de Marcos*, Comisión General de la HOAC, Madrid, 1976.

METZGER, B. M., *A Textual Commentary on the Greek New Testament:* A Companion Volume to the United Bible Societies' Greek New Testament (4th rev.ed.), Deutsche Bibelgesellschaft, D-Stuttgart (2nd ed.), 1994.

MOUNCE, W. D., *Basics of Biblical Greek* (2nd ed.), Zondervan, Grand Rapids - Michigan, 2003.

PONTIFICAL BIBLICAL COMMISSION, *The Interpretation of the Bible in the Church* (document), Rome, April 23, 1993.

PUERTO, M. N., *Marcos*, Verbo Divino, Navarra, 2006.

SCHMID, J., *El Evangelio Según San Marcos*, Herder, Barcelona, 1967.

SILLS, D.L. (ed.), *Enciclopedia Internacional de las Ciencias sociales*, Vol. 1 & 2, (V. C. Tomás, ed. española), Aguilar, Madrid, 1974-1977.

______, *International Encyclopedia of the Social Science*, Vol. 1 & 2, The Macmillan Company & The Free Press, NY – London, 1972.

SIMPSON, J. A. – E. S. C. WEINER (eds.), *The Oxford English Dictionary* (2nd ed.), Clarendon Press, Oxford, 1989.

STUHLMUELLER, C. (ed.), *The Collegeville Pastoral Dictionary of Biblical Theology*, TPI, Bangalore, 2005.

THAYER, J. H. (ed.), *Thayer Greek-English Lexicon of the New Testament* (electronic edition), IBT, 2000.

TROADEC, H., *Comentarios a Los Evangelios Sinópticos*, Actualidad Biblica-17, Madrid, 1972.

WITHERINGTON, B., *The Gospel of Mark: A Socio-Rhetoric Commentary*, Eerdmans, Grand Rapids – Cambridge, 2001.

ZERWICK, M., *Analysis Philologica Novi Testamenti Graeci*, Sumptibus Pontificii Instituti Biblici, Romae, 1960.

Secondary Literature

AHEARNE, KROLL, P. S., *Who are My Mother and My Brother? Family Relations and Family Language in the Gospel of Mark*, Journal of Religion, 81 (2001, 1).

ALLEN, O. W., *Reading the Synoptic Gospels: Basic Methods for Interpreting Mathew, Mark and Luke*, Chalice Press, Missouri, 2000.

ASSMANN, J., *Religion und Kulturelles Gedächtnis : Zehn Studien*, Beck, Munich, 2000.

AUERBACH, *Mimesis: The Representation of Reality in Western Literature*, (trans. W. R. Trask), Princeton University Press - Princeton, NJ, 1953.

BARTON, S. C., *Discipleship and Family ties in Mark and Mathew*, Cambridge University Press, N.Y., 1994.

BAUCKHAM, R. (ed.), *The Gospels for All Christians: Rethinking the Gospel Audiences,* Eerdmans, Grand Rapids, 1998.

BEAVIS, M. A., *Mark's Audience: The Literary and Social Setting of Mark 4:11-12*, (JSNTsup.) JSOT Press, Sheffield, 1989.

BEST, E., *Following Jesus: Discipleship in the Gospel of Mark*, JSNTsup.4, Sheffield, England, 1981.

______, "The Role of the Disciples in Mark", *NTS* 23 (1977).

______, *Mark: The Gospel as Story*, T & T Clark, Edinburgh, 1983.

BIRD, M. F., "The Markan Community, Myth or Maze? Bauckham's "The Gospel for All Christians" Revisited", *JTS* 57 (2006).

BLANCO, A., – A. CABALLERO – D. L. La CORTE, *Psicología de los Grupos*, Prentice Hall, Madrid, 2005.

BOTHA, P. J. J., "The Historical Setting of Mark's Gospel: Problems and Possibilities", *JSNT* 51 (1993).

BROADHEAD, E. K., *Prophet, Son, Messiah: Narrative Form and Function in Mark 14-16*, JSOT Press, Sheffield, 1994.

______, *Teaching with Authority: Miracles and Christology in the Gospel of Mark*, JSOT Press, Sheffield, 1992.

BROWN, R. E., *An Introduction to the New Testament*, TPI, Bangalore, 2000.

BULTMANN, R., *The History of the Synoptic Tradition* (trans. J. Marsh), Basil Blackwell, Oxford, 1963.

CARNEY, T. F., *The Shape of the Past: Models and Antiquity*, Coronado Press, Lawrence – Kansas, 1975.

CARROLL, R. M. D. (ed.), *Rethinking Contexts, Rereading Texts: Contributions from the Social Sciences to Biblical Interpretation*, (JSOTsup.) Sheffield, 2000.

CERESKO, A. R., *The Old Testament: A Liberation Perspective*, St. Paul's Publications, Bombay, 1992.

CHANCEY, M. A., *Greco-Roman Culture and the Galilee of Jesus*, Cambridge University Press, Cambridge, 2005.

CHAPMAN, D. W., "Locating the Gospel of Mark: A Model of Agrarian Biography", *BTB* 25 (1995, 1).

CLIFTON, B.C., *The Disciples According to Mark: Markan Redaction in Current Debate*, JSOT Press, Sheffield, 1989.

CROSSLEY, J. G., *The Date of Mark: Insight from the Law in Earliest Christianity*, (JSNTsup.) T & T Clark, London, 2004.

DEWEY, J., "Mark as Interwoven Tapestry: Forecasts and Echoes for a Listening Audience", *CBQ* 53 (1991).

______, "The Literary Structure of the Controversy Stories in Mark 2:1-3:6", *JBL* 92 (1973).

DOISE, W., *Psicología Social y Relaciones entre Grupos: Estudio Experimental* (1ª ed.), Vol. I & II, Rol, Barcelona, 1979.

DONAHUE, J. R., "Windows and Mirrors: The Setting of Mark's Gospel", *CBQ* 57 (1995).

DOWNING, F. G., *Making Sense in (and of) the First Christian Century*, (JSNTsup. -197) Sheffield Academic Press, Sheffield, 2000.

DWYER, T., *The Motif of Wonder in the Gospel of Mark*, (JSNTSup.128) Sheffield Academic Press, England, 1996.

EFRAT, B. SHIMON, *Narrative Art in the Bible*, (JSOTsup.-70) The Almond Press, GA (USA), 1989.

ELLIOT, J. H., *What is Social Scientific Criticism?*, Fortress Press, Minneapolis, 1993.

ESLER , P. F., "Ezra-Nehemiah as a Narrative of (Re-invented) Israelite Identity", *BibInt* 11 (2003, 2-4).

______, *Conflict and Identity in Romans: The Social Setting of Paul's Letter*, Fortress Press, Minneapolis, 2003.

______, *Conflicto e Identidad en la Carta a los Romanos: El Contexto Social de la Carta de Pablo* (trans. J. Pérez Escobar), Verbo Divino (Estella), Navarra, 2006.

______, "Jesus and the Reduction of Intergroup Conflict: The Parable of the Good Samaritan in the light of Social Identity Theory", *BibInt* 8 (2004, 4).

______, "Ludic History in the Book of Judith: The Reinvention of Israelite Identity?", *BibInt* 10 (2002, 2).

______, "Making and Breaking an Agreement Mediterranean Style: A New Reading of Galatians 2:1-14", *BibInt* 3 (1995, 3).

______, "Social Identity, the Virtues, and the Good Life: A New Approach to Romans 12:1-15;13", *BTB* 33 (2002, 2).

______, *The First Christians in their Social World: Social-Scientific Approaches to New Testament Interpretation*, Routledge, London – USA - Canada, 1974.

FAULKNER, A., *Jewish Identity and the Jerusalem Conference: Social Identity and Self Categorization in the Early Church Communities*, www. sharp.arts.gla.ac (an authentic electronic publication of the University of Glasgow), eSharp Issue 6: Identity and Marginality i (Autumn 2005).

FERNANDEZ, CYPRIAN E., *Identity in Conflict: A Socio-rhetorical Reading of the Markan Story of Jesus*, Asian Trading Corporation, Bangalore, 2016.

______,"Memory and its Social Vitality; A Biblical Understanding", *LW* 121 (2015), pp. 8-28.

______,"Architectural Space and Operational Base of the Primitive Jesus-movement Revisited: Con-textual Readings", *LW* 121 (2015), 399-423.

FIONE. B. S.J., "Covert Allusion in 1 Cor 1-4", *CBQ* 47 (1985).

FISHER, K. M., - U.C. VON WAHLDE, "The Miracles of Mark 4:35-5:43: their meaning and function in the Gospel frame work", *BTB* 11(1981).

FLEDDERMANN, H., "The Discipleship Discourse (Mk 9:33-50)", *CBQ* 43 (1981, 1).

FRENTRESS, J., – W. CHRIS, *Social Memory: New Perspectives on the Past*, Blackwell, Cambridge – Mass., 1992.

FREYNE, S., *The Twelve: Disciples and Apostles; A Study in the Theology of the First Three Gospels*, Sheed and Ward, London – Sydney, 1968.

GEDDERT, T. J., *Watchwords: Mark 13 in Markan Eschatology*, JSNTsup., JSOT Press, Sheffield, 1989.

GEHRING, R. W., *House Church and Mission: The Importance of Household Structures in Early Christianity*, Hendrickson Publishers, Massachusetts, 2004.

GRASSI, J. A., *The Rediscovering the Impact of Jesus' Death: Cues from the Gospel Audience*, Sheen &Ward, Kansas City, 1987.

GUIJARRO, S., *La primera biografía de Jesús*, UPSA, Salamanca, 2006 La presentación de la clase.

______, *Fidelidades en Conflicto: La Ruptura con la Familia por causa del Discipulado y de la Misión en la Tradición Sinóptica*, UPSA, Salamanca, 1998.

______, "La Familia en el Movimiento de Jesús", *EstBib*, 61 (2003).

______, *Los Primeros Discípulos de Jesús en Galilea*, in Los Comienzos del Cristianismo (Coord. S. Guijarro), UPSA, Salamanca, 2006.

GUTHRIE, D., *New Testament Theology*, InterVarsity Press, England, 1981.

HAENCHEN, E., "Die Komposition von Mk viii 27. ix 1", *NovT* 6 (1963).

HAGEDOM, A. C., - J. H. NEYREY, "It was out of Envy that they handed over: the Anatomy of Envy and the Gospel of Mark", *JSNT* 69 (1998).

HALBWACHS, M., *La Mémoire Collective*, Presses Universitaires de France, Paris, 1950.

______, *La Memoria Colectiva* (tras. I. Sancho – Arroyo), Prenas Universitarias de Zaragoza, Zaragoza, 2004.

______, *Los Marcos Sociales de la Memoria* (trans. M.A. Baeza – M. Mujica), Anthropos, Barcelona, 2004.

______, *On Collective Memory* (ed. & trans. L. A. Coser), University of Chicago Press, Chicago, 1992.

______, *Morphologie Sociales*, Armanda Colin, Paris, 1946.

HANAUER, J. E., *The Holy Land: Myths and Legends*, The Sheldon Press, London, 1907.

HASLAM - S. ALEXANDER - P. J. OAKES, C. McGARTY - J. C. TURNER - K. J. REYNOLDS - R. A. EGGINS, "Stereotyping and Social Influence: The Mediation of Stereotype Applicability and Sharedness by the Views of In-group and Out-group Members", *BJSP* 35(1997).

HATINA, T. R., "Who will See 'The Kingdom of God coming with power' in Mark 9:1 – Protogonists or Antagonists?", *Biblica* 86 (2005, 1).

HAWKIN, D. J., "The Incomprehension of Disciples in the Markan Redaction", *JBL* 91 (1972, 4).

HENDERSON, S. W., *Christology and Discipleship in the Gospel of Mark*, Cambridge University Press, N.Y., 2006.

HENGEL, M., *Seguimiento y Carisma: La Radicalidad de la Llamada de Jesús* (trans. J. A. Jáuregui), Sal Terrae, Santander, 1981.

______, *The Four Gospels and the one Gospel of Jesus Christ: An Investigation of Collection and Origin of the Canonical Gospels*, Harrisburg, Trinity Press International, 2000.

______, *Problems of a History of Earliest Christianity*, Biblica 78 (1997, 1).

______, *Studies in the Gospel of Mark*, SCM Press, London, 1985.

HOLMBERG, B., "Jewish versus Christian Identity in the Early Church", *RevBib* 105 (1998).

HORSLEY, R. A., *Archaeology, History, and Society in Galilee: The Social Context of Jesus and the Rabbis*, Trinity Press International, Pennsylvania, 1996.

HUTARDO, L .W., *Lord Jesus Christ: Devotion to Jesus in Earliest Christianity*, Eerdmans, Michigan-Cambridge, 2005.

IERSEL, B. M. F. VAN, "Failed Followers in Mark: Mark 13.12 as Key for the Identification of the Intended Readers", *CBQ* 58 (1996).

INCIGNERI, B. J., *The Gospel to the Romans: The Setting and Rhetoric of Mark's Gospel* (BIS 65), Brill, Leiden, 2003.

IVERSON, K. R. *Gentiles in the Gospel of Mark*, (LNTS) T & T Clark International, London, 2007.

JEFFERS, J. S., *The Greco-Roman World of the New Testament Era*, InterVarsity Press, Illinois, 1999.

JEREMIAS, J., *Jerusalén en tiempos de Jesús*, Cristiandad, Madrid, 2000.

JOYNES, C.E., "The Returned Elijah? John the Baptist's angelic identity in the Gospel of Mark", *SJT*, 58 (2005, 4).

KEALY, S. P., "Recent Reflections on the Gospel according to Mark", *BTB* 35 (2005, 3).

KEE, H. C., *The Community of the New Age: Studies in Mark's Gospel*, The Westminster Press, Philadelphia – Pennsylvania, 1977.

KELBER, W. H., *The Kingdom in Mark: A New Place and a New Time*, Fortress Press, Philadelphia, 1974.

______, *The Oral and the Written Gospel*, Fortress Press, Philadelphia, 1983.

KIRK, A. – T. THATCHER (eds.), *Memory, Tradition, and Text: Uses of the Past in Early Christianity*, (Semeia Studies 52) SBL, Atlanta, 2005.

KOESTER, H., *Ancient Christian Gospels: Their History and Development*, SCM – Trinity, London – Philadelphia, 1990.

______, "Mark 9:43-47 and Quintilian 8.3.75", *HTR* 71 (1978).

KRENTZ, E., *The Historical-Critical Method*, (Guides to Biblical Scholarship: OT Series) Fortress Press, Philadelphia, 1996.

LATOURELLE, R., *A Jesús El Cristo por Los Evangelios*, Sígueme, Salamanca, 1992.

LEGRAND, L., *The Bible on Culture*, TPI , Bangalore, 2001.

LIPPONEN, J., – J. LESKINEN, "Condition of Contact, Common In-group Identity, and In-group Bias toward Contingent Workers", *JSP* 146 (2006, 6).

MACK, B. L., *A Myth of Innocence*, Fortress Press, Philadelphia, 1991.

MALBON, E. S., *Narrative Space and Mythic Meaning in Mark*, Harper and Row, San Francisco, 1986.

______, *In the Company of Jesus: Characters in Mark's Gospel*, Westminster John Knox Press, Louisville – Kentucky, 2000.

______, *Narrative Space and Mythic Meaning in Mark*, Harper and Row, San Francisco, 1986.

MALINA, B. J., *The New Testament World: Insights from Cultural Anthropology* (3rd ed. revised & expanded), Westminster John Knox Press, Louisville - Kentucky, 2001.

______, "The Social Sciences and Biblical Interpretation", *Interpretation* 37 (1982).

______, "Let him deny himself Mk 8:34", *BTB* 24 (1994).

MANIPARAMBIL, J., *Synoptic Gospels*, Claretian Publications, Bangalore, 2000.

MARCUS, J., "The Jewish war and the Sitz im Leben in Mark", *JBL* 111 (1992).

______, *Mark 1-8*, The Anchor Bible 27, Doubleday, N.Y- London – Toronto – Sydney – Auckland, 1999.

MARXSEN, W., *El Evangelista Marcos: Estudios sobre la Historia de la Redacción del Evangelio*, Sigueme, Salamanca, 1981.

MATEOS, J., *Los "doce" y otros Seguidores de Jesús en el Evangelio de Marcos*, Cristiandad, Madrid, 1982.

MATERA, F. J., "The Incomprehension of the disciples and Peter's confession (Mk 6,14-8,30)", *Biblica* 70 (1989).

MATHEWS, V. H., "The Determination of Social Identity in the Story of Ruth", *BTB* 36 (2006, 2).

MICHAEL, L. WHITE, *De Jesús al Cristianismo* (trans. J. P. Escobar), Verbo divino, Navarra, 2007.

MOSCOVICI, S., *Influencia y Cambio de Actitudes: Individuos y Grupos* (1ª ed., trad. D. Rosenbaum), Paidós, Barcelona, 1985.

MRÁZEK, J.,– J. ROSKOVEC (eds.), *Testimony and Interpretation: Early Christology in its Judeo-Hellenistic Milieu*, (JSNTsup.) T & T Clark, London-NY, 2004.

MYERS, CHED, *Binding the Strongman*, Orbis, Maryknoll, 1994.

NEIRYNCK, F. (ed.), *The Minor Agreements of Mathew and Luke against Mark*, Leuven University Press, Leuven, 1974.

NEYREY, J., "The Idea of Purity in Mark's Gospel", *Semeia* 35 (1986).

OLICK, J. K., "Collective Memory: The Two Cultures", *ST* 17 (1999).

PAINTER, J., "When is a House not Home? Disciples and Family in Mark 3: 13 – 35", *NTS* 45 (1999).

PERRIN, N., "The Composition of Mark ix 1", *NovT* 11 (1969).

PETERSON, D. N., *The Origins of Mark: The Markan Community in Current Debate,* Brill, Leiden, 2000.

POWELL, M. A., *What is Narrative Criticism?*, Fortress Press, Minneapolis, 1990.

REGODÓN, J. NÚÑEZ, *El Evangelio en Antioquia*, UPSA, Salamanca, 2002.

RHOADS, D. - J. DEWEY - D. MICHIE, *Mark as Story: An Introduction to the Narrative of a Gospel* (2nd ed.), Fortress Press, Minneapolis, 1999.

______, *Marcos como Relato: Introducción a la Narrativa de un Evangelio* (2nd ed.), Sigueme, Salamanca, 2002.

RHOADS, D., – K. SYREENI (eds.), *Characterization in the Gospels: Reconceiving Narrative Criticism*, (JSNTsup.) Sheffield, England, 1999.

RICHES, J. K., *Conflicting Mythologies: Identity Formation in the Gospels of Mark and Mathew*, T &T Clark , Edinburgh, 2000.

ROBINSON, J. M., *The Problem of History in Mark*, SCM Press, London, 1971.

ROHRBAUGH, R. L., *The Social Location of the Marcan Audience*, BTB 23 (1995).

ROSKAM, H. N., *The Purpose of the Gospel of Mark in Its Historical and Social Context,* Brill, Leiden, 2004.

SALDARINI, A. J., *Pharisees, Scribes and Sadducees in Palestine Society: A Sociological Approach*, Eerdmans, Grand Rapids–Cambridge, Michigan – U.K., 2001.

SÁNCHEZ, J. C., *Psicología de los Grupos: Teoría, Procesos y Aplicaciones*, McGraw – Hill, Madrid, 2002.

SANDERS, E. P., – M. DAVIES, *Studying the Synoptic Gospels*, SCM Press – Trinity Press, London – Harrisburg, 1989.

SANDERS, E. P., *Jesus and Judaism*, SCM Press, London, 1985.

SCHENKE, L., *La Comunidad Primitiva: Historia y Teología* (trans. M. O. Gaztelumendi), Sígueme, Salamanca, 1999.

SCHMID, J., *El Evangelio Según San Marcos*, Herder, Barcelona, 1967.

SCHMIDT, T. E., "Mark 10:29-30; Mathew 19:29: 'Leave House...and Region'?", *NTS* 38 (1992).

SCHWARTZ, B., "The Social Context of Commemoration: A Study in Collective Memory", *SF* 61 (1982).

______, *Abraham Lincoln and the Forge of National Memory*, University of Chicago Press, Chicago, 2000.

______, "Postmodernity and Historical Reputation: Abraham Lincoln in Late Twentieth-century American Memory", *SF* 77 (1998).

SENIOR, D., ""With Swords and Clubs ...": The Setting of Mark's Community and His Critique of Abusive Power", *BTB* 17 (1987).

SHERIF, M., - C. W. SHERIF, *Social Psychology*, Harper and Row, NY, 1969.

SHERIF, M., *Intergroup Relationship and Leadership: Approaches and Research in Industrial, Ethnic, Cultural and Political Areas*, John Wiley & Sons, NY, 1962.

SMITH, A., "Tyranny Exposed: Mark's Typological Characterization of Herod Antipas (Mark 6:14-29)", *BibInt* 14 (2006, 3).

STETS, J. E. – P. J. BURKE, "Identity Theory and Social Identity Theory", *SPQ* 62 (2000), (also available as electronic material online page www.wat2146.ucr.edu).

STRANGE, W. A., *Children in the Early Church*, Wipf & Stock, Oregon, 2004.

SUH, J. S., *Discipleship and Community: Mark's Gospel in Sociological Perspective*, (Nexus Monograph Series 1) Claremont, CA, 1991.

TAJFEL, H., *Grupos Humanos y Categorias Sociales: Estudios de Psicologia Social* (trad. C. Huici), Herder, Barcelona, 1984.

______, *Human Groups and Social Categories: Studies in Social Psychology*, Cambridge University Press, Cambridge, 1981.

TANNEHILL, R. C., *The Disciples in Mark: The Function of a Narrative Role*, Journal of Religion 57 (1977, 4).

TELFORD, W. R., *The Theology of the Gospel of Mark*, Cambridge University Press, UK, 1999.

TERRY, D. J., – M.A. HOGG (eds.), *Attitudes, Behaviour and Social Context: The Role of Norms and Group Membership*, Lawrence Erlbaum Associates, NJ, 2000.

THEISSEN, G., *Colorido Local y Contexto Histórico en Los Evangelios* (trans. M.O. Gaztelumendi), Sigueme, Salamanca, 1997.

______, *The Gospels in Context: Social and Political History in the Synoptic Tradition*, (trans. Linda. M. Maloney), T & T Clark, Edinburgh, 1992.

______, *El Movimiento de Jesús*, Sígueme, Salamanca, 2005.

______, *Estudios de Sociología del Cristianismo Primitivo*, (trans. F. Ruiz – S. Vidal), Sígueme, Salamanca, 1985.

TRAINOR, M. F., *The Quest for Home: the Household in Mark's Community*, Liturgical Press, Minnesota, 2001.

TURNER, J. C., *Redescubrir el Grupo Social* (trans. P. Manzano), Morata, Madrid, 1990.

TYSON, J. B., "The Blindness of the Disciples in Mark", *JBL* 80 (1961).

VAAGE, L. E., "El Evangelio de Marcos: Una Interpretación Ideológica Particular dentro de los Cristianismos Originarios de Siria-Palestina", *RIBLA* 29 (1998).

______, "En otra Casa: el discipulado en Marcos como ascetismo doméstico", *EstBib* 63 (2005, 1).

______, *Galilean Upstarts: Jesus' First Followers According to Q*, Trinity Press, Pennsylvania, 1994.

WAETJEN, H., *A Re-ordering of Power; A Socio-political Reading of Mark's Gospel*, Fortress Press, Minneapolis, 1989.

WANSBROUGH, H., "Mark III.21- Was Jesus out of His Mind?", *NTS* 18 (1972).

WEEDEN, T. J., "The Heresy that Necessitated Mark's Gospel", *ZNW* 59 (1968).

WENHAM, D., "The Meaning of Mark III.21", *NTS* 21(1975).

WIJNGAARDS, J. N. M., *Background to the Gospels*, TPI, Bangalore, 1996.

WILLIAMS, J. F., *Other Followers of Jesus: Minor Characters as Major Figures*, (JSNTsup.) JSOT Press, Sheffield, 1994.

WRIGHT, A. G., "The Widow's Mites: Praise or Lament?- A Matter of Context", *CBQ* 44 (1982).

YZERBYT, V. (Coord.), *Emotions and Social Identity: Toward an Integrated View of Intergroup Conflict:* European collaborative Research Network, Catholic University of Louvain, Belgium, 2004, Doc. A1-10, Electronic resource: www.esf.org/generic. (accessed 16-10-2006)